THE
MOVEMENT
MADE US

THE MOVEMENT MADE US

A FATHER, A SON, AND THE LEGACY OF A FREEDOM RIDE

DAVID J. DENNIS JR.

In collaboration with David J. Dennis Sr.

HARPER

An Imprint of HarperCollins*Publishers*

HarperCollins books may be purchased for educational, business, or sales promotional use. For information, please email the Special Markets Department at SPsales@harpercollins.com.

FIRST EDITION

Designed by Nancy Singer

Library of Congress Cataloging-in-Publication Data has been applied for.

ISBN 978-0-06-301142-7

22 23 24 25 26 LSC 10 9 8 7 6 5 4 3 2 1

CONTENTS

THE
MOVEMENT
MADE US

US

There's a video of James Baldwin interviewing a stranger with my daddy's face that will one day be my face.

The VHS tape of this interview has been in my family for forty years. The cassette itself is blank with the exception of a half-faded sticker on it that reads "James Baldwin Interviews Civil Rights Workers (1981)." Baldwin himself gave it to my dad, who doesn't recall ever watching it. The tape stayed at my mother's house after the divorce, collecting dust until I started researching my father's life a few years ago. When my mother gave me the video, she told me that she'd shown it to me when I was a child and I kind of remembered that without remembering the specifics.

The interview with Dad comes toward the end. The man whose face appears on the screen above the grainy words "David Dennis, CORE Activist" is my father, but not the one who figures in my memories from childhood. The man in the video with my daddy's face was scowling, the lines around his eyes red, his fingers pressed against his temples, and the skin around his jaw drooping. As he talks about the 1964 Freedom Summer and the murders of his friends and the way the search for their remains uncovered more mutilated, decapitated, desecrated bodies of long-forgotten and nameless Black Mississippians, his nostrils flare and he looks like he wants to set the world on fire. So many of my favorite times spent with Dad were day trips traveling through Mississippi, watching him deliver speeches at various memorials, anniversaries, celebrations, and funerals. I've sat in rooms while he was being interviewed for documentaries. I'd seen him mourn his friends, cry over them, share his guilt and regrets. I've seen him sad. I've seen him angry. But I'd never seen him look like he did sitting across the room from James Baldwin.

I was raised by Dave Dennis Sr., the Civil Rights veteran. The man who spoke about his demons on those trips. The man who worked tirelessly with Bob Moses to reignite their Movement throughout my childhood. That was the man I admired even as he became a father I deserved more from. I'd thought that the Dave Dennis behind podiums with his fingers to the sky and crying freedom for our future was the man who emerged from the Movement. The Baldwin tape tells a different history and answers a question I never asked.

In this grainy video, the stranger Dad is lost in his own fury. When he talks to Baldwin, all that's left is a hardness. A calloused, impenetrable husk.

The video is one of the only interviews my dad had done from the end of Freedom Summer up until the 1990s, when I was a kid. He'd wrapped himself in a cocoon of survivor's guilt and regret to the point that he would refuse interviews and try to hide from any spotlight his heroism brought. The few interviews he did in the 1980s were combative, short, and full of inaccuracies that come from him simply not giving enough of a damn to care about his answers. The one exception is the interview he did for *Eyes on the Prize* in 1985—five months before my birth—but even that interview was distant and only done because one of the people working on it, Judy Richardson, had been a SNCC worker and, after multiple attempts, finally convinced him to participate in the documentary.

When I ask my dad about that man talking to Baldwin he tells me about his "period of insanity." The vaguely detailed lost 1970s and '80s spent running from ghosts, diving in and out of financial despair, drugs, a ruined marriage to the woman who survived the Movement with him, a move to Lafayette in southwest Louisiana, a marriage to my mother and my birth when he was forty-five years old. The years that more resembled those of a soldier returning from Vietnam than a hero of American democracy collecting praise as a foundational member of the Movement for Civil Rights.

My dad was on the way to another catastrophic collapse in the late 1980s when he'd gotten a call from Bob Moses. The two hadn't spoken since the 1960s, when they presided over the Council of Federated Organizations (COFO) together and spearheaded the 1964 Freedom Summer. The distance wasn't out of any sort of animus, but because they both needed so completely to flee the Movement and anyone associated with it. Bob had gone to Tanzania to start a family and teach math. My dad hid within himself.

Bob had a vision for a new Movement, one built on erasing the educational gap. One built around math literacy and Black kids. It was an invitation for my father to return to what he and Bob saw as unfinished business. To right the wrongs they felt they had left unfixed. The prospect invigorated my father as much as it terrified him. Bob, or "Uncle Bob," as I'd come to know him, was persistent.

Finally, one day in 1992, my dad was driving through the Mississippi Delta after a meeting with Bob, whose pitches were wearing him down. It had been Dad's first time in Ruleville, the home of Fannie Lou Hamer, since the '60s. It was on that drive that Mrs. Hamer, who had been dead for fifteen years, spoke to him. Dad pushed on the gas, but it was too late. She was in the car. In the back seat. Playing on the radio. In the rearview mirror. "Why you leave us, Dave? Where you been? You know better than that. We needed you in here. These kids out here ain't no better off than we were and you running? You couldn't even come tell me goodbye, at least do something for these babies."

Dad stopped in Jackson—his home base during the Movement—for a few days. Then he came home and told everyone we were moving to Mississippi. Dad was taking on Bob's charge to help lead the Algebra Project. He was rejoining the Movement. I was six years old when all this happened. I didn't know the full story. I just remember one day he came home and it felt as if the next day we were moving.

My dad is explaining the story behind our move on a Zoom call, which is how we have to communicate during a pandemic mismanaged by a white supremacist president. Our plans to talk face-to-face had been derailed, but we were committed to finally talking through our lives: me to talk about what it was like being his son and him to explain to me why he was the father he was.

"So, all those trips we took to all of those speeches when I was a kid. Those were the first times you were going through and revisiting those places?"

"Yeah, I guess so." It all feels so heavy. I'd always assumed that by the time I'd been gone on those trips with him to talk about his ghosts, he'd been decades-deep in reckoning and coping. I thought he was smoothing over closed wounds. I never realized he was opening them anew. I was being raised by a man who was facing demons for the first time. This changes everything I thought I knew about my life. Everything about us and what made us.

"So my whole childhood was shaped by you returning to the Movement for the first time in thirty years?" I lean back in my chair and look to the ceiling. I feel like it's about to fall on me. "Jesus, you were fifty years old."

"Going back to Mississippi saved my life. I'm an organizer at heart and that's my calling. It really is. That's what I'm good at. Being there for my people, finishing what we started there. I was myself again. I was back in my groove. I was finally happy."

I want to scream. "Dad, you know those years were horrible for me, right?"

My dad spent the 1960s willing to sacrifice his life. He spent the '90s willing to sacrifice his family. Our relationship was a casualty of his crusade, my mother coming home from work, holding our family together with duct tape, weary smiles, and promises that Dad would be here if he could. Dad was always traveling—the Delta, McComb, Chicago, New England—anywhere but with me. He treated our home like a Freedom House where the friends he reunited with stayed almost every night—me giving up my room and sleeping on our couch all through elementary school, never knowing who was coming or going. I loved these people, but all I really wanted was my dad.

I knew Uncle Bob as the soft-spoken math genius who would sit on the floor with me to test out his new algebra models and who bought me a *Home Alone* video game for my eighth birthday. I knew Hollis Watkins as the wise storyteller with a singing voice that melted steel. Uncle Rudy Lombard was the smartest man I ever knew, and Uncle Don Hubbard always had a joke. They were not symbols of freedom to me, but the elders who covered me and watched over me and continue to watch over me. I knew and loved them before I was aware of what this country tried to do to them.

But it's Miss Euvester Simpson I can't stop thinking about. She would come to the house, laugh, and eat whenever my dad cooked. It wasn't until I started working on my father's story that I learned that she was one of the kids assaulted with Mrs. Hamer in a Winona, Mississippi, jail. It seems impossible that someone who survived that brutality could ever smile again. A beautiful, dimpled, wide-mouthed smile that screams back decades and cries out, "I'm still here."

I feel blessed to have known these people outside of the context of the Movement. To know them as parents, uncles, aunts, spades players, storytellers, mathematicians, and huggers who loved with their whole faces, listened with their whole torsos, and comforted with their entire beings. Each happy day, a miracle of their own resolve.

These are the people who also taught me about Dave Dennis. They'd tell me how my dad led them through what felt like unwinnable battles and was willing to jump on grenades for them. They told me about his fearlessness and his natural skill as an organizer, always rallying troops and devising contingency plans. Growing up with these people taught me that to be Black in America and part of the Movement was to have fought a war on American soil. A war where the United States government, state legislators, white vigilantes, and terrorists alike collaborated to bomb churches, murder workers, hide bodies, misinform the public, spy on freedom organizations, creating a treacherous and deadly path to liberation. The freedom fighters aren't just Civil Rights veterans. They're heroes who saved this country as a by-product of simply trying to save themselves. And they did so while fighting an oppressive regime that wanted to eradicate human rights and lace Black bloodlines with explosives. Their stories are war stories.

Through these people, I came to understand what kind of hero Dave Dennis was. I admired him and wanted to be like him, staring down the evil white men who would stop us from getting free. My Movement family would tell me how I looked just like my father, from our bluish-green, droopy eyes, to our wide noses, even down to our crooked pinkies. "Boy, he spit you out" would be the common refrain in our house. They'd ask me if I wanted to be a troublemaker like him or how I'd carry on his legacy. My dad would lean back in his chair, glass of Crown Royal in his hand, and smirk. Watching his pride in what I could be made me feel like I had a sun in my chest, burning hot and unfading.

I loved Dave Dennis. But I didn't know my dad.

This book chronicles Dave Dennis's Movement stories from 1961 to 1964, from the moment he joined to the end of Freedom Summer. They're told as my father remembers them, the blanks in his memory just as important as the details he can recall with vivid precision. I researched and interviewed his friends to uncover stories he'd caged up, in an effort to jog the moments back to his consciousness. Some came back. Some didn't. The spirit of decades-old conversations are preserved even if the direct quotes were polished. Blue houses may be orange and beige carpets may be green. But the stories are true to my father and felt in our lineage.

I wrote these words not knowing if America was going to waltz into an autocracy that stripped away our voting rights, how this country would strike back against the largest nationwide protest

for Black lives we've ever seen, or if my own dad would survive the pandemic. I wrote these words because, through it all, I
wanted everyone fighting to see what Black people in America are
capable of no matter what weapons are used against us. I wanted
people on the streets in Minneapolis to know how Mississippi
sharecroppers could rewrite the Constitution or how college kids
from New Orleans could stand in front of gun barrels and refuse
to back down. How Black folks across the South risked their
families, homes, and livelihoods for their beliefs. I want these
stories to be a lighthouse.

But I also wrote these words because I wanted to know how
my father and I became who we are. I wanted to know what this
Movement did to us as a family. I want to know where the cal-
louses form and which scars become transferable. I want to know
who I want to make proud, who I want to love me, and how
much of the twentysomething-year-old man who got on a Freedom Ride thinking he'd die; who said goodbye to Medgar for the
last time; and who should have been in the car with Goodman,
Chaney, and Schwerner was left to become my dad.

This is the story of the Movement. And a father and son who
never stopped fighting for freedom and each other, reaching
across a wall of Black fighters and ghosts who have been there for
generations and days, our fingertips centimeters away from one
another. Longing. Loving. Scared. Fighting. Us.

I.

DILLARD

I spent a year of my life thinking I'd never see another woman as beautiful as Doris Castle.

In 1960, I was twenty years old and a first-semester freshman at Dillard University, an HBCU (historically Black colleges and universities) in New Orleans, founded in 1930. I was surrounded by stunning women but seeing Doris on campus made them all disappear. She was standing below an American flag that was fighting the sun for her attention. Yes, she was gorgeous—a confident, captivating smile and big round eyes that dared you to look away. But it was her assuredness. Standing in the middle of all those students with a megaphone in her hand, she was magnetic.

Doris was saying something about Civil Rights and equality. Something about a group called CORE and fighting segregation. I didn't care what she was talking about. That Movement stuff wasn't for me. I just wanted a date.

• • •

I was the first person in my family to graduate from high school, so that felt like the pinnacle of my educational accomplishments.

As far as I was concerned, the rest of my life was set. I didn't hope to attend college; that was what rich kids did. Black boys from Shreveport didn't go to those places. I was convinced I would get a job and live a quiet life at home.

Then I spent a day with Mr. Jack.

Mr. Jack was my gray-haired next-door neighbor in Shreveport. He watched me grow up and took a liking to me at an early age. One day the summer after I graduated, Mr. Jack came to me with a plan in his eyes.

"Hey, Sonny, what you gonna do now that you out of school?"

"I don't know, Mr. Jack. I have this letter from Dillard, but I don't think I can afford it. I think I'll just go to a trade school and—"

"You don't need all that, boy. Them schools don't got nothing for us but a piece of paper that makes you feel better about workin' fa white folk. Me? I ain't need school to work for myself."

Mr. Jack drove a Nehi soda truck, which means he worked for white folks. But if you asked him, Mr. Jack worked for Mr. Jack. He worked alone all day, delivering crates of Nehi bottles to local restaurants, doctors' offices, stores, and other Black-owned businesses, because he couldn't deliver to white establishments. He set his own routes and break times. He felt like he ran his own Black business and carried himself accordingly.

"Look, Sonny. You're a good kid." It felt like Mr. Jack had his speech prepared. "I've had my eye on you since your momma brought you to this neighborhood and I'm proud of the man you are. I'm about to change your life. I'm retiring in a few months. I get my watch and my retirement check and I want you to take my place. Wattaya say?"

"You mean . . . ?"

"Come deliver these Nehis with me! Just one day. I'll show you my routes and how to do it. It's easy. You'll have a job for the rest of your life. Just like me. Well, until I get my watch."

I didn't really want to drive a Nehi truck and deliver boxes of soda bottles for a living, but I didn't have a plan either. My mother would leave the Dillard letter on the kitchen table every day, never pushing me to go but reminding me that the offer was there. I don't think she really knew what I could get out of college but thought that it could keep me safe for as many years as I would spend there.

I didn't want to offend Mr. Jack. My momma would lose it if she knew I turned him down, especially knowing I'm walking past that college letter every day.

"I can't wait," I told Mr. Jack through gritted teeth and a forced smile.

"Great! See you tomorrow!"

Riding around with Mr. Jack, I saw that he was right. His job was easy, in theory. All you had to do was go to a warehouse, sign a sheet, load a truck full of crates, and drive to a bunch of houses and businesses. There was a serenity to Mr. Jack's routine. He'd roll his windows down, keeping his radio off so he could hear the tires crunching the tiny rocks on the dirt roads. The dust would kick up and cake around his elbow, which hung out of his window, but he didn't seem to mind. He drove with a big, toothy grin. I don't know if he drove like this every day for decades or if his happiness came from knowing he was on his last lap. The drives are always happier, it seems, when the call of freedom is at its loudest.

When we got to our first stop, I walked around to the back of the truck and pulled one of the crates toward the edge of the trunk, closer to my chest. I struggled to get the leverage I needed to lift it. I was already in a bigger fight with these sodas than I thought I'd be when I agreed to ride along. By the time the crate scooted out of the trunk, the truck no longer supporting its weight, it dove to the ground like it had been planning its escape the whole drive.

I expected to hear the bottles breaking when the crate hit the road, but they didn't. Instead of the crate hitting the ground, it landed on my fingers. The sudden drop ripped my shoulders out of their sockets, feeling like they'd left my torso completely. The momentum also forced me to suddenly bend over, straining my lower back in the process. So there I was with crushed fingers, yanked shoulders, and a cracked back. My first crate.

"You good back there, Sonny? It's not too heavy, is it?"

"No, sir! Just really excited to be here!"

The walk from the truck to the Jenkinses' store felt like I was walking in lava, the bottoms of my feet burning through my shoes, my knees tearing with every step, and the tendons ripping in my shoulders.

I spent the next four hours delivering boxes.

For lunch, we sat on the back of Mr. Jack's truck. Mom had made us a couple of sandwiches for my big day—a thick slice of bologna between two thicker slices of Wonder Bread.

Mr. Jack scooted close to me, our hips almost touching as our legs dangled off the back of the truck. He hadn't left the truck all morning, but his jeans were as dirty as mine—old, generational dirt that clung to every inch of the denim. Dirt that somehow survived years of washing and walking. I looked at my own jeans. They were pristinely blue when my morning started but not anymore. How many years would this rookie soot stay with me, weighing down my every walk? I was trying to knock off the stubborn clumps of dirt with my hand when Mr. Jack started talking.

"You see this, Sonny?" He opened his fist to reveal a gold pocket watch in his palm. "I got my watch a whole month early. Forty years. You deliver these bottles for forty years and you get a retirement and this."

I stared deep into the bezels of his watch and the second hand that moved to the beat of Mr. Jack's voice. I looked beyond, at the unending dusty road ahead of us, and the businesses that seemed to be sprouting up in front of us, adding more stops, tendon tears, and crushed fingers.

By this point, Mr. Jack's words were fading out of my consciousness. I didn't care about the tiny sunshine in his palm. I could only focus on my own arms. I was holding my sandwich, just barely outside of the brown paper bag nestled between my legs. My hands were shaking, pain shooting up my wrists and biceps. I couldn't move the sandwich from the bag to my mouth.

"You are going to have a family. A wife. Kids. And all you gotta do is carry. That's all you gotta do."

"Mr. Jack. Look. You've been so nice. I . . . . I just can't do this."

I loosened my fingers so that my sandwich could fall back into the paper bag.

"Here. I'm sorry. I can't carry anymore. I just can't. Thank you for the opportunity, but I just can't carry this all my life. It hurts too much. You can keep my earnings for the day. And my sandwich. I . . . I quit."

I hopped down from Mr. Jack's truck, feeling the tiny rocks on the ground stubbornly pushing themselves through the bottoms of my shoes to my feet, and limped home.

"Mom, where's that letter from Dillard?"

• • •

"You gonna stand over there and stare or you gonna come talk to me?"

I thought I was playing it cool, just another onlooker captivated by Doris's words, but clearly I wasn't doing a good job at acting.

"Excuse me?"

"I mean, you over there staring like I'm a glazed ham, you gonna do something about it? Mr.?"

This would be the thing I remember about Doris. The way she could be confrontational and endearing at the same time. She made you feel secure in who you were but made you want to make yourself better. I don't know how she did it.

"Dave. I'm Dave Dennis."

"I'm Doris Castle. Very nice to make your acquaintance Mr. Googly Eyes."

"Now . . . I just couldn't help but be moved by your words and . . ."

"Negro, you ain't hear a word I said. Don't lie to me."

"Okay, you got me." I moved closer. "I'm not so much into all that activism and getting arrested. But I'm a good date. How about din—"

"Oh, hell no. It don't work like that, baby. I'm here for CORE and CORE only."

"Core of what?"

"Congress of Racial Equality. That's what this is all about."

"Core. Root. Apple. We can talk about it all over dinner?"

She looked me up and down. Then she walked even closer.

"Look, I only go on dates with men. Real men. And a real man fights for Black people. You want to go on a date? Here. Take this pamphlet. Meet us for a CORE meeting and we'll talk there.

Now go clean the grass from the bottom of your jaw, boy. I'm fine but I ain't *that* fine."

• • •

I was fourteen in 1955 when I saw the picture of Emmett Till in his casket, his face looking like one of the old torn-up baseball gloves we'd play with as kids. It was a revelation for America and the answer to a mystery that lasted my entire childhood. I'd suddenly known where the Black people on the plantations I grew up on would disappear to. Men and women would be there next to us picking cotton and then the next day they'd be erased so thoroughly from the living that nobody even dared to acknowledge they were ever alive. Their absences would just hang in the air.

I was aware of racial terror, like any Black kid, especially in the South. I sat in the back of buses. I picked cotton for white men who owned the land we sharecropped on. I heard them call me "boy" and "nigger" and I knew that speaking up would get me and my family killed.

But it wasn't my job to fight that racism. My job was to go to school, become an engineer, make money, retire when I wanted to and not have to wait for a gold watch. I appreciated the fights others took on, but I didn't want any part of it.

New Orleans had already been buzzing about those negro student aggressors who had integrated the McCrory's five-and-dime store a few months earlier. We talked about them in our classes and in our dorms. I believed in what they were doing, but not enough to jeopardize why I had come to Dillard. There was no future in Movements. The only result of fighting is having people who love you looking down at coffins, fighting back the urge to scream out your name.

Doris and the rest of those people were fools. Brave and admirable. But fools.

Still. I wanted that date.

So I went to the New Zion Baptist Church, where the Southern Christian Leadership Conference had been formed three years earlier, for my first meeting with the Congress of Racial Equality. The meeting was led by Rudy Lombard, Jerome Smith, Doris, and her older sister, Oretha. Jim McCain was there representing the national office. Lolis Elie, a Black lawyer in New Orleans, was present to offer legal advice. He was the first Black lawyer I'd ever seen besides Calhoun from *Amos 'n Andy*.

There were about a dozen other people in the meeting listening to Rudy and Oretha lay out the plans to make CORE's presence further known at the segregated counters by showing up, demanding to be served, and leaving as soon as the cops were called. The process was called a "hit-and-run." They were talking about how this would help aggravate the store owners and disrupt the businesses. The people who showed up to the meeting, many with their eyes fixated on Doris, seemed solely concerned about the consequences.

So do you get arrested? What happens if you get arrested? How long do you stay in jail? What do the police do to you?

Like me, they were kids who just wanted to finish school or get jobs. But now the prospect of risking the security of a diploma and a career for something larger than themselves was threatening to tear their lives apart. I could see they were scared.

I wasn't scared at all. Because I knew no matter what anybody in that meeting said, my ass was not going to be doing a sit-in or a hit-and-run or anything that would land me in jail. I was *finishing* school. These people were out of their damn minds.

After that first meeting was over, I wanted to talk to Doris, but it was clear I'd have to fight for her attention with a handful of other guys she'd convinced to come to the meeting. So I figured

I'd have to try again another day. At the next meeting. Then the next meeting. And the one after that.

The more I went the more I found myself compelled by what was being discussed. Each week I'd enjoy listening and learning. I'd eventually be willing to help by preparing pickets, training students for sit-ins, and doing any auxiliary work necessary to help, all with the understanding that I had no interest in putting myself at any risk of being arrested.

"Hey, Dave," Doris said after a few weeks. "You not the feds or anything are you?"

"What?"

"I mean, you just come here and help train and make signs and all that, but you don't ever wanna go out in the field. You looking like you working for Hoover. You wearing a wire?" Doris. Always challenging and inviting. "I'll tell you what, you've been here every week and helping out. We kinda like you. A few of us usually meet up at my house after. Come hang out . . . And no . . . *this isn't a date!*"

The Castle sisters lived in a white shotgun house on 917 North Tonti Street in the Treme area of New Orleans. To get to the kitchen in the back, we had to walk through the master bedroom and the Castle sisters' rooms. We usually ended up stepping over Mr. Castle as we made our way through. He was a longshoreman and slept through the day, only rolling over and putting a pillow over his head as we walked by. It was in the Castles' kitchen, the aroma of red beans and rice in the air, where the intense strategic planning for New Orleans CORE would take place. It was also there where I'd gain a new family.

There was Oretha, Doris's older sister, the vocal leader and heart of the enterprise. She was just a year or two older than we were, but she felt like an elder. She knew when to

dial up the emotion, chiding us when we weren't being asser-
tive enough and being the voice of reason when we needed to
calm down. She'd already become a legend for the time when,
during a sit-in at Woolworth's, a white man in a blue business
suit, brown suspenders underneath his coat, and a matching
hat walked up to harass her, as was customary. The demonstrators had been trained to deal with having food poured on
them and having their hair pulled. This white man wanted to
take things a step further. He hocked up a loogie in his throat
to spit on Oretha.

She calmly stood up from her seat, took a step toward the
man, and looked him in his eyes, and said: "Good sir, I'm sure
you're having a good time doing this to us. And I'm sure you've
heard how we are nonviolent, which is mostly true. But if a drop
of water leaves your mouth and touches any part of me, I swear to
God I will stick my foot so far up your ass I'll be cleaning that ball
of spit in your mouth up from the bottom of my shoe."

The man took a beat, buttoned up his jacket, turned around,
and swallowed his spit.

Oretha could move mountains when she talked. To us and
anyone else.

Rudy Lombard was a Xavier student from Algiers and a bit
older than the rest of us too. He was a strategist, the genius who
always had a plan. If Oretha was the engine, Rudy was the foot
on the gas. He founded the New Orleans CORE chapter, and his
mantra, "We is us," was the spark that led the group to stage its
initial sit-in at McCrory's on Canal Street. Rudy towered over the
room, commanding attention when he spoke, though he rarely
raised his voice. He'd sit with his legs crossed, head leaning back,
soaking in the information before he would say something that
was so profound that everyone else would wonder why they

hadn't thought of it first. He would become my best friend after the Movement years.

Initially, though, I was closest to Jerome Smith. He was lanky like a basketball player but chiseled, with strong cheekbones and these large hands. He talked with a speed and confidence that was accompanied by a severe stutter that flared up the more excited he became, and he always had a scheme that was a bit less thought out than anything Rudy would come up with. But he made up for it with his passion. Jerome always seemed to have a new book under his arm every week, was constantly quoting Frantz Fanon, Gandhi, James Baldwin, and W. E. B. Du Bois, injecting political discourse and nonviolent philosophies into every conversation. He had a way with words, speaking with the rhythm of an improv jazz set. It was like he'd put words together by how they sounded more than how much sense they made. Once while giving a speech at the HBCU Southern University, he got word that the police were heading out to arrest him, so he interrupted his speech, leaned into the mic, and declared, "I must elite from this den of iniquity." I never knew what he meant, but it didn't matter. It sounded so powerful. Jerome was raw emotion and sincerity, a loyal and loving brother who would have everyone's back no matter what.

The Thompson sisters, Alice and Jean, as well as their cousin Doratha "Dodie" Smith-Simmons were all fire. They were as fearless as they were tiny, never hesitating to confront anyone who dared speak to them the wrong way. The men in CORE would complain about dealing with white folks on missions with the Thompson sisters around because the two would always get in some racist's face, dragging the men into an ass whooping with them. Don Hubbard was our age, but he had a wife, kids, and a job driving cars downtown. He couldn't jeopardize any of it, so he was even more determined to not get arrested. He'd happily drive people to McCrory's, but there was no way he was getting out of his car. Don was soft-spoken but wise and always offered up a joke to cut any tension.

I had grown to love these people, so I kept going to the meetings at Oretha's house as often as I could. Mostly, though, I'd stay quiet. There wasn't much room to talk with Jerome's philosophizing, Rudy's strategizing, and Oretha's rallying of the troops. I went to Oretha's house for the Movement and the people. But I also went there for the food.

Oretha and Doris's mother, Virgie Castle, worked at a Black-owned New Orleans restaurant called Dooky Chase's a few blocks away from their house on Orleans Avenue. The restaurant, which opened in 1941 as a sandwich shop, eventually became a hub for soul food, politics, and Black leadership. It was the place where most Black families, especially in the Creole section of the city, would go for their Sunday dinner of fried fish, shrimp, oysters, chicken, seafood platters, shrimp and crawfish etouffee, stuffed mirlitons, gumbo, and jambalaya. Prominent Black folks like Thurgood Marshall would meet there when they were in New Orleans. By the 1960s, Dooky's became the central strategic meeting place for Dr. King and other activists when they came to town.

Beyond its historical importance, Dooky Chase's was a place that made us feel like we belonged. Eating in the dining room felt like being at a family reunion with strangers who looked like us. The restaurant housed the spirit of New Orleans. The soul of the city's Blackness rested everywhere, from the carpet to the ornate chandeliers. We felt like we deserved the best the world could give us when we were at Dooky's.

Mrs. Chase would send Doris and her mother home after work with extra batches of fried chicken and po-boys because she knew Oretha was headed to a strategy session with the rest of the upstart group of CORE members.

I think back on those Thursday nights at Oretha's with fondness. I gained a family in those months while learning about how to organize and articulate our need for freedom. I felt a passion for the Movement, but not enough to put my life in danger. Instead, I felt a greater passion to my friends. I wanted us to win because I wanted them to win. They were owed a victory for how much they cared.

"Dave, when you coming out there with us, man?" Oretha would ask.

"Oh now y'all know Dave too learned to be galivanting with us raucous cityfolk," Jerome would chime in.

"His grades aren't even good enough," Don would say. "He might as well join us."

"Us?" Oretha would shoot back at Don. "You coming out there now?"

"Yeah, you don't see my spirit in there with y'all?"

They'd all laugh at my expense, poking at me to join them in the field, knowing I'd never relent. But Doris was working on me.

"Dave, I get it, honey. You want to go out in the world and get a job and have a family and be a man. But that's not what's gonna make you a man. A man is going to put his life on the line for something bigger. You're a man? You gonna have that job and think you a man. But you gonna change the world here and really be one."

• • •

My grandfather's hands were like granite. Growing up, he'd do this thing where he'd call me over to him and tell me to hold out my hand. Then he'd grab it and squeeze. I'd feel my bones collapsing on themselves from the power of his grip. I'd fall to the floor crying.

"Get up, boy. The day you stand up to me when I squeeze is the day you're a man."

I agonized over those squeezes for my entire childhood. I knew they were coming and I could hear the sound of my bones straining even before he ever would touch me. I'd look at my hands constantly, wondering if they were strong enough for me to be a man. I'd curse them if they got injured and celebrate them when they punched some kid in school and didn't break. I needed my grandfather's approval. He was the only real dad I'd ever known.

One day when I was sixteen my grandfather came back home from working the field. Before he said anything, I walked right up to him and I put my hand out. He squeezed. I bit down until it felt like my teeth would push through the bottom of my jaw. But I didn't flinch.

"Now. You're a man."

My eyes never left my grandfather's. He walked away. As soon as he left the room, I sobbed.

I was his equal now. I was a man.

He never hugged me again. But he respected me.

I'd spent so much of my life looking forward to that moment. That gratification of having my grandfather call me a man. To hear Doris challenge that manhood years later at the CORE meetings triggered an anger and a spite inside of me. How dare *she* challenge me as a man? She'd never felt the pain of that vise grip or the pain of that grip letting go. How could I be anything but a man?

Doris's words gnawed at the tender parts of my flesh. They kept me up at night. They spoke to me louder than my professors in class and ate through my stomach in the cafeteria. Then I went home for Easter, where her words screamed even louder.

II.

JAIL

My roommate, Samuel Sepeku, came home with me for Easter.

Sammy was the first person I met when I got to Dillard. When I walked into our room, my suitcases and bags behind me, Sammy was already there and had made his half of our space his own. There were fabrics over his bed that had colors I'd never seen before—the brightest yellows tiptoeing along these singing greens and tiny red stripes. On the wall was a picture of some man who looked like a priest of some sort, his hand raised before a congregation that looked like they were cheering him on. It looked like church from back home, but different. Sammy had nailed many Jesuses on the Cross to the walls around the room, too. Two Jesuses sat on his desk, along with a leather Bible with the satin bookmark string hanging down.

He was sitting upright at the desk with perfect posture, his gray slacks riding up to his shins, a tucked-in white shirt, and a red tie. He had on the shiniest damn dress shoes I'd ever seen. He made me want to burn my dingy white-collared shirt and gray-black shoes with the flapping soles. I did one of those soft half tap half knocks on the already-open door. Sammy closed his Bible, shot up from his chair with his hands by his side.

"Hey, I think I'm your roommate," I said, trying to read this kid.

He extended his whole arm without bending it. The rest of his body didn't move. "Greetings, sir. My name is Samuel Sepeku. I am pleased to be your roommate." His voice was deep and rhythmic. Like the first syllable of his word came from his chest and the second syllable came from his nose. He wasn't from Louisiana. I looked around at the room and tried to understand what was going on.

"Hey, I'm Dave Dennis. I'm from Shreveport. Uh . . . you?"

"Ah, Shreveport. That is close, no? Louisiana. Country boy! I, too, am a country boy. From Tanganyika."

"Tang . . . hmmm . . ." I was too ashamed to tell him I didn't know what he was talking about, but he could tell. I was still looking at all the Jesuses.

"It's in East Africa. My father, John Sepeku, is the archdeacon of Magila. Which is in . . . Dave . . . are you okay?"

I was staring at him now. "Magila, you say? And that's in Africa?"

"East Africa, yes."

"That's . . . that's far."

"Yes. I've flown to New Orleans alone. My entire family is still there, but I think I like it here. You look like you have another question for me."

"Well, I mean. In Shreveport we used to go to these picture shows. The colored ones would show this movie called *Tarzan*. You ever heard of *Tarzan*? Well, he swings around in the jungle and there are all these, uh—"

"Savages?"

"Well, yeah. These savages and they're all Black and they're all from Africa and they wear face paint and have bones hanging out their noses and they make animal noises and—"

"And you believed that."

"I don't think so. I mean, no. Of course not. But I never really thought about what people from Africa were really like. I knew you didn't make animal noises, but I didn't know you all wore slacks and church shoes and had all these Jesus pictures. I didn't even know y'all knew who Jesus was." I felt sillier with every word.

"You said something back there." He ignored what I had said and moved on. "A 'colored' theater."

"Yeah."

"You know, I wonder why you Black Americans don't just rise up and fight against these things. Colored water fountains. Colored this. Colored that. I come here and am less free than at home." I had no clue if he was right and had no way of checking. I just assumed if there were more Black people there than white folks here then he might have a point. "If I get arrested or fight, they'll take my visa and I'll go home. I can't do those things, but you can. Why don't you do something? Are you afraid of Tarzan?"

As he laughed at me, three more freshmen walked by us in the hallway. They were all bald. Then another one stopped by the door. "Oh, you two are probably next, huh? Get ready!" He rubbed his head.

"What is the meaning of this?" Samuel asked.

"This is orientation, baby! The upperclassmen are shaving our heads. This is how we get initiated."

"Sir, did you want your head shaved?"

"Nah, not really, but they held me down. I like it, though. It's school spirit!" He turned and ran down the hall again, cheering with his friends.

I started rubbing my hair. "I don't think I want to do that shit, man. Pardon my language. No offense to the Jesuses."

"I, too, refuse! Let's handle this now. Come with me."

Before I could blurt out a "wait," I was following Sammy to wherever he was going. We walked through the dorm. Down the stairs. Across campus and into the Student Union where upperclassmen were hooting and hollering and freshmen were nervously trying to join in. Sammy walked to the corner of the cafeteria and grabbed a broom, put it over his knee, and broke off the brush. He stood up on a cafeteria table. I just stood slack-jawed hoping nobody would notice me with him.

"Can I have everyone's attention? My name is Samuel Sepeku and this is my roommate, Dave Dennis." Shit. "We understand that there is a thing where you are shaving heads for some school initiation. I am unfamiliar with these traditions, but I want to let you know that my roommate, Dave Dennis, and I will have no part of it. And if you even try, you should do it before I fashion this stick into a spear. As you all know I am from Africa and can do such things!" He then winked at me.

Nobody mentioned shaving our heads for the rest of orientation.

That was Sammy. He did what he wanted and just watching him not take anyone's mess made me wonder why I'd spent so much of my life just reading *colored* signs and following the rules. I loved spending time with him when I wasn't hanging around with the CORE crew at North Tonti, which I'd been doing for six months by the time Easter came around. Sammy couldn't fly home for the short break, of course, so I suggested he come with me. I wanted him to meet my family, and I wanted my family to meet someone from Africa. I also wanted Samuel to see Shreveport.

• • •

"You ever had fried chicken, Sammy?" Mom had a full spread for us when we got to her house. A big pot of greens, yams, and cornbread. That's how she said she missed me.

"Why, yes ma'am, I have. Especially in New Orleans. Dave brings me some from his meetings."

"Meetings?"

"Yes, they have lots of extra chicken at those CORE meetings."

"CORE?"

"Yeah, Mom. It's the Con—"

"I'm familiar with CORE." She was suddenly ice.

Nobody spoke. Soon my mother's fork was punching the plate, stabbing the greens like they were trying to run away. We'd never talked much about the Movement and she never told me not to get involved, but I just knew she wanted me to finish college and the belief was that these kids getting arrested didn't care about their educations. I didn't know exactly what she was thinking. But I knew enough. She didn't look at me.

"You know, Sammy. The chicken in New Orleans isn't like it is here. Chicken don't have to travel so far to get here." She managed a chuckle. Sammy responded in kind. I just kept eating. "So what do you plan on doing this weekend?"

"Well, ma'am, I want to go to church Sunday for sure. This is my first American Easter and I want to celebrate the Resurrection."

"Oh, you know we are gonna have a big thing at First Baptist. We're gonna have a repast and—"

"I'm sorry to interrupt. But I was hoping to go to a Presbyterian church around here as that is the church of my family. My father is part of the clergy, soon to be bishop."

I was still eating. I knew what was coming.

"Oh, y'all really left y'all brains in New Orleans. Sonny, you didn't tell him?"

"I did let him know, Mom, but the guy wants to go. It's Easter. They can't turn us away."

"Yes, I am well aware of the history of segregation in that church, but they must honor my wishes as the son of a high-ranking member of the church. They have to grant me access."

"So you Martin King now? Going to meetings and integrating the church? You gonna come save Shreveport next? Lemme start collecting my bail money while we're all out here volunteering to catch an ass beating," my mom said.

"It's not like that. Sammy just wants to go to church and if they say no, we'll leave."

"But I assure you, ma'am. They will say yes. They have to respect our request."

I'll never forget the way Sammy's face dropped and how he squeezed his eyes so his tears wouldn't come out while we stood outside the church listening to a white man tell us we couldn't walk in for Easter service. Sammy had laid out his suit the night before and written his family back home about how excited he was to go. He wanted to show me how he worshipped. He wanted to worship in America. But a white man was explaining to us that we were children of God who weren't welcome in his white chapel with fancy windows and crucified Jesuses.

Samuel wasn't having it. He just kept quoting Bible verses to the man. Something about showing no partiality. And one about dividing walls of hostility and loving your neighbor as your-self. He was throwing out Marks and Deuteronomies and Johns and he just wouldn't stop. Every time the white man opened his mouth to explain, Sammy had a new verse to finish his sentence.

And he was talking about his dad. "My father is John Sepeku. He is an archdeacon, soon to be a bishop. You are not going to allow the son of a clergyman to worship with you? My father is a member of your clergy and you are telling me we can't honor the same God in the same place?" He was speaking like he was giving a lecture in class, but I could feel the heat of his words.

More white men were gathering by the entrance, and I imagined they were moments away from calling the police. I didn't know what would happen next, but at that moment I was ready to go to jail. It wasn't about the Movement or lunch counters or Doris or meetings. It was about standing at God's doorstep and watching my friend's heart break because he was made to feel lesser than, all because of the color of his skin. I was willing to face any consequence for Sammy's stand.

Finally, Samuel just walked away. The police were coming and he knew he couldn't get arrested and lose his visa. He didn't say anything on the drive back to my mother's house. But she was waiting there for us, and without saying a word she grabbed Sammy and hugged him this deep motherly hug. I just watched.

"Ma'am. If it is okay with you, I'd like to go to my room and pray for a little bit. Thank you for trying to warn me. I should have just listened. You know this place better than I." He walked away with his hand rubbing the back of his head like he was kneading dough, leaving just my mother and me alone in the kitchen.

"Mom, I hated it. I just can't . . ."

"I know. Jesus. I know." She reached out to my hand, nearly touching it, before walking away. "I know."

• • •

I came back to Dillard in a cloud of confusion and doubt. Like I was midair after jumping high off a diving board but unsure whether I wanted to fall into the water or try to grab the board on the way down. I knew that if I needed to, I'd be willing to get arrested. Being in front of the church with Sammy taught me that. But I didn't think I wanted to be put in a position to have to make that decision again. The seal inside of me was cracking from the force of Doris's words and the lava in Sammy's eyes, but I wasn't fully invested in risking my future.

Meanwhile the City of New Orleans was starting to budge on its strict arrest policies. The hit-and-runs CORE was putting on were taking their tolls on local businesses, and the police wanted to work out a deal. A compromise also benefited CORE, which was straining to provide bail and legal fees for all the arrests. The city would allow up to four picketers in front of Woolworth's and McCrory's on Canal Street without any worry of arrest.

"So you're saying we won't get arrested no matter what?"

"Yes, Dave," Rudy assured me. "We have a deal with the city. Come on out and you'll be fine."

So on April 17, 1961, I put on my only suit, gray, with a black tie and white shirt, and those same dusty dress shoes, and stood by the designated entrance of McCrory's and held up a picket sign that said DON'T BUY AT THIS STORE NEGROES ARE NOT WELCOME AT ALL COUNTERS. This was easy enough. I was actually enjoying myself a bit, the feeling of nervousness subsiding with every minute. I felt silly that I was ever scared to do this. I allowed myself to think about what was next. How I'd be able to help CORE through college, then become an engineer and help fund the Movement. How my wife and kids would eat at this very lunch counter one day. How my friends and I would all laugh about how I was so worried. How we'd grow old.

Then Doris, who was on lookout across the street, called me over.

"Dave, them shiftless negroes are doing that thing again." I knew what she meant. Some of the middle- and upper-class Black folks in the city were interrupting our boycotts by sneaking in the back of the stores so that the boycotters wouldn't see them. "I need you to go around back and hold up your sign. Put a lil more shame in their boots."

I did it without thinking. What I didn't realize was that my move to the back of the store was a violation of our agreement with the city.

I was there for about five minutes before I felt a hand on my shoulder.

"Nigger, you're going to jail."

Now, we had been trained in what to do when confronted and arrested by police. I'd taken part in the training, sometimes playing the racist white man or the angry cop, pulling a girl's hair or throwing food on her dress or roughing the guys up and hand-cuffing them. I'd felt prepared. But it's different when the hand is on *your* body. I wasn't *supposed* to be getting arrested. The sureness I felt in front of the church, ready to fight for Sammy, was gone. I panicked. I saw my diploma vanish. My life, over. The cop squeezed my arm and was tightening his grip on my future.

"What the hell?! Officer! No! You're not supposed to arrest me! You're not supposed to arrest me!" I was yelling and squirming so much that another officer grabbed me, my arms locked behind my back, and threw me in a paddy wagon. Jerome, Alice, Doris, and I were arrested that day for disturbing the peace. I, however, had another charge: resisting arrest. Jerome, out of pure solidarity, raised a fuss too and also had a resisting arrest charge. *The one damn time I decide to join in*, I thought to myself.

"Well, Dave. You busted your cherry. You might as well enjoy it now, baby," said Jerome, who was used to the arrests by now.

His laughs ricocheted off the paddy wagon walls we shared on our way to jail.

A fully formed rage grew inside of my rib cage that day. That cop's hand on my arm. Those cuffs. The way they treated us as subhuman. Throwing me into a jail and calling me a nigger. Making Sammy feel like less than what he is. The pictures of Emmett Till they showed us one afternoon at church. The way they stole my grandparents' land. I didn't know what I'd do next, but I knew that I never wanted another Black person to feel like we'd felt—like trash tossed in a dumpster, vulnerable to the whims of a white man, disposable. It was the final bend that snapped my spine. I had to fight.

In jail, Jerome convinced me to join with him and the rest of the group in participating in the Gandhian practice of "jail, no bail." The idea being that posting bail only poured more money into an oppressive system. Bail, we felt, also conceded guilt. So not only was I in jail, but I was in lockstep with Jerome, who was now sending out messages to the *Louisiana Weekly* that we were refusing bail.

"I guess I'm in this thing with you guys for the damn long haul."

Jerome couldn't stop laughing. "Welcome to the fight, my man!"

My actual time in jail didn't last long, however. After a few days, a guard came to my cell.

Dave Dennis? You're free to go. Your bail's been posted.

What? How? Who?

Your daddy, David Dennis Senior, is here to bail you out.

III.

DADS AND FATHERS

I grew up on the Miles Family Plantation in the rural part of Shreveport, Louisiana. It wasn't our plantation in that we didn't own it. But it was ours in that we, and the rest of the Black share-cropping families, cultivated it to make it sustainable and turn that otherwise confounding land into an economic boon that helped transform the city into one of the most popular in the state. My grandfather David Perry, whom I called Dad, was Mr. Miles's number one worker, eventually moving up to overseeing the cotton production of the dozens of other sharecroppers. We lived in a green house overlooking the bayou—Dad, my grand-mother, Bessie, our dog, Mootsie, and me. The land allowed us to grow our own crops—squash, beets, sugarcane, tomatoes, and every type of green imaginable. We had berry bushes along our yard, acting as a barrier to the rest of the sharecroppers' land. Our green house was an electricity-free palace. We had a large wood-burning stove in the middle of the house to keep us warm and three bedrooms surrounding it. It was by far the biggest, most upscale house of all the sharecroppers' homes. Dad loved that

land. He loved growing food and cooking. He loved that house.
He was happy there.

But happiness only lasts so long on a plantation. When I was
about six, white folks were starting to build a subdivision across
the lake from our house and the new neighbors didn't want to
look out their windows at my Black family tending to our land.
Our lives were an eyesore. So we were told we had to move.
That's also when dad learned that he wasn't earning equity in the
land like he thought he was and had no legal right to stay there.
Our fertile land of fig trees, sweet potatoes, and fresh water was
gone. Instead, we ended up on the other side of the plantation in
a one-bedroom tin-roof shack in the middle of dry, dusty land,
where joy dies as quickly as any crop dad tried to grow there. All
the fulfillment he got from living off the work he'd done with is
bare hands had dissipated. He was a different, sullen, angry man
in that shack.

One day, when I was little, I saw him trying to plant and I
wanted to help. I didn't quite understand that he was trying to
find blood in a barren stone.

"Boy, go on back in that house, this land ain't for you to grow
nothing. I gotta do it."

"But Dad, I want to!"

"Get!"

I was a child, angry and confused, so on my way back to the
house, I stomped on some tiny potatoes that were clinging to life
on a small patch of dirt. All I heard behind me was the swooshing
of my dad's overalls and him snatching a switch off a tree. It was
the only time he whooped me. But he wasn't whooping me. He
was swinging down on our trashy house and our muddy yard and
our plates of food that had morphed from feasts to bare survival.
I felt the sting of every blow.

Since I was little, Aunt Kat and Aunt Coot would come by on weekends from spending their weeks anywhere from downtown Shreveport to Los Angeles. They'd show up in shiny purple and yellow dresses that smelled like the gardens on the far side of the plantation. They looked like stars from the movies they'd take me to see when they'd come to pick me up. They'd show me a city life that felt like a new world. Aunt Coot would say the same thing to me every time before we'd go out.

"Remember, now. You make sure you keep calling me Aunt Coot while we're out here, okay?"

I don't remember how many trips we took and how many times she told me to keep calling her Aunt Coot before I realized she was saying this because she didn't want anyone to know she was actually my mother.

I don't know much about my father, Tom Dennis. All I know is that he was a sharecropper and renowned on the plantation for how fast he picked cotton. All Dad would tell me about Tom was that he could pick three hundred pounds of cotton a day, a super-human amount. He met my mother when she was seventeen. They got married and then I was born. Then he left the plantation to become a catfish farmer, traveling across the country before resettling in Texas when I was older. There's a picture of him, my half sister, and me together when I was a kid, but I don't remember taking it.

The only time I remember seeing him was in 1962, a few months after I'd started making headlines as a Freedom Rider. My mother called to say that my father wanted to see me. I had no desire to see him. He'd made his choice. I was busy. He was a distraction.

"You only got one father, Sonny," she said, calling me by my family nickname. Hearing that name at that moment chilled my veins. "And you'll always only have one father."

When I got to my father's house, he greeted me with a big smile, his shoulders hunched over as he waved me in. He was older than the one picture I have of him. Now his dark cheeks were drooping, and his eyes were worn. But he was jumping around with an enthusiasm that betrayed his age.

"Just you wait right there, Sonny. You want some water? Some liquor? You good? It's good to see you, Sonny. You look great, man. J-just you wait right there, boy it's good to see you. You sure you okay?"

I just sat on the couch, watching his mania. We never actually caught up. He never told me about himself. Where he went. Why he left. He never asked me about my childhood. Never asked if I had a family or if I'd left them like he did. He just told me to wait. Then he left.

Some minutes later my father showed back up with about half a dozen men. He gestured for me to follow him and the men to the back of his house. We walked into his bedroom, where he had newspapers and *Ebony* and *Jet* magazine clippings with pictures and stories about me and the Freedom Rides on his wall. It was like a shrine.

Then he pointed at me and finally said what I knew was coming: "See fellas, I told y'all this was my son!"

That was the last time I saw him alive.

• • •

I've had a scar on my lower back since I was a child. I was told that it came from falling off a wagon when I was about seven. I was told that I was goofing around and playing cowboys and Indians when the wagon hit a ditch, knocking me to the ground. I was paralyzed.

That was the story I believed for sixty years.

We had a cousin who cleaned in the Shriners Hospital, so she used her connections to beg the white folks to admit me—the only colored boy to be treated there. The doctor performed some experimental surgery that he'd come up with to fix issues such as mine. The operation was successful, but he died in a car accident weeks later, leaving nurses and doctors to try to figure out what to do with me next, with no blueprint on how to proceed with my recovery.

I stayed in the back of the hospital in what was essentially an inside porch—floor-to-ceiling windows, a bed, and nothing else, isolated from the white patients. Nurses would come in for a few minutes a day, bending and extending my legs and trying to get me to walk. Then, at night, they'd strap me facedown on a gurney to straighten my back. But mostly, they'd just leave me alone.

This was my life for a year. The only person who could come visit me was my grandmother, because she was light skinned enough to pass as white. She was the sole companionship I had during my whole time in the hospital.

One day, she brought me a radio to keep me company. It was the first electrical device I'd ever seen up close. The back of the radio had these tubes that I'd mess with, taking them out and putting them back just to watch them light up. But one night, I accidentally knocked over a glass of water on the radio while I was fiddling with it. Suddenly, sparks started flying everywhere. My hands began trembling in rhythm with the electricity. All I could see was a bright light flashing from my eyes to my ears. My mouth tasted like plastic. Next thing I know, I was running down the Shriners Hospital hallway looking for help.

That's how I found out I could walk again. A few weeks later, I was out of the hospital.

Here's what I learned when my mother died in 2009: I didn't end up in the hospital because of a fall. It was tuberculosis, the disease that had torn through Black communities in the South, especially those that had been cut off from adequate health care through the early parts of the twentieth century. The stigma and contagiousness of the disease had already forced my family to be exiled from St. Maurice, Louisiana, before I was born, having killed my uncle and collapsed Aunt Kat's lung. My family couldn't risk another move, so they kept my diagnosis a secret. The secret lasted most of my life.

When I got out of the hospital, I came back to a world where the family dog, Mootsie, was the only friend who was familiar to me. My family's lives were in upheaval. We'd had to move to the city of Shreveport to find work. Dad had been sucked into what I can only now describe as a depression, still not over being evicted from our green house. He rarely smiled and was short with everyone. He was moving from one factory job to another and watching over people's land, but he hated not feeling as self-sufficient as he used to. My grandmother was struggling in her new role, needing to find work to supplement our income. She cleaned white folks' houses to get by. My mother had moved in with us after marrying a man named Mr. Aaron.

I never called my stepfather my stepfather. I called him Mr. Aaron, even when I liked him and especially when I grew to hate him. Mr. Aaron was a jitney driver in Shreveport, which means he would spend most of his days hanging out at the train stations and bus stations picking up Black folks and driving them around because they weren't allowed in taxis. Jitney drivers knew everything happening in the city, listening to the gossip from whomever they drove, and they knew which Black people were coming in and out of town. That also meant knowing what was going on within the Black community. Mr. Aaron would feed secrets about Black folks to police officers so they could keep tabs on them. He'd also let the police know when and where to go in the Black parts of town to find drugs, gambling, and women. In short, he was a snitch and an Uncle Tom. He loved to yell "Yassuh!" and laughed along when they made fun of his paralyzed right hand, damaged when he tried to stop a man from beating a woman on the street. In the midst of the confrontation, the woman grabbed a knife and stabbed Mr. Aaron through his palm.

Mr. Aaron's endearment to white folks meant he could go places a lot of Black people couldn't. Often he'd take me to rodeos, fairs, concerts, and many other events held in Shreveport. I saw Elvis in a barn one weekend and fell in love with professional wrestling the next. I appreciated Mr. Aaron taking the time to bond with me, but I kept him at a distance, especially after he got Mootsie killed.

One day, my grandmother and my mother were heading to the corner store, and I wanted to walk with them. Mr. Aaron was outside washing his car like he did every day, even when it rained. He washed and scrubbed the outside, swept the inside and picked up every crumb. That car was his livelihood. My mother didn't want to leave Mootsie in the house alone, so she asked Mr. Aaron if the dog could just sit in his car until we got back. Mr. Aaron just grumbled and nodded. I should have known then that he'd let Mootsie out of his precious car while we were gone. On our way back, we found Mootsie on the side of the road, folded over, bloody and alone. She'd tried to follow us to the store. I ran to her, holding her head up. I sobbed, screaming to the navy-blue clouds. I'd lost my best friend.

The next morning, I did what I did every morning before. I set out Mootsie's food and water. The morning after that, I emptied out her full bowls and refilled her containers again. I did this same routine the next day. And the next. Until my grandmother sat down with me, her hand in mine, and talked to me about death.

"Why are you still feeding Mootsie, Sonny? Do you think she's coming back, baby?"

"No, I just want to feel like she's here. I should have stayed with her and not left her with Mr. Aaron. It's my fault!"

She started rubbing my hand. A knowing, tender caress.

"I'm gonna tell you now. You gotta let the dead leave, baby. You let your mind and your body force them in places they don't wanna be, you just gonna keep putting yourself through pain and riling up their spirits where they don't belong. You gotta love the dead more than you want them alive. You not gonna free yourself until you let them go where they gotta go."

I wish I had listened to her.

She put her forehead against mine, and hummed the melody to "When the Saints Go Marching In" until the pain went away.

I don't think I ever forgave Mr. Aaron for Mootsie, but I'd soon have more reason to hate him.

One night, I was startled out of bed by a commotion. I stumbled to the living room to see Mr. Aaron screaming at my mother. His nose was at hers. Spittle bouncing off her face. Then my grandfather walked out of his bedroom to see what was going on. He seemed unfazed by the intensity of the argument, but that was his typical stoicism.

He walked in the living room and calmly asked them to be quiet, before retreating back to his bedroom. The yelling didn't stop. My grandfather came out again, quietly asking them to calm down. They kept arguing. Five minutes later, Dad came out of his bedroom with a shotgun pointed at Mr. Aaron, who ran out of the house like his clothes were on fire.

A few days later, my mother and Mr. Aaron moved into another house in the Hollywood area of Shreveport.

I went with them.

I didn't go because I wanted to be with my mother, whom I'd just started calling "Mom" instead of Aunt Coot. I went because I was a teenager and I felt like I should be there to make sure she was safe in case Mr. Aaron tried to do anything to her. I slept on her couch every night. That's where I was when Mr. Aaron hit my mother for the last time. They were arguing again, and he'd hit her in the mouth with his disabled hand, which, because of the dead nerve endings, made it more solid than it would be otherwise. My mother's blood landed on the kitchen countertop. She was on the floor in tears while Mr. Aaron stood over her. I didn't know what else to do, but I knew I couldn't let him land another blow.

So I grabbed a cast-iron skillet and swung, a firecracker going off in the kitchen as it smacked the back of his skull. Mr. Aaron fell to the floor, bleeding along with my mother. Both of them looked up at me, their eyes wide and hands bloodied over their wounds.

Mr. Aaron never hit my mother again. At least not in front of me.

Dad. Tom. Mr. Aaron. The dads in my life. The men whose presences, absences, and lives shaped mine. Three men, incomplete in their guardianship but creating the totality of my references for manhood as a child.

It wasn't any of those three men however, who came to pick me up from my cell in New Orleans after the picketing.

Your daddy, David Dennis Senior, is here to bail you out.

I walked out of my cell, out through the booking area, still perplexed about who could have bailed me out. "My daddy? We don't have that kind of money."

When I got to the jailhouse lobby, I saw a tall, brown-skinned man with a belly protruding through his suspenders. He looked like a beardless Black Santa Claus. I'd never seen him before. He had a smile on his face. I had a smile on mine too. He could tell by how wide open my eyes were what I was thinking.

"You know I'm not really your daddy, right?"

"Oh, I know," I lied. In the back of my mind, I was hoping this man would tell me he was my actual daddy. My smile disappeared.

"Let's get something to eat."

The man took me to a diner and bought me my first real meal in days: shrimp po-boy, fries, and a soda. I knew scarfing the food down so fast after not eating for days would make me sick, but it didn't matter.

"The guards were right, you know. My name is Reverend Dave Dennis. I wasn't lying or nothing. I'm the president of Local 1419 of the International Longshoremen's Association. You know what that means, kid?"

He knew I didn't.

"That means I represent thousands of colored men and millions of dollars in labor and contracts. I'm one of the most powerful Black men in this country, kid. I saw your name in the paper and, as you know, that's my name. I figure, what are the odds? Someone with my name and he's in jail! Ha! I can't have you sullying my name like that, right? Anyway, I kept up with what you were doing and you sure got a rabbit's foot up yo' backside because now you're out of jail and you got yourself a lifeline. Y'all need some money or something, I got you. That is, if you gonna continue on with this lil crusade you crazy lil college kids got going."

I didn't respond because, well, I didn't know what to say.

"You are gonna keep doing this stuff, right?"

It was the first time I was confronted with the question of what's next. Where does the Movement go and where do I fit in? How far will I take this? I still wanted to finish college, but I could also still feel the cuts the handcuffs had left on my wrists.

Reverend Dennis just laughed.

"Yeah, that's all I needed to see. You're in this thing for good whether you know it or not."

IV.
FREEDOM RIDES

I never knew what Dad and Mr. Hank had been arguing about that day in front of our house in Shreveport, but I do know that in 1950s Louisiana there wasn't much in this world more terrifying than pulling an unconscious white man out of a ditch.

Mr. Hank owned a bit of land on the outskirts of Shreveport in a place called Crooked Bayou and had hired Dad to watch over it, giving my grandfather something to do that reminded him of the time he was happy on the plantation. Something went wrong to the point that the two of them began shouting at each other so loudly that my grandmother and I ran outside to see what was happening. Mr. Hank was always nice to us, but he was a white man. Which means we had to show him the utmost respect at all times. Even Dad had to call him "Mr. Hank" while Mr. Hank just called us by our first names, or more typically "boy" and "girl." The two men were in each other's faces, and then I heard my granddaddy say, "Watch your mouth, don't curse in front of my wife and my grandson. You not gonna disrespect me in front of all I got."

Don't give me that shit.

My granddaddy's fist hitting Mr. Hank's jaw sounded like the cracking of a whip. Then we heard a splash as the white man in his overalls collapsed into a puddle of mud at my granddaddy's feet. My grandmother lost it.

"David! You gotta run! Run!" she screamed at him.

"I'm not going anywhere, Friend." That's what he called her. Friend. Never by her name, unless he was angry or wanted to put his foot down. Then he walked over to Mr. Hank and started lightly slapping his cheeks to wake him up.

Dad grabbed Mr. Hank up from the ditch, cleaned him up with some towels, and dragged him, half limp and woozy, to the front porch. My grandmother and I watched them talk from inside our house. After a few minutes, Dad walked back in the house. "We'll be back. Mr. Hank gonna take me for a ride. We gonna hash this out."

"Are you out of your damn mind? You get in that truck with him and you not making it back! They gonna kill you!"

"I'm taking Mr. Hank and that's the end of it. All right now, Bessie. That's enough."

I thought that'd be the last time I'd see my granddaddy, watching him walk to Mr. Hank's truck.

An unspoken fear held my grandmother and me while we tried to busy ourselves in the house, thinking about all the horrible things that would happen to Dad while pretending we weren't thinking about all the horrible things that were going to happen to Dad.

That night, we heard Mr. Hank's pickup truck speeding up to our house before coming to an abrupt stop. My granddaddy came stumbling out of the truck. He and Mr. Hank were laughing in between slurred, barely coherent sentences. Dad yelled back at Mr. Hank: "Drive home safe, Mr. Hank!"

Mr. Hank yelled back, "Sure thing! Mr. David!"

My grandmother waited until Mr. Hank pulled away before hugging her husband so tightly she almost squeezed the alcohol out of his pores.

"See, nothing a bottle of gin can't solve," my granddaddy laughed.

"What were you thinking?!"

"I wasn't. You just don't curse in front of my family."

My grandmother just nodded and kept hugging him.

A few years earlier my grandmother and I got on a segregated bus in Shreveport: Blacks in the back, whites in the front. When we got on the bus, my grandmother sat in the front. She could. Her hair was red and curly. She could pass for white. I was half a shade darker with kinky hair and could not. So I walked to the back.

She turned around and saw me at the back of the bus and mouthed to me to come sit by her. I pretended I didn't see her. I wasn't going to sit by her in the Whites Only section. They would have killed me *and* her. The whole ride she just stared knives into my chest.

I kept looking out the window.

When we got to our stop, she walked out through her exit door and I walked out through mine.

She slapped me as hard as she could.

"Boy, when I tell you to do something, you do it."

"But that seat's for white folks."

"I don't care. You listen to me. Don't you ever be more scared of them than you are of me, you hear me?!"

Her words left a stone in my stomach that hurt more than her slap. I really thought that if I sat with her I could have been killed. But I always wanted to take that moment back, horrified that I had allowed my grandmother to feel that I let my fear take up the space that belonged to her.

• • •

I returned to Dillard from my first bid in jail proud that I had done a good thing, but wholly unconvinced that I'd continue in this upstart resistance Movement. The cool spring wind coming into New Orleans off Lake Pontchartrain was giving way to wet, humid heat that made us feel like we were trapped inside a soda bottle—suffocating from the lack of air, desperate for any hint of a breeze to come from above. But the only thing looking down was a sun that seemed to hate us. It also felt like the whole city was being shaken up. The explosion was coming.

I thought about Mr. Jack and his crates of soda bottles a lot when I first got back on campus. I thought about the things we spend our whole lives carrying. The responsibilities we hold on to even if they tear at our limbs and rip our fingers from their sockets. I got back to Dillard only wanting to take my exams, but I felt the heaviness of a larger responsibility. Every "Colored Only" sign was a new crate. Every news image of a person who looked like me being beaten at a lunch counter calloused my fingers and put splinters in my palms. These were the clumps of dirt that gathered around the knees of my slacks and reminded me of the things I carried.

Still, I'd served my time. I went to jail. I supported the cause. I just wanted to finish my freshman year, become an electrical engineer, and leave the thankless job to other people who wanted to spend their days loading and unloading the weight of this country's hatred.

• • •

I'd first heard about the idea of the Freedom Rides during our CORE meetings. In 1947, Bayard Rustin and CORE responded to a Supreme Court decision that outlawed segregating interstate travel by conducting bus rides across part of the South. They called it the Journey of Reconciliation. By the time I got to New Orleans, there was a renewed fervor for these demonstrations to take place. This incarnation of the rides would feature a group starting in Washington, D.C., and traveling all the way down to New Orleans. Jerome and Julia Aaron were supposed to join that bus, but their arrests for picketing at McCrory's meant they would have to miss out.

We knew there was the potential for aggression, but we honestly thought the event would go off without too many problems. There was even a banquet planned at Dooky Chase's for May 17 to greet the riders when they made it to town.

That all changed in Alabama.

"Dave, we need you at nine-seventeen right now." Jerome's voice on the phone was unusually shaky and solemn. But clear. "They bombed 'em. The motherfuckers bombed 'em."

When I got to Oretha's house, it wasn't Oretha's house anymore. It wasn't the place for fried chicken, jokes, and planning. It was a MASH unit prepping for patients.

The kitchen was a situation room. Rudy was standing beside a large easel pad listing the names of New Orleans hospitals. Oretha was pacing from the phone to the kitchen. The rest of us were trying to adjust our eyes to the chaos.

"Here's what we know." Oretha held her hand on her stomach as if she were trying to use her palm to calm the anxiety building up inside of her. "The riders were attacked in Anniston and Birmingham. There was a bombing. There are injuries."

In Anniston, a bus full of riders was set upon by a mob, their Greyhound firebombed so that they had to evacuate, but when they got out of the bus, white men with bats and beer bottles were waiting. They whaled on those poor kids while the police looked on. In Birmingham, another mob of hundreds were waiting for another bus of Freedom Riders. The local government and police had agreed to let the mob do what they wanted for ten minutes before they'd intervene. The mob used that time to rain hell on as many riders as they could. Pipes. Knives. One man had a pitchfork.

"Are they . . ." someone in the room asked.

"Alive. They're all alive." Oretha said it as if she needed to hear it for herself one more time. "But there's a problem. There are serious injuries and none of the hospitals there are willing to treat any of them. We're the hub. So we have to handle it."

Rudy, the strategist, took over. He explained that the national CORE office would buy plane tickets to get the riders to New Orleans so they could get treated. It would be hard to find proper medical care for them in the city, as any doctors willing to help would surely find themselves ostracized, terrorized, and their lives threatened.

"We have to see if any doctors will take them, then we have to see where they can stay the night," Rudy explained. His plan was to see if Xavier University, a Black Catholic HBCU in the city, would be able to use any space it had to house the Riders until the next day. "Dave is coming with me."

I locked eyes with Rudy, walking toward me, and saw his mouth moving, but I didn't hear what he was saying. It was like I was on the other side of a fogged window trying to decipher what was happening. It was all going so fast. What the hell is all of this?

"Dave, Dave . . . Let's get going."

I didn't move. I felt body-cast stiff, unable to make my feet follow Rudy.

"Dave." He put his hand on my chest, snapping me out of it.

"Bombed?" It was all I could say, my teeth feeling heavy like grand pianos in my mouth.

"Yes, David, they use fucking firebombs. Let's go."

• • •

Rudy and I would spend the rest of the night driving around New Orleans, begging doctors and hospitals to take the injured riders from Alabama. One after another turned us away. Doctors and nurses avoiding eye contact with us as they told us they couldn't close the wounds on men and women who were fighting for equality. Hospital administrators looked at the ground and told us they didn't have enough staff to stitch up heroes.

We were saved by Flint-Goodridge Hospital, which was attached to Dillard and housed most of the city's Black physicians. They agreed to take in the riders and treat their wounds, even though nobody was sure about the extent of their injuries. Rudy somehow arranged for riders to be housed in empty dorm rooms at Xavier, informing the school's Dean of Men, Norman Francis, only after the rooms were occupied. Francis, to his credit, agreed to let the riders stay. We thought we'd done the impossible and had the situation in hand thanks to Rudy's planning. But the night was still young.

When we got back to Oretha's house, there were sleeping bags on the floor with barely enough space to walk without stepping on a pillow or blanket.

"You can put the sleeping bags up, Oretha. We got places for the riders to sleep," Rudy said loud enough for everyone in the house to hear him. "Me and Dave handled it." That was a lie. I just rode along, providing Rudy company while he did all the strategizing. In fact, I'm not sure he was paying any attention to me on the road, he was so deep in his own machinations.

"Those aren't for the riders, Rudy. They're for us. We got a long night ahead of us."

While we were out, the injured riders were supposed to have been on a plane to New Orleans, but their flight got canceled. Someone had called the airport and threatened to bomb the plane if it was allowed to take off. There goes that word again. *Bomb.*

I would become acquainted with bombs plenty of times over the next few years, to the point that they just became part of the hazard of being Black in the South. Bombs were as common as batons and police dogs.

Bombs didn't just take lives, but their use as a tactic of intimidation and death in the 1960s made all of it feel more like war than activism. When I went to McCrory's, I expected a slap on the wrist and an angry phone call from my mother. But bombs? For riding buses? On American soil. And a bunch of twentysomethings had to figure out how to survive, with rolled-up sleeping bags and the smell of leftover red beans and rice in the air while trying to sneak in some studying for final exams.

The bomb scare was nothing more than an empty threat with no other goal but to disrupt, which is what it did. The wounded riders had to be flown in later that night. I was groggy and in a haze, sleepwalking. I tried to envision what it must have been like to walk out of a burning bus onto a muddy field of boots, baseball bats, and empty beer bottles. I wondered how sure they were they were going to die. I wondered who they prayed to. I wondered if they felt like fools dying over buses. I wondered if they felt dingy nails and aluminum tearing at their skin and welting their heads and wished they were at home, oppressed but alive. I wondered if they wished they had guns of their own to kill those white people for what they were doing.

I tried to imagine it all. But it didn't seem real until I saw those riders get off the plane. Walking, limping, nearly broken. A man with bandages all over his face, arms, and legs; a woman barely able to straighten her back, her shoe creating a rift in the dirt as she dragged it.

"Dave . . . they can't . . . this is . . . ," Jerome tried to whisper but he couldn't find the words.

"I know." I didn't know what I knew. But I knew.

My eyes were fixed on James Peck, a white member of CORE from New York who was part of the original rides in the 1940s. He got the worst of the beating. He arrived in New Orleans with a bandage on his head, dried blood caked up above his eye. He reached his hand up to his forehead to check whether he was bleeding through, his hand shaking as he did it. He didn't look relieved. He didn't look like he felt happy to be alive. He was just there.

I wanted to ask them how they felt, but that would have been a worthless question. "Not dead," they'd probably say. I'd always thought that being close to death would make me cherish my life more. Their eyes told me a different reality. I didn't yet understand what it feels like to be living when you know you should be dead.

We'd gotten word that Martin Luther King and a group of activists had arrived in Montgomery, Alabama, to decide whether they would continue the rides. The violence shook everyone, and there was a need to weigh the potential victory of a completed ride against any possible loss of life. The students—namely a Student Nonviolent Coordination Committee (SNCC) group from Nashville and our CORE group from New Orleans—were determined to continue the rides and had decided to travel to Montgomery to convince King and the rest to let us carry on.

The New Orleans group would consist of Jerome, Julia, Oretha, and Doris. And whoever else would volunteer.

As determined as they were to get on those rides, I was doubly fixated on staying at home.

"Jerome . . . I have to go to class," I told him as I was leaving 917. We'd been up all night making sure the Riders had places to stay and were situated, and I was dead tired but still trying to make sure I finished my freshman year without this damn Movement ruining my grades.

I could feel the disdain emanating from his pores. Everyone at CORE always respected my desire to finish school and stay out of trouble. They always knew I'd go only so far. Jerome, though, was the one who was always nudging me to become more committed. Each time I mentioned school, it felt like I was betraying him and the time we spent together in that jail cell.

"D-dave . . . your cherry, bro. It's busted. You got in jail once, you're in now, man." He saw my unabashed refusal to budge, but he also just really wanted me to go with him.

"Okay, that's fine. Go to your classes. But come back afterward. We're having a get-together back here tonight to see us off to Montgomery."

Jerome turned away before I could agree to do what he said. He tried to hide it, but I saw, even in a room barely lit by the morning sun traipsing through partially opened blinds, that he was shaking his head.

• • •

The mood had shifted by the time I got back to 917 that night.

"Look who it is." Doris shot me a grin that was as intoxicating as it was mischievous. I still had our date in the back of my mind. "My daddy wanted to see us off properly, so he brought something. And it happens to be your favorite."

She reached behind her kitchen counter, grabbed a brown paper bag, and pulled out a bottle of Johnnie Walker Red, my signature drink. "If you're going to see us off to Montgomery, you're going to see us off in style, baby."

We spent the next few hours eating po-boys from Dooky's and drinking. Well, I was doing most of the drinking. As the night went on, we cracked jokes and sang Freedom Songs. Namely "We Shall Overcome" and my favorite, "When the Saints Go Marching In." There was something about that song. It was celebratory and defiant, somber and happy. And it reminded me that I was surrounded by the bravest people I knew. Soon I found myself singing as loudly as anyone else.

"Dave, you singing like you coming with us," Oretha teased me.

I nodded.

"Wait, you coming?"

I didn't say anything. They kept singing. I kept drinking. I drank until the room spun. I drank until I could barely hold my glass. I drank until I drowned my heart, which was beating somewhere near my tonsils.

Apparently, at some point that night, I pounded my fist on the counter and yelled, "Dammit, I'm coming!" A few hours later, we left 917, packed our bags, and got on a train. But I don't remember any of that. The liquor had taken over. The next thing I actually remember is coming to on a train and seeing colossal trees speeding by me so fast they looked like one continuous blur. They were so peaceful, strong enough to hold my weight if I wanted to cower in the branches away from the world around me. I was leaning toward them when my forehead crashed against the reinforced window between me and Mother Nature. As I rubbed my forehead, I heard the loud squeal of a train hitting the brakes.

I looked to my right. Jerome was smiling.

"Hey, man. We're here. Thanks again for you volunteering. I believed in you, brotha."

"Volunteer? For what? What the hell is going on, Jerome?"

"Come on, we gotta hurry."

I took one step off the train and saw six white boys in suits with what seemed to be sticks in their hand and guns on their sides.

"Fuck, Jerome, what the fuck?"

I turned around and ran back on the train and jumped into my seat. "What the fuck?!"

Jerome was right behind me. "Dave, what are you doing?!"

"Who are those people? Where are we? Take me back to New Orleans! The hell, man?"

"Calm your nerves, Dave. They're here for us."

"I know they're here for us!"

"No, not for us. *For* us. It's JFK. He sent federal marshals to meet us. We're good." He put his hand on my chest. "Calm down, man. We're good. We're in Montgomery, Alabama."

The whole world had changed while I was passed out.

The night before I got to Montgomery, King delivered a speech in support of the Riders at Ralph David Abernathy's First Baptist Church. He almost didn't survive the night. Another mob, including several Klansmen, surrounded the church and threatened to beat or kill anyone who left. King and the members of the congregation were held under siege in the church until dawn the next morning, when federal marshals and the Alabama National Guard finally escorted them out after Governor John Patterson placed the city under martial law.

President Kennedy had gotten word of the situation and the potential for a massacre in Alabama, so he tried to ensure that everyone involved with the rides could get to the city as safely as possible. Oretha had informed Robert Kennedy, to his disbelief, that five New Orleans CORE members were en route to Montgomery.

The guards were there, waiting to protect us.

"Dave, look. We're going to get off this train. We're going to let these white boys escort us to convince King and them to let us get on those buses. And when they tell us yes, and we take that ride, then you can be scared. But right now, I need you to get the hell up so we can go."

It probably would be a better story to say that my decision to go to Montgomery was made in a moment of bravery. That I stood firm with my brothers and sisters and would not leave their sides. The story I remember, though, is Jerome shoveling alcohol down my throat until I was drunk enough to go along with him. Jerome, to this day, swears that I have the wrong version of the story. That I found some semblance of fortitude in my spine and I stood up in Oretha's house declaring that I wouldn't let anyone get on the buses without me beside them. "Don't no liquor make you do nothing you weren't gonna do no way," he'll say.

When I accuse him of getting me drunk enough to change my life, we laugh about it, like we're still in our twenties on another wild-goose chase for freedom. I don't think about Jerome as someone who dragged me to trauma. He was a friend who was probably afraid deep down too. We had been in jail together at a time we didn't know when we'd get out. We shared meals, stories, and looked at each other as the only anchors to the outside world. If we were going to be riding silver coffins across the Deep South, I can't be furious at him for wanting company.

V.

GOD AND FEAR

Dr. Richard Harris was a renowned Black pharmacist in Montgomery. Like many prominent Black people in the medical field, he used his wealth and resources to help out the Movement. In this instance, Harris offered his home for our big meeting. A meeting I was never supposed to be part of.

When I walked into Dr. Harris's living room—now the headquarters for our future—I saw heroes I had no business being around. There was John Lewis, who was my age, but already an understated giant. He projected an air of class and steadfastness. He was just so sure of everything he said and walked with a confidence that made him seem as much of a leader as King himself. There was Andrew Young, C. T. Vivian, Wyatt Tee Walker, and so many other people who felt larger than life.

And then there was King. Dr. Martin Luther King Jr. To me, he was royalty. He dressed like us, sure, but being around him felt like being around a music star and the president himself. Even in Dr. Harris's house, speaking in hushed tones given the seriousness of the meeting, his voice still captivated the room. My eyes just gravitated toward him even when he didn't speak. He was MLK. A god. I'd realize later that I only saw him as such because I wasn't in the work. I didn't see him as a man because I didn't realize that the folks putting their lives on the line were just like the rest of us.

The tension in the room was suffocating; we felt it as soon as we walked in to join a meeting already in progress. James Farmer, the director of CORE and one of the principal organizers of the rides, was quite frankly making an ass of himself. Farmer had already lost many of the people in the room by being so adamant about calling the rides off after the Anniston attacks. Now, sensing the fervor to continue, his tone had changed from hesitation to making sure CORE was front and center in receiving recognition. He made sure to call the rides "CORE rides" and ensure that CORE activists would be in front of as many cameras as possible.

"Now, Mr. Farmer, let's not get ahead of ourselves." King, ever the diplomat, knew how to diffuse the tension aimed at James while redirecting the conversation. "We need to first make sure that this demonstration is taking place. I cannot in good conscience ask any of you to take part in these rides. This is dangerous. If you do this, the many days ahead that you have to continue to fight may not be as plentiful as you thought before this day began."

Diane Nash and John Lewis had taken the lead in speaking on behalf of the students. I didn't have much to say—I was in over my head amid these Civil Rights icons and I was still trying to figure out how the hell I ended up in Montgomery in the first place. I just wanted to play the shadows and get on the first train back to New Orleans without anyone noticing. If they needed me to make calls or help organize, I'd be happy to do so. But I knew I wasn't getting on that damn bus. No one in my family even knew where I was.

Julia Aaron was one of the more honest and fearless CORE members we had in New Orleans, and she took that fearlessness to Montgomery: "So, Dr. King, how are you going to tell us about the dangers of these rides if you're not even willing to go?"

King looked around the room. He knew that this was the moment he could lose the youth support. But deciding how to respond was not an easy matter.

"As you know, Dr. King has a warrant from a bogus charge in Chicago," someone said. "He's under probation and if he gets arrested again that's years in jail. We . . . we can't afford that."

Julia shot back: "Hell, I'm out on bail in New Orleans as we speak."

Another person: "I'm on probation too, he ain't special. Hell, most of us on probation or got warrants." The unrest was building.

The question wasn't whether or not King was chickening out on us. We knew better. He'd put his life on the line far too many times for us to think he was suddenly afraid. But his objection signaled something far worse than fear: superiority. I saw the room turning against him, despite the fact that he was making a salient point about the hard truths of the Movement. King couldn't afford to be in jail for years. He was the leader and losing him could derail everything everyone had worked so hard for. But it was impossible for him to make that point without making the rest of us in the room seem sacrificial. The master orator would misspeak and earn the resentment of some of us forever:

"Look, if you want me to go I'll go, but I think I should decide when I face my Golgotha." Golgotha is where Jesus was crucified, and for many in the room, Dr. Martin Luther King Jr. had just compared himself to Jesus. So what were we? His disciples? His followers? Mere mortals trying to save Black folks at the feet of the messiah?

"Ohhhh, de Lawd has spoken," one student yelled, a nick-name that King never lived down in some circles.

This man who, minutes before, seemed like an infallible hero to me was being chopped down inch by inch. I don't know what came over me, but I decided to speak.

"Everyone, I know this isn't a popular opinion, but maybe he's right. Maybe he is too important to go to jail. Maybe . . ." I looked at Jerome, his face buried in his hands. Doris looked like her soul was fleeing her body from embarrassment. My sentence trailed off and a silence overcame the room that seemed to last a decade. I should have kept my mouth shut. I was an island—the young activists looked at me as though I'd turned on them and the older ones had no clue who the hell I was.

"Okay, so, Martin isn't going, fine," said James Farmer. "But these rides are happening. Show of hands: who's going on those buses?"

As soon as he spoke, I heard a voice from somewhere in the room say, "Okay, now, make your choice, because there's not enough space in this room for both God and fear."

God and fear.

For some reason that one sentence made me drop every bur-densome fear that had held me back. The strain on my shoulders from holding on to the dream of finishing school instead of fight-ing for freedom went away. I didn't think about coming home for the summer and hugging my mother. I didn't think about another night in jail. I didn't think about going back home and holding my grandmother in my arms. I didn't think about anything beyond the next few hours.

I no longer was carrying the terror of risking my life for this Movement. I loosened my grip on survival, and the weight of my fear falling from my shoulders cracked the ground below me, breaking through it and sending me crashing into a reservoir of disregard I didn't know existed before. I was free. And in that moment I became someone willing to die.

I grew up playing with army figures and was fascinated by the soldiers who had bayonets on the front of their guns. I always wondered what compelled someone to be first in line for war, knowing that there was a good chance they'd die as soon as the fighting started. What compelled someone to run headfirst to death? Pride? Legacy? Ignorance? I never understood the inclination.

But all of that changed after hearing about "God and fear." I understood that all of us in the Movement were much more like those soldiers on the front line than I had wanted to admit, and more than this country has wanted to admit in the years since. To decide to face the Klan in the Delta; the police in Jackson; the bombers in Montgomery; the governors in Georgia; the FBI in Washington; the white men who wanted to make themselves feel superior by seeing our bodies swinging from oak branches; the mothers who packed up cold cuts and gathered their children to watch lynchings at the park, we had to understand that dying was as sure as the first bead of sweat on a Mississippi afternoon. And yet we march toward it.

I knew at that moment that I was willing to welcome death with the same passion that I desired freedom. That the end of a noose could come before the end of segregation. That a gun pressed against my temple would be as likely as a Mississippi sharecropper casting a ballot.

Just as I knew Dr. King's role would be to lead us and thus he needed to be protected from assassination and jail, I knew that my role in the Movement would be that of the sacrificed. That the reluctant changemaker is the perpetuator of stasis. I needed to commit fully or not at all and not at all was never an option. I had to be the foot soldier charging ahead for what could be the last few dozen steps I'd ever take. I still don't know what makes those soldiers charge with their bayonets, but I know why I charged. I charged so that the people behind me, those that would follow, could have clearer paths to their freedoms.

I see the Black boys and girls in places like Ferguson or Minneapolis or Atlanta, chased away by smoke bombs and armored police cars, beaten and terrorized. Have they come to terms with their mortality? Did they think their last days would come when they decided to take to those all-too-American streets? Did the sting of the tear gas reveal the specter of death? When I look at their eyes, I see that some of those children have made the same decisions I did. At some point they decided that they'd have to sacrifice all they've ever been to change this country. Still. The world I had hoped to create was one in which these young men and women would be able to both carry morsels of innocence with them and hold the ability to experience fear. Because to have that fear means that you are still carrying the desperate desire to live.

I lost that desire that night in Montgomery. I knew that in order for me to commit I'd have to leave my dreams of living behind. I rejected fear and chose God. And I was sure I'd see Him in a matter of twenty-four hours.

I raised my hand. I was going to join the Freedom Rides.

Neither Jerome nor Doris ever really expected me to volunteer for the rides. They'd always hoped I would, though deep down I think they always felt like their egging me on was ultimately fruitless. But he looked scared for me as he saw my arm shoot up.

"Dave, you don't understand. We're going to die tomorrow."

I looked at him and smiled.

"What the hell, right?"

• • •

There was still the matter of James Farmer. He was already being criticized for missing the first rides that got attacked in Alabama, though he had a legitimate reason: his father passed away right before he was supposed to join. But the rumors that he'd chickened out had outpaced the truth. Now, instead of raising his hand, he said that he needed to do some other work and help to manage the rides. In fact, later he'd say that he was "scared shitless" of going. We all could smell the fear on him, because someone else's musk is always easier to detect when your own goes away. I'd felt differently about Farmer than I did about King. Farmer wasn't as important as King, and if he was going to champion the CORE rides then he couldn't stay behind and enjoy the ensuing fame as he dropped roses on our graves.

We all felt that way, but it was Doris who would speak up later that night, cornering James away from the group but loud enough for us to hear.

"That's bullshit, James! What kind of paperwork you got that you can't do on a bus? Paper travels, James. And if we all die then paperwork is the least of your problems!"

"I need to make sure everything goes smoo—"

"It's not going to go smoothly. Smooth is in New York. You in Alabama. Ain't nothing smooth on these buses. Either you get your ass on that bus or you can forget trying to lead us again."

I woke up the next morning with a happiness that caught me by surprise. "Hey, let's go get this dying over with, okay?" I joked with Jerome on my way to the bus. By the next morning, President Kennedy had decided that we'd have the National Guard provide security by riding on the buses with us to Jackson, where we'd be safely arrested by local authorities and put in jail for the crime of desegregating buses. "Oh, good, they're gonna have armed white men on the bus with us the whole time. Don't you feel safe, Jerome?"

He and Doris couldn't believe the person they were talking to. "Dave? You good?"

"Yeah, I didn't want to take my bio exam anyway."

The legend that students were writing their last will and testaments that night may be true, but I certainly wasn't one of them. I did not have anything but love to will to anyone, and you did not need any notarized documents for that. I didn't think about what I was leaving behind. Or where I was going.

I don't know who made the decision to put me on the first bus, and at the time I didn't care. Dr. King greeted all of us at the door of the buses, stopping short of apologizing for not coming with us. I could tell he wanted to do something, and he was still smarting from the lashings he had taken during the meeting. But I always respected him for standing there, looking us all in the eye as we got on.

Doris ended up on the bus behind me. As she was pulling off, she saw Jim Farmer standing on the sidewalk bidding riders farewell also.

"Jim, come on! You need to be on this bus!"

To our amazement, he relented and joined.

• • •

I wish I could tell you about what it was like to be on that first Freedom Ride bus, but I simply don't remember much of it. I think I just didn't bother to remember anything because, really, what is the point of remembering if you're certain you won't be alive to relive those memories?

But some of the memories come back when I force them to the front of my mind.

I remember that the National Guard cleared the roads, but there were protesters on the highway medians the whole way to Jackson.

Angry white men and women—and their children—with picket signs, shotguns, and nooses, lined the roads, all yelling at us as if we could hear what they were saying from a speeding bus with closed windows. At any moment, one of them could have tossed a bomb at us, and what were the guards and their big guns on our bus going to do then?

I remember one of the guards was standing over me, leaning to his side, with his bayonet mere inches from my face.

"Sir, you gonna move that thing?"

"Excuse me?"

"That pointy thing at the end of your gun. You gonna poke my eye out, sir."

"You think I'm that careless?"

"No, suh." I loved adding that whenever I wanted to get under a white man's skin. "It's just that one false move and you're going to stab me. You get reprimanded for stabbing negroes on their way to jail?"

"Fine." He moved his bayonet a few inches upward, away from my face but close enough that I could hear the blade clicking against the barrel of the gun, reminding me that the line between protection and aggression was as thin as the point of his weapon. At that moment, the bus suddenly hit the brake and my face shot forward. If the blade had been where the guard originally had it, he would have stuck me directly in my left eye.

I looked up at him and laughed. "See?"

I remember singing and joking the whole ride to Jackson. I remember someone had to pee really badly. I remember fleeting moments where I thought I'd make it to Jackson safely then feeling foolish for allowing myself to hope.

Then. Suddenly. Jackson. My first time in Mississippi.

We were directed off the bus through the back of the station directly into a paddy wagon that was waiting to take us to jail, all part of the deal Kennedy made with the Mississippi government that allowed him to provide us with escorts. I made the walk with a smile on my face. Jail didn't scare me anymore. In essence, we were under arrest as soon as we left Alabama. We went calmly, partly because we had been briefed that this would be the procedure if we made it to Jackson alive.

All of us marched in a single file as if we were on a school field trip. Except for one woman who started screaming. The police and a couple of the riders grabbed her to try to calm her down, but she wouldn't stop screaming.

"No! No! I'm not supposed to go to jail! I'm not supposed to be here!"

She twisted her wrists and balled her fists and dug her feet in the ground to try to get away. She gritted her teeth and struggled against everyone trying to subdue her.

"I was supposed to die! I was supposed to die! I'm supposed to be dead! Why didn't I die?!"

I'm supposed to die!

I'm supposed to be dead!

LETTER 1

Dad,

I've been thinking a lot about the way your voice sounded that one night in 2016 when I was driving four hours up 85 from Atlanta to Charlotte. I don't know if I expected you to sound proud or happy. Instead you sounded nervous and made a joke about having bail money on standby for me. I remember the way your voice trailed off, sounding like disappointment. Were you disappointed that I was going to continue a cycle of putting myself in danger that you wanted ended? Or were you just disappointed that I even had to make a choice to begin with. Maybe you were just disappointed in America.

Two days earlier, Charlotte police officer Brentley Vinson shot Keith Lamont Scott in the back, killing him. As soon the news spread across the city, Black folks gathered around the crime scene and started protesting. I knew that I had to join them.

I lived close to Charlotte for four years in college at nearby Davidson, so I felt a responsibility to this place. A place where I was pulled over by cops, denied entry into clubs because of "attire" and my braids. Charlotte needed a reckoning and I had to be there to tell the story of that reckoning.

"Please, just be careful," you said, sounding like your heart was breaking.

• • •

"He was dead! He was dead! He was dead!"

My friend from Davidson, Braxton Winston, had been at the center of the Charlotte protests. He'd marched to the scene of the killing hours after Keith was shot and stood between police and protesters. An image of Braxton—his shirtless back to the camera, his locs tied in a bun with a couple of strands hanging down to his shoulder blades, his fist defiantly in the air as he stared down police in riot gear with nightsticks in their hands—had become an iconic symbol of defiance overnight. When I got to Charlotte, I immediately attached myself to Braxton to follow him through the closed-off streets, smattering of protesters, and armed police guarding businesses and clubs they felt were less expendable than Black humans. Braxton's strong New York accent delivered in a smirk made him as disarming as any de-escalation tactic. He'd been in the streets for two days and had gotten to know every cop, city councilman, and activist on a first-name basis. His conviviality betrayed the pain he was feeling over what had happened the second night of protests, before I got to town.

A group of marchers had gathered in front of a hotel, where police had barricaded themselves. Police responded by firing tear gas into the crowd. One of the protesters, Justin Carr, fell, bleeding from his head. Braxton and others grabbed him as he collapsed. They tried to put gauze on his head and hold his hand and tell him to breathe. They told him he'd be okay as his eyes rolled back in his head. Justin Carr died that night.

Police charged a Black man, Rayquan Borum, in the killing, saying he fired a shot into the crowd. Forensic scientists and coroners said a gunshot killed Carr. At least ten people I talked to the night after said it was one of the police's rubber bullets that hit him in his temple at close range. A bullet from a gun was never found at the scene.

I saw Justin's dried, faded blood on the pavement right at the edge of my feet. In this dull maroon Rorschach I saw America. Below me was all that was left of someone who was killed for protesting. In front of me was a group of marchers forcing back the agony of the murder they witnessed. Still. I stood at the fulcrum of our fight. The blood of our yesterday, the persistence of now, and the fight for tomorrow.

I spent much of the summer of 2020 thinking about that moment in Charlotte. I thought about Justin Carr's blood when I watched thousands take to the streets of Minneapolis for George Floyd and Kentucky for Breonna Taylor and I thought about Justin Carr when I drove through the Satilla Shores neighborhood where Ahmaud Arbery took his last breaths as Spanish moss fell by his side. I thought about Justin Carr as Stacey Abrams and LaTosha Brown carried on the legacy of the Movement's push for Black voting rights, redefining what's possible for Black voters in the South. I thought about Justin Carr because all these steps to freedom came in the midst of a police war on Black people, a president who wanted as many of us eradicated as possible, and a pandemic that threatened to choke our airways as we gathered. I thought about Justin Carr in these moments because standing in Charlotte I knew that this country will never be able to wash away the bloodstains that paint this land or stop our footsteps from stomping past monuments of what hatred has wrought.

I also know that the organizing that removed Donald Trump from office at the end of 2020 has revealed the depth of the American commitment to white supremacy. The Movement ended Trump's presidency and made way for what was supposedly the most progressive government in American history and yet that government still refused to convict the former president for a race riot insurrection that killed people at the U.S. Capitol. That same government couldn't stop a resurgence in Jim Crow laws that led to some of the most oppressive antivoting legislation we've seen since the days of the Mississippi Freedom Democratic Party. The country is giving more money to police, and Black people are still being killed by those police, poverty, and mass incarceration. In the very midst of what is supposed to be the American Dream is the persistence of anti-Blackness, despite what we are told are victories. The fight has, at times, felt unending and the obstacles have felt insurmountable.

It's in these moments when resolve threatens to give way to despair that I lean on what you've taught me about getting free. About what it takes for us to overcome the type of oppression that's baked into the very fabric of Americana. About how Movement work is coalition work where each individual contributor must be met where they are without shame or guilt over how much or little they suffer, sacrifice, or risk for freedom. That this work takes everyone doing what they can for the shared goal of liberation. That the word "activist" should be inclusive, not one used to parse out different hierarchies of freedom fighting where the pain we've endured becomes our work's currency. These are lessons I forget far too often.

Sometimes we curse ourselves by measuring our worth in the fight by how much trauma we endure. I do this too, Dad, as you know. I hear people call me an activist and the word scalds me in a way that feels cold until the burning starts. I recoil and cower within my own insecurities. The word feels like sacrilege because I so often compare my pain to yours. *You're* the activist—the person who had to deliver eulogies for his friends and who was handcuffed and jailed and beaten and scarred and has nightmares and funerals and demons and our family.

After all, just a couple of years before I went to Charlotte, I'd wrecked myself with guilt over my original sin: I didn't go to

Ferguson when Mike Brown was killed. I watched my friends pour milk on their eyes to wash out tear gas and scuff their knees when cops tossed them on the pavement. I sat at home, writing, trying to spread the word of what was being relayed to me, but I wasn't there. I was too scared. Not of police or jail. I was scared of putting your grandchildren through what I went through myself: a father who dove into the Movement with no regard for whom he leaves behind. I didn't want my family to feel sacrificial. I didn't want them to wonder when I would be coming home. I didn't want my trail to freedom paved with promises I'd forgone. I didn't think it was possible to be part of a Movement and be the parent that my children deserved. Just as you couldn't separate a commitment to the Movement from a willingness to die, I can't separate a commitment to the Movement from a willingness to sacrifice my family. Maybe that's why the word "activism" burns like it does. Because of what that word meant to your son, and could mean for my children.

But watching my friends feel the physical wrath of hatred felt like a different kind of torture, a self-diagnosed cowardice.

You've done this, too. You've told me how you never considered yourself a part of the Movement until you decided you were ready to die on the Freedom Rides. But prior to that you had been holding trainings, participating in meetings, and helping strategize. You would have made an invaluable contribution even if you'd just kept doing that and never went to jail and just went about your life as an engineering student. Yet you call the moment you were willing to die the start of your activism. "That's just when I knew there was no turning back," you'll say. "That's when it started for me."

But sometimes it feels like the fact that you survived makes you want to diminish your significant role. And that guts me. I want you to be proud of your efforts to organize behind the scenes during Freedom Summer. I want you to feel the rumblings below your feet that started when you shook up Shreveport. I had to hear these stories from your friends and sift through them in documents you've long let slip through your fingers. I want your grandchildren to hear your good stories directly from you. Because you did a good thing. You punish yourself for what you did just as I punish myself for what I didn't do. Being beaten and jailed and killed isn't part of activist work. It's part of white supremacy reacting to activism. And these reactions are for white folks to hold, not us. We deserve better.

Your son

VI.
SHREVEPORT

I want to tell you some more about Shreveport, my hometown.

There were 3,494 homicides in Louisiana in the ten years following the Civil War—566 of those occurring in Shreveport's Caddo Parish. Seventy-one percent of those Caddo Parish victims were Black people killed by white people. Between 1877 and 1950, Caddo Parish had 48 lynchings, the third most in the nation at the time. As a result, Caddo Parish earned the name "Bloody Caddo."

Shreveport was the Louisiana state capital during the Civil War after Baton Rouge was occupied by Northern forces. It was also the last city to surrender to the Union. The former agricultural town was known as the gateway to the West, bordered by Texas, Arkansas, and the Red River. In the heart of Shreveport's historical center is the city's courthouse, which sits on 2.5 acres of land, including the Forty-Six Confederate Veterans Reunion Monument on the building's east side, memorializing Confederate soldiers killed during the Civil War. In order to walk into the courthouse, you have to pass by a twenty-foot-tall southern live oak tree where the whites in Shreveport did some unknown number of their hangings.

I spent most of the summer of 1961 walking by that tree on my way to the courthouse, wondering when it'd be my body swaying under constellations of the Louisiana night.

• • •

When I left Shreveport on my way to Dillard, I was destined to become the first college graduate in my family. Less than a year later, I got called into the president's office, where I was told it would be best if I took a leave from the school. They told me it was because my time in jail in Jackson left me too far behind in my work to catch up for the semester. In truth, some schools didn't want the stench of harboring a Freedom Rider—painted as public enemies in America—on campus. Suddenly, I had no long-term prospects for what my life would look like. It didn't matter. I was still riding the adrenaline rush of an interstate trip that should have killed me. I had abandoned the idea of planning for a future because that felt like setting myself up for disappointment.

By the time I got to my mother's doorstep, I'd already made up my mind to start a CORE chapter in Shreveport. Doing that would take all my energy and guarantee that I'd never be able to get a job in the city. That didn't concern me. Freedom would be my career. The Movement had taken up residence in my marrow and refused to leave, and I was going to let it course through my being for as long as my body was above ground.

I'd spent my entire Movement life—a whole eight months or so by this point—in the big city of New Orleans, which presented its own violence. But I'd learn that smaller towns are where white terrorists waged their most vicious wars on Black residents. The terror in these towns benefited from their being too small for the national media to report on and too inconsequential for federal investigations. National Civil Rights organizations, already spread thin by a burgeoning Movement, simply didn't have the resources to deploy workers in large number to places like Shreveport. Or the Delta. Or Bogalusa. Or Anniston. CORE had already let me know that they did not have the money to support a Shreveport chapter like they did in New Orleans. If I wanted to start a CORE chapter in Bloody Caddo, I would have to find a way to do it locally.

The police and Klan in Shreveport were differentiated by name alone. Black people were lynched with no recourse. White terror uprooted Black communities and destroyed families. Corpses were sometimes left hanging out in public as a monument to untouchable white vigilantism. Terror reigned and the Black residents had to fend for themselves.

I'd spend the next few years in the Movement traveling to new cities and learning how to create noise and disrupt the white establishments in those communities. Shreveport was where I learned that the most important part of the work was to truly understand the communities in which I'd be working. I had to get to know the local leaders putting their lives in danger to protect as many people as they could, fighters who would never get statues erected in their honor or mentions in history books. I had to become their extended family and figure out how I could help local leadership. The worst thing I could do was try to bulldoze the Movement structures already in place locally. I had to work symbiotically with the people on the ground, who were as unheralded as they were unaided.

The groundwork being done by local Black businesspeople, sharecroppers, domestic workers, jitney drivers, sex workers, farmers, barbers, beauticians, mothers and fathers, whose daily tasks placed them alongside the white people who could readily identify and kill them at will, is a hugely significant part of the Movement that has not been sufficiently recognized. These people put their lives on the line. Their houses were being burned down. Their churches were being bombed. Their businesses being destroyed. Their loved ones disappearing in the middle of the night. These heroes didn't have national organizational emergency funds to bail them out of jail. They didn't have savings to replace their lost wages when they were fired from their jobs for demonstrating. They didn't have check-ins to make sure they made it home safely every night. Some did not have electricity, telephones, running water, or sewerage. They just had each other, and they were changing this country before any of us showed up, knocked on their doors, and asked them to continue risking their lives.

When I returned home to Shreveport, I had to relearn my city through the eyes of the activists already in place. But I didn't know where to start.

So I asked my mother.

"Boy, you not trying to get a job?"

"This is my job. This is how I'm going to change what's going on here. And then, when I'm done, I can get a job." I lied, of course. I didn't think I'd make it to the end of this.

My mother didn't say anything. She just stared at me. I waited for her to say something. To tell me how disappointed she was in me for getting kicked out of school and ruining my dreams. I expected her to tell me that I had to leave her house. I expected her to call me a fool for throwing my life away.

What I didn't know then and didn't learn until almost fifty years later, after my mother died, was that she was part of a group of beauticians in Shreveport who used their resources to organize communities and offered their salons as headquarters in their efforts to reshape the city. These women were organizing underground voter registration drives in northern Louisiana, using their influence as some of the city's most important business owners to get Black locals to buy in. My mother never talked about it. Maybe she didn't think about her work as Movement work. This was just what she and her friends did.

"You need to get your teeth cleaned," my mother finally said after eyeing me from head to toe.

"What?"

"Your teeth. They look a mess. You need to go to the dentist."

"So, you're just not going to help me? I—"

"Go to the dentist. Get those dirty teeth cleaned and I'll help you find who you need."

"Okay."

"Good, I already got you an appointment with your old dentist: Dr. C. O. Simpkins."

Cuthbert Ormond Simpkins was the preeminent Black dentist in Shreveport and that's all I knew about him when I got to his office, having begrudgingly prepared for some appointment that I didn't feel I needed. His office was empty when I got there, just Doc.

"Hi, Sonny. I've been very excited to talk to you since you have been back."

"Talk? To me?"

He walked over to a door in the rear of his office. He pulled out a set of keys and unlocked it.

"You coming?" Simpkins led me into a hidden room, the walls covered by picket signs, flyers, and newspaper clippings. He explained to me who he really was.

C. O. Simpkins was a community organizer and one of the most powerful leaders in Shreveport and the entire state of Louisiana. He ran for a seat on the Caddo Parish School Board, making him the first Black person to run for office in Shreveport since Reconstruction. He was president of the United Christian Movement, a group of activist preachers and others who held sit-ins and voter registration drives before they became national pillars of the Civil Rights Movement. Simpkins also became one of the founding members of the Southern Christian Leadership Conference and was friends with Dr. King, who gave one of the early iterations of his "I Have a Dream" speech in Shreveport years before the March on Washington.

Simpkins's life was in the crosshairs of the Klan and police during his entire struggle. One night, he was pulled over by three police officers. They all had their guns trained on him. Simpkins stepped out of the car, German Luger in his hand, and calmly told them, "You may kill me, but I'm taking some of you with me."

Doc told me these stories not to deter me from trying to take on the Klan and the police but to let me know the danger I was facing and how to keep myself safe. Years later, Simpkins would have to heed his own warnings and leave town with his family after both his home and a house he was building were bombed. Nobody was ever charged with the crimes.

"The best weapon you can have is information, Sonny," he told me in that room. "You have to control that information. Do you know what this is?" He pointed to a large contraption in the middle of the room.

"I don't have any clue, sir."

"This, son, is a mimeograph machine. It lets us copy pages and make our own newspapers. That's right, I bought my own information disseminator. We need to tell our people the truth, and I needed someone to be that truth teller. This is how you start your Movement in Shreveport."

This was the beginning of the *Freedom Voice*, a local bimonthly newsletter for the Black communities in Arkansas, Texas, and

Louisiana. Suddenly, I had direction and a way to understand Shreveport and stay under the radar until I could develop a plan of action. Dr. Simpkins was giving me his shoulders to stand on.

My mother was in her kitchen cooking chicken and dumplings when I got back from Dr. Simpkins's office. Before I could say a word, she looked at me and smiled, but I could see the weight on her eyelids.

"Your teeth look clean, Sonny. Too clean to hide."

• • •

Dr. Simpkins gave me entrée to all the most powerful Black preachers and the leadership of the underground Civil Rights movement in Shreveport and northern Louisiana. I knew that if I could get them on board for sit-ins and picketing, then the rest of the Black community would follow.

CORE was continuing the Freedom Rides throughout the South. One ride went from St. Louis down to New Orleans and would be led by the CORE field secretary B. Elton Cox, a tall, fast-talking pastor from North Carolina who talked like a snake's tail rattles. It was his oratorical brilliance and charisma that earned him the attention of the NAACP and CORE in North Carolina. He survived the Freedom Ride attack in Birmingham, rode to Jackson with us, and became CORE's lead man for this next phase of the rides.

Cox, along with Bliss Ann Malone, a St. Louis schoolteacher; Annie Lumpkin, a St. Louis student; Janet Braun-Reinitz, a New York housewife; and New York pastor Reverend John C. Raines, would make an overnight stop in Shreveport on the way to New Orleans. We saw their layover and the subsequent attention a group of Freedom Riders arriving in town would garner as an opportunity to put together a protest to galvanize the community. We'd planned for Cox to lead a group of local pastors—the figureheads of the community—in a sit-in at the segregated bus station lunch counter. He'd get arrested with the pastors following suit. We'd use their arrests as a lightning rod to get the community behind the cause, marching and protesting for everyone's freedom. But that was later. First, I had to make sure Cox and his crew survived their arrival to Shreveport.

I spent the night before Cox came to town thinking about the bombings and beatings in Alabama, knowing full well that any stop a freedom bus made had the potential for more terror. I could still see the blood seeping through bandages, the vacant eyes staring back at me. Now, I had to make sure Cox and the others didn't suffer the same fate. But I needed a car to pick them up. I had only one option.

My grandmother's apple-green 1951 Pontiac was the only one like it in all of Shreveport. She had saved up her earnings from cleaning white families' toilets and kitchens to buy that car because she wanted it, and that's all the reason she needed. She was going to get something out of all that labor. She moved around in that car feeling like the baddest woman in northwest Louisiana. Green Pontiac. Her prized possession. Every Black person in Shreveport who saw that car knew it was hers and every white family she cleaned for knew her by that car. That was Bessie's car. I knew I was supposed to be incognito, but it was the only car I could use.

"What you need my car for? You got a date or something, Sonny?"

I couldn't lie.

"Or something!" My dismissive laughter could always disarm my grandmother.

"Boy, you take my car, you follow two rules," she said, dangling a key in my face. "You don't embarrass me doing something stupid, and you don't put a single scratch on it. You just my grandson, but this? This is my baby."

I sat in Grandma Bessie's car a few hundred feet away from the bus station, waiting for Cox and the others' bus to show up and trying to figure out how not to chip a centimeter of bright green paint. As I waited, I saw the mob forming like a rash. News had spread that Freedom Riders were coming to town and dozens of angry white men, women, and children gathered around the station entrance. They were screaming, holding signs and with pockets full of rocks and bullets. News cameras were there to capture a massacre. The police were there with their backs turned to the mob, not even trying to calm anyone down.

Pickets are only as unlawful as the people holding them.

I had seen those same enraged white people on the sides of the road all the way from Montgomery to Jackson. I knew that they would have killed me if the National Guard weren't by our sides. There was no National Guard in Shreveport to protect the five riders. I was the only person there who wanted them to stay alive.

As soon as I saw the crew getting off the buses, I pressed my foot on the gas like I wanted my toes to touch Hell. I drove my grandmother's car between the mob and the Riders. I swung the passenger side door open. "Get in! Hurry!" We sped off, kicking up dirt and dust at death.

Miles away, far removed from the fracas downtown, where spacious mansions and old money ruled, a white husband and wife were sitting on blue lounge chairs in front of a black-and-white television watching the news. They had been served cold glasses of sweet tea and warm slices of cornbread on tiny trays with red roses drawn on them. This was what the couple did every day after the man got off from work. Today, they watched in disgust as news anchors spoke in slow, deep tones about Freedom Riders invading Shreveport.

"Look at these niggers thinking they can come here and disrupt our city," he said to her.

"I hope they get what's coming to them. They should have learned in Al'bama," she responded.

The woman called out to the kitchen behind them. "Bessie! Come out here and see this! You won't believe what these niggers are doing!"

My grandmother came out to the living room through a swinging door. She had beads of sweat on her forehead from clearing out dishes in a kitchen where only a breeze from a cracked window was giving her a little respite from the heat.

When my grandmother walked into the living room, she saw her two white employers looking at her, their heads now turned away from the TV. They were waiting for her response to what they had been watching on the news.

"Bessie, you believe these Freedom Riders coming and messing up our city?" They looked at her with big, nodding smiles.

In these white homes, this was a common test of obedience. White folks loved quizzing their Black workers about race issues, not for any actual debate or exchange of ideas but to see what they could get the Black employees to agree upon. Especially if the white person had control of a majority of the domestic worker's salary. If the Black people working for them agreed that these Black "outsiders" were in the wrong, it made the white folks feel better about their racism. My grandmother was used to this hazing and would usually bite her jaw and nod along with whatever the white woman and her husband would say. This time was different. This time she felt her entire body stiffen.

All she could see on the TV screen was her Pontiac darting through a crowd of white people to rescue those riders. She could nod her head in quiet agreement as usual, but that would only elicit a chuckle before the couple did an about-face. And if they saw her car, they'd know it was hers and spread the word to the other white elites in the city. If one white couple knew she had anything to do with Freedom Rides, her whole family would be a target. So my grandmother acted fast.

She made a beeline to the television—the white couple following her with their eyes the whole way—blocked their view, and saved our family.

"WHOO LAWD I CAN'T BELIEVE THOSE NIGGAS CAUSING ALL THIS TROUBLE SOMEONE NEEDS TO STRING THEM UP I SWEAR IF I WERE THERE I'D RUN THEM OVER." Her arms flailing, she pulled her dress wide to make sure the couple couldn't see any of the screen. "WE NEED TO GET THOSE NIGGAS OUT THE CITY, I SWEAR SOMEONE NEEDS TO DO SOMETHING!" She did this until she heard the man on the TV behind her start the weather report.

Grandma Bessie hitched a ride with a friend of hers to my mother's house that night and walked straight into my room, where I was writing up notes for a report to the CORE national office. I stood up with her keys in my hand.

"Don't worry, your car is in one piece and it doesn't have a scra—" Before I could finish, she grabbed me by my shoulders then pulled me toward her, squeezing my whole body like Dad used to squeeze my hand.

She started telling me the story of how she had to dance in front of that TV for those white folks until she could hear her knees creaking. And we laughed a big, gasping-for-air laugh until our eyes started tearing up. The whole time she was holding me. Never letting go.

• • •

Cox and the rest had made it into town safely, but we still had to test the bus station lunch counter. I'd spent weeks, with the help of Simpkins, working on the local pastors and getting them on board to join Cox in going to the station and getting arrested. The pastors hadn't taken this task lightly. They understood that arrests could always escalate to something far more violent. Especially in Shreveport. The night before, they held prayer circles and asked God for eternal protection. Some asked Him to look over their families if they got killed. Our relationships with Black pastors were essential in every city, and having them commit in this way signaled the progress of the Movement in Shreveport. But B. Elton Cox ruined everything.

The plan was for me to drive Cox to the bus station so he could go in first, assert that he was planning to get served, get denied, and get arrested. Then the other pastors would follow suit and get arrested. My job was to be on lookout because I would be needed once the pastors were in jail. I'd use their arrests to get their congregations amped up to participate in marches. They would rally behind their jailed leaders and form a unified resistance unlike anything Shreveport had ever seen before. But plans only go as far as resolve allows.

Walking into those bus stations was walking into a deathly uncertainty. There was no protection from any of the violence that would strike down a demonstrator. And that violence would come from angry white people and police alike. The only way to succeed was to swallow the fear, no matter how much it clogged up your throat. Easier said than done, but whole Movements depended on that bravery.

When Cox entered the station, he was met by Police Chief Harvey Teasley, a round giant of a racist whose fingers were never more than centimeters away from either his gun or his baton. He had a square cement jaw that his Southern drawl would gargle out of, along with droplets of chewing tobacco. Nobody knows exactly what happened between the two men, but after a few moments of talking to Teasley, Cox was walking right back out of the station over to the colored side, the four riders who came to town with him right behind him.

"What the hell is he doing?"

The pastors stood outside, flat-footed and bewildered, waiting for a cue to enter that never came. I didn't know what to do either. I couldn't tell them to go in alone without someone like Cox to watch over them. I watched the men and their maroon suits and wide-brimmed church hats from my car, a block away. They looked at Cox, who refused to make eye contact with them as he walked right onto a bus headed for New Orleans. Not knowing what to do, the pastors just dispersed and went back home.

I saw the whole Movement falling apart as I watched Cox walk out of that bus station. I knew what was coming next. Those pastors trusted us to fulfill a goal. They'd housed Cox and the other Riders in their homes, risking their lives in the process. They'd said final goodbyes and prepared for the worst. They put their lives in our hands and we failed them because we made them feel like it was all for nothing. I failed them. Cox was on the bus out of town. I had to stay back and answer for our inaction.

"What kind of operation do you all have here?" the pastors would ask at the next meeting, disenchanted with the entire idea of us trying to organize.

I had to save face and get the pastors back on board. So three weeks later, we returned to the site of the Cox retreat. Even if the pastors wouldn't join us en masse, a show of faith could go a long way in regaining their trust. We managed to get two reverends to come: Harold Lee Bethune and Harry Blake. We also had Levert Taylor, a Grambling student on summer break, Delores McGinnie, who had just graduated from local Notre Dame High, and her little sister, Marie. Again, I was the driver, dropping the demonstrators off and monitoring the situation from a block away so that I could organize the ensuing protests and manage any legal fees we'd need to scrounge up. Reverend Blake would stay in the car with me.

The police department had already gotten word we were coming. This was common; every meeting I had in the Movement had at least one informant present. We would never know who these people were, but we expected that most plans would be intercepted by local police or the FBI. So Bethune, Taylor, and the McGinnie sisters were met by twenty police officers when they got to the bus station, and they were arrested immediately. Though they didn't make it to the lunch counters, they at least showed that they were willing to get arrested. It was a start. Blake and I observed the arrests and started to drive off.

Then we heard a tap on the window.

There were two officers outside the car.

We tailed you after you dropped those niggers off at the station. You're under arrest for aiding, counseling, and encouraging those criminals to break the law.

Again, I was going to jail when I wasn't supposed to. For merely being a block away from a group of Black kids trying to eat. The arrest and the couple of weeks I'd spend in jail wouldn't be the worst part. I'd been in jail before and knew the drill. No, the worst part would come the day after my arrest. The front page of the *Shreveport Times* would cover our integration attempt in an announcement that got the attention of every white person in Shreveport, especially the Klan and the police: *One of the original Freedom Riders is right here in town.* That one sentence might as well have been followed by: *You know what to do.*

By the time I got out of jail I had gotten word: the Klan had put a bounty on my head.

VII.

AMERICAN TERRORISM

My time of relative anonymity in Shreveport was over. The Freedom Rides were still all over the national news as CORE battled with the state of Mississippi over the cases following our arrests. White folks around the country were outraged that we had disrupted and integrated the buses and received National Guard aid to do so. We were the most hated group of kids in America. And now there was a lone, sitting duck in Shreveport, away from the watchful eye of national news, federal protection, or anyone who would notice I was gone. I was in jail two days before the guards came in and took my mattress. I was in jail a week before the newspaper published my home address. Shreveport was a death trap for Black people, and I was in the middle of it.

I didn't care.

I never acted like someone who was in between a shotgun and a ditch. Once I got out of jail, I still went everywhere by myself: bars, restaurants, grocery stores. I went on dates. I drove around at night alone. I'd stare white men in the face while they looked back at me, shocked I had the audacity to be seen. Only a maniac or someone who was protected would take these kinds of risks as often as I did.

I'd convinced myself that I needed to show the rest of the Black folks in Shreveport that I wasn't afraid, so I had to show my face. Honestly, I was still shell-shocked from my Freedom Ride and too numb to be scared. Grandma Bessie would say that God watches over children and fools. I was both.

Meanwhile, I was using the momentum from the arrests and the attention it brought to regain the pastors' trust. But they were just one cog. It takes a whole community to make a Movement. I reached out to local Black businesses asking them to lend their resources whenever we needed them. That's where the Freeman & Harris Cafe came in. The restaurant served the best fried food in the city and was the place where Black businesspeople hung out and where families gathered after church for Sunday dinners. Pete Harris, who owned the restaurant, wanted to help out as much as he could and would provide free chicken for most of our big meetings. Thinking back to my early days in New Orleans, I was banking on the hope that people would attend meetings for the free food and then be lured into Movement work.

We had a passionate group of young people, like Levert Taylor and the McGinnie sisters, working with us and a new group of young ministers like Reverend Blake, Reverend Blade, and Reverend Jones, who were making names for themselves and providing new leadership. They had joined forces with some of the elderly ministers like Reverend McLain, who was working with Dr. Simpkins.

Then I reached out to the people I grew up with, kids I went to school with and their siblings. Some were in high school. Some were on summer vacation from college. Others had been swallowed up by the streets. Shreveport had gangs all over the city, mostly grouped together by neighborhood. There were the Hollywood, Cedar Grove, Allendale, and Lakeside gangs.

I tried to sell these young Black men on the idea that if we got rid of segregation then maybe they wouldn't have to take to the streets. The nonviolent part was the hardest sell. "Dave, man, you lettin' them crackers kick your ass all day? We not letting niggas beat us up without getting shot so we not letting white folks do it," one of the Allendale kids would say, his hands on his belt buckle on Levi's that were down low on his hips and cuffed at the bottom above his patent leather shoes with the heels cut down so the toe of his shoe would stick up, as was the style for the corner boys back then.

"This is bigger than you," I'd try to argue, still not totally sold on nonviolence myself. "If you just help us and we win this thing, you won't have to do any of that stuff you're doing out here."

"I got more of a chance out here in these streets than you do in those bus stations."

When all philosophical debates failed, I would rely on my wild card: "Look, please. Just come to one meeting. . . . We're gonna have Freeman and Harris chicken."

Our churches would be filled with these cross sections of the Shreveport community. Gang members sitting with elders. Business owners with beauticians. College kids with clergy. These churches were our organizational headquarters. They were community centers. They were second homes. They were bunkers.

At the end of August, I invited Hank Thomas to come speak at Evergreen Baptist Church on Allen Avenue. I'd admired Hank as one of the bravest among us. It was one thing for us to have hopped on a Freedom Ride not knowing what the experience was going to be, jumping into a fear of the unknown. But Hank had survived the bombing in Anniston and, like John Lewis, volunteered to go back on the rides to Jackson. That's a different kind of fearlessness. I knew he could inject that fearlessness into our community.

Evergreen was one of the larger Black churches in the area, and the white folks in Shreveport were already fuming over my being allowed to walk around the city alive. But now I was holding meetings and inviting more Freedom Riders into town. There were seven hundred of us in that church. We were energizing the Black community. White folks outside of those walls were matching our energy. An overload was coming.

I introduced Hank, then sat in the back of the church, just trying to observe and make sure everyone was as safe as possible. A mother and her daughter, no older than seven or so, tried to quietly slink out of the church. The mother looked at me and mouthed a "thank-you" while putting two clasped hands against the side of her face to signal to me she was too tired and needed to go home. The girl smiled, her dimples taking up the entirety of her cheeks. I returned a nod and a thank-you for coming as they walked out of the sanctuary into the lobby and out of the church. Seconds later I heard a pair of high-pitched screams coming from the lobby. I rushed toward the sound, quickly closing the sanctuary doors behind me.

"Eyes! My Eyes!" The little girl was sobbing, tears streaming from her face as her eyes went from slammed shut to wide open. Her mother was holding the girl's head close to her chest.

"My baby! They attacked my baby! Something's in her eyes!"

I grabbed them and tried to get them to the bathroom near the exit to get a better look at what was hurting the girl and to quiet their screams so as not to alarm the rest of the congregants. As I walked them back, my own eyes and nostrils started burning.

"Dave, they—they're out there. The Klan. They're here. We can't leave!" The mother was in hysterics.

I found a towel in the cabinet under the sink, wet it, and handed it to the mother to pat her daughter's eyes while I went upstairs to get a better view of outside. There were dozens of white men, women, and children with bats, guns, canisters of what was either gas, acid, or who knows what. Even more police officers were scattered among them, Teasley included. They were just standing there. Silent. I'll never forget the freckly-faced white man in overalls, a baseball bat in his right hand, his left hand resting on his son's shoulders. While inside a little girl the same age as that boy, with purple hair bobbles and church socks up to her shins, was crying in agony because something had burned her entire face.

I didn't know what to do next. Hank was finishing his speech and if any of us left Evergreen it would be the last thing we ever did. I had to keep us inside without raising anyone's concern. I needed divine intervention. That's when my guardian angel started singing. My grandmother, who had been sitting in the back of the church as she did for all our meetings, was standing up now. And she was singing the songs that raised me.

Oh when the saints, go marching in
When the saints go marching innnnn . . .

Her voice hung from the chandelier, bounced off the pulpit, and high-stepped down the aisle, lifting everyone on its way. By the time she started the second verse the entire church was singing, dancing, and clapping. As my grandmother stood, she looked at me and nodded, letting me know she was going to provide cover all night if she had to. I don't know how she knew this was what I needed.

The wheels in my head were turning as I tried to figure out how to get us out of there alive, but at least we had time. And the spirit. Then I got a tap on the shoulder.

It was the kid who was part of the Allendale gang. His pants were pulled up this time and his white dress shirt, faded and splotchy, was tucked in.

"Dave, I know they're out there."

"Yeah, but please don't tell anyone until I figure this out."

"Look, don't worry. We knew they would come. This what them crackers do. My crew waiting in the bushes and some of them alleys over yonder and we already got these motherfuckers surrounded. Just give us the word."

He turned away to walk to the rest of his guys in the church. I knew what he was thinking, so I grabbed his shoulder.

"No, man, you can't do what you want to do. We're not doing that."

"Them words ain't gonna save nobody. Them songs ain't gonna get us out of here. You gonna need us to get rid of these crackers and we'll do it. I swear we will."

Now I had more lives to save. This was going to be a bloodbath. I don't know why I did it, but I turned around and walked out of the church and stared at the sea of loathing in front of me.

"I need to talk you," I yelled across to Teasley, who was leaning against his cop car off to the side, out of the way of the mob.

Slowly, he walked toward me, his hands on his belt, a smirk on his face. He reveled in my desperation. He'd take two steps, spit out his tobacco and take two more, looking around admiring the trees around us as he walked. He wanted me to be scared. He was waiting for me to beg.

Sounds like you might need some help out here, boy. You doing all that protestin' and who do you call when you need help? You need us to save you? I'm not so sure if I can.

He was baiting me. His collar was wilted and damp from sweat. I wanted to grab him by it.

"With all due respect, sir, I'm not calling for help."

Oh, really? Well, I'll just leave y'all to it then.

"Look, sir. I am in a church. A church where we accept saints and sinners. And we have some saints in here. And we have some sinners. I am trying to make tonight peaceful. I'm not calling for you to help us. I'm calling for you to stop some bad things from happening to a whole lot of people. And it won't just be the negroes in this church. What happens next is on you. Sir."

He towered over me, the sun at his back, blacking out his face. I knew I had to stand my ground.

He spit a line of tobacco right at the front of my shoes. Then he looked right at me. The white people behind him were squeezing their bats and cans of whatever burned the girl's eyes. The fire edging toward the dynamite.

Teasley turned around and walked away. I walked back into the church.

I didn't know what was coming next. I was essentially telling the chief of police that there were armed Black people nearby. He could come and arrest us all. Or worse. My grandmother was still shaking the church's columns with her voice. I was pacing around the back, my knees rattling. I didn't know if I just killed or saved us.

Then came the knock.

I opened the door and saw only one officer walking away. There was nobody with him. No other cops. No rioters. No bats or guns or violence. Most of the people at our meeting never knew what really had happened.

That wouldn't be the closest I came to death in a Shreveport church.

We would have another rally two weeks later. This time at St. Rest Baptist Church, about half a mile north of Evergreen. Now it was my turn to be the headliner. The community stepped up even more to ensure we could have our meetings in peace. Freeman & Harris had delivered their regular supply of fried chicken, and because of what had happened at Evergreen, the deacons from several local churches began patrolling the area an hour before the meeting to make sure we were safe. However, just after the rally began police cars showed up and all the deacons were arrested and taken to jail. I didn't know this was happening, but I'd find out.

We were a few minutes into our meeting when we heard the explosion. Then we smelled the smoke coming in from the room to the left of us. Someone had tossed a firebomb into the Sunday school building attached to the sanctuary. It sounded like the building's bones were breaking.

Unlike the Evergreen church situation, I couldn't hide anyone from the imminent danger. Panic started to fill the church as fast as the smoke. Two of the men in the back were coughing. A wide-eyed woman in a yellow dress was standing up, no expression on her face, in shock.

Somehow, outside of my own body, a plan manifested.

I'd known that it was a common battle tactic for Klan members to smoke out inhabitants of a building so they could pick everyone off with batons and bullets at the front door. I couldn't risk that happening to us. We had to sneak out the back.

"Hey, y'all. Who wants some chicken?"

"The hell you talking about, Dave, we gotta get out of here!"

"Look, if you all come this way, you should leave with one of these boxes of Freeman and Harris. We don't want Pete to be mad at us for leaving his chicken to be burned up by these white folk. Just come this way calmly."

I was standing at the church's back exit, boxes of chicken piled up next to me. And one by one everyone in the church came to me, grabbed their chicken, and walked outside. We stood in the back-yard, eating our food while the church filled with smoke behind us.

The next day, the newspaper reported the bombing with a description of two cars the terrorists tossed the bombs from: a 1960 black Ford sedan and a 1953 Ford pickup truck with three white men on the flatbed. The manhunt for those terrorists didn't last long because a week later Teasley held his own investigation that uncovered something else, which he reported to the *Shreveport Times*: *I received information that the firebombing of the church was an inside job by some members of the group who were seeking publicity and sympathy.*

Of course he hadn't received any information. It didn't help that the local newspaper had published pictures of Black people watching the church burn while smiling and eating. The paper accompanied those pictures with claims that we were having a picnic and had staged the whole thing.

Sixteen of us were arrested and charged with vagrancy and littering. For bombing our own church while we were inside.

Teasley didn't even believe his own story. He didn't care who actually had bombed that church. He cared about keeping us off the street and away from organizing any protests while the State Fair was in town.

Shreveport had been hosting the State Fair of Louisiana for forty-five years. The event was one of the biggest income generators for the city as traders, vendors, and families traveled from Texas and Arkansas to bring in money. The fair was also a segregated event. I grew up going to the fair, but only on "Nigger Day": One day out of the week when we'd have to pay to get in, but most of the games, rides, and exhibits were closed. Black people could just walk around and breathe the same air white people had breathed the day before. We'd had the opening of the fair circled on our calendar for weeks as the perfect large-scale segregated event we needed to disrupt. Teasley was no fool. He knew what we were planning and couldn't afford that kind of scandal on his watch.

Black Shreveport was ready to take down the State Fair. First, Shreveport CORE had to spread the word within the Black community that we were boycotting "Nigger Day." The beauticians and barbers made sure all their customers knew not to go. We put notices of the boycott in the *Freedom Voice*. Black kids were traditionally let out of school on "Nigger Day," so we had to figure out something for them to do to keep them away. Practically every Black church in the city organized field day events like arts and crafts, board games, and sports to keep the kids entertained. Freeman & Harris provided free boxes of food to any family that brought their kids to these field days. White Shreveport stood perplexed as the fairgrounds looked like a ghost town. But that wasn't enough for us. We wanted to shut down the entire fair.

Every year, there was a big ceremony during the fair in downtown Shreveport. The white high school bands would play while white businesses, social clubs, and organizations would parade their floats down the streets. It was northern Louisiana's own Mardi Gras. Our idea: during the fair, the Black kids, schoolchildren and gang members alike, would strike with only their words to weaponize white fear against itself. Joe Jernigan, a childhood friend of mine who didn't hesitate to take on the Movement work, organized some of the teens to spread out in small groups among the white parade-goers and deploy their misinformation.

"Hey, you heard about them CORE negroes?" Joe would say to his friend as a white mother pushed her baby's stroller.

"Yeah, man, I heard they got some big shit planned. It's gonna get ugly here," another would say as a dad walked by with his son on his shoulders.

"I'm taking my ass home tomorrow, chief. These niggas crazy and I heard they gonna do some wild stuff," as two white kids zipped by hand in hand.

"Real wild shit," someone would say, standing behind a white couple who would grip each other's hands a bit tighter.

Meanwhile, one of the McGinnie sisters dropped flyers on the ground with messages about a "strike" at the fair or a "clash" and as many fear-mongering words and phrases as possible.

• • •

"CORE Shreveport chapter, how can I help you?" It was the next day and I knew the phone call was coming to the front desk of our makeshift headquarters in the back of Dr. Simpkins's office.

I done warned you niggers about pulling any shit here, boy. I've seen your fucking flyers and heard your plans to do something at my fair. You try that shit and you're leaving in bags!

"Who am I speaking to? How may I direct your call?" I said with the calm of a well-trained secretary. That probably pissed him off more.

You know who it goddamn is, boy. You hear me? Try me.

"Oh! Sheriff Teasley! I'm so happy to hear from you, but I haven't the slightest idea what you're referring to. I don't have any plans for your fair. We're patiently waiting for Coon Day to enjoy it like we're supposed to."

I thought about his calm, smug walk to the church and how helpless he thought I was. I wanted to laugh in his face.

White visitors were so worried something was coming that they kept calling the police department asking about a riot. The next day the front page of the paper ran a story about calming the fears of would-be fairgoers. The city's eyes were glued to prime-time newscasts speculating about protests and unrest. Fear about

Black folks in Shreveport planning *something* during the fair had reached everyone's front porch.

The next day, the fair was relatively empty. The only people there were police from surrounding cities, state troopers, and deputized Klansmen on horseback with heavy artillery and police dogs. They looked like they were preparing for battle, not a joyous event. This visual deterred families from wanting to attend as much as anything we could do. Police stayed on patrol the entire remainder of the fair, which only prompted more unease from potential patrons, who saw riot gear as further reason to stay home and stay safe. I don't know how many people eventually refused to go to the fair or the economic impact from the no-shows that followed. I just know this: we won. The State Fair was integrated the next year.

The State Fair bluff embarrassed Teasley. He couldn't control the negroes in his city long enough for the biggest event in the state? There was egg on his face and his rage could have boiled it. Teasley wasn't going to stop until he got his revenge.

• • •

I already knew who was coming and what it meant when we got a knock at my mother and Mr. Aaron's front door one night a couple of weeks after the fair ended. I was in my bedroom and was prepared to go answer the door and take whatever was coming for me. When I got to my bedroom door, Mr. Aaron was there. He simply put his hand up and said, "Stay in here. Don't come out for anything." He walked to the front door and opened it. There were three plainclothes officers on our front porch.

"Can I help you, sirs?"

"Hey, Aaron, we just wanted to take your son to the station for questioning. There's been an incident we think he may be involved in."

Mr. Aaron. My stepfather. The man whose hand cracked my mother's eye like a brick crashing through glass. The man I stood over with a bloody cast-iron skillet. The man I'd never forgive. The jitney driver. The Uncle Tom. The snitch. The man with no affiliations to any Black person in Shreveport. If anyone was going to give me up it was going to be him.

"Well, sirs, it's after midnight and I'm not even sure where he is. But I'm sure whatever it is, it can wait for sunlight, right? I'll see you fellas tomorrow." Mr. Aaron started to close the door, but one of the officers stopped it with his foot.

"Aaron, yer kiddin'," the officer said with an incredulous chuckle. "Now move, boy." Aaron didn't budge. "You sure you want to do this? You still don't have your license, right? How you gonna keep your lil business going without it?" Mr. Aaron didn't budge.

"W-well if that's the case we can just take it up in the morning." I heard his voice trembling from inside my room. "A-and I'll just have to reveal *all* my records, including any white folks I happen to see late at night on my routes in Black neighborhoods playing the numbers and messing around with colored girls. O-officer."

All I heard after that was the door closing. Then Aaron walking past me to the living room to his cigar cabinet, where he grabbed a long stogie he could barely unwrap with his hand shaking so much. He didn't light it. He just sat on the couch chewing it, brown paper sticking to his lips. We sat in silence the rest of the night.

They would have killed me that night. I know it. I would have been swinging from that tree in front of the courthouse for everyone to see. Or they would have hidden my body. My mother knew it. Aaron knew it. I always saw Aaron as the man who killed my dog and hit my momma. The man I needed to protect her from. I never even went to his funeral. I never thanked him. I never forgave him. But he saved my life.

Two weeks later, I got a call from the national CORE office. They wanted me to move to Baton Rouge and help with the CORE chapter there. Students at Southern University were turning the city on its head and we were on the verge of something special, they said. Still, I didn't get why they wanted me to leave Shreveport. We were organizing and the State Fair win was a huge moment. What the hell was going on?

"Sonny, have you gotten any calls lately?" my mother would ask a day later. That's when I knew. Sometimes when CORE leadership would come to Shreveport, they'd stay at our house. Momma became close with some of them and would check in with them when she was worried. It was clear she'd made a call— many calls—to get me out of town. She, too, was trying to save my life.

I tried to protest the decision with CORE, but they must have known the danger I was in even if I didn't. My mother knew what was coming. She got me out right in time too, because a few weeks later, when I was already in Baton Rouge, I saw our Shreveport house on the news.

A cross was burning in the front yard.

"Mom, I'm on my way!" I was in a panic.

"Sonny, don't you even worry. Joe Jernigan and his boys are here as well as all my beautician friends. They already got me covered."

"I shouldn't have left, I gotta come back, I—"

Joe had grabbed the phone from my mother. "Sonny, look. We got someone with a gun in every room in this house. We got your momma taken care of. You go on. You got bigger things to focus on. You change the world. We got you taken care of in Shreveport, Sonny. We got you."

VIII.
BATON ROUGE

I finally had a job.

CORE made me a field secretary when I moved to Baton Rouge, which meant I was on their payroll. A whole twenty-five dollars a week.

On September 22, 1961, the Interstate Commerce Commission issued a ruling prohibiting interstate buses from using segregated terminals. Buses and terminals now had to post notices that patrons could use their facilities without discrimination based on race or national origin. All bus terminals had until November 1 to comply. The national CORE office wanted to make sure the law was being enforced, so members would travel across Louisiana, Texas, and Mississippi to test whether the local bus stations had complied with the edict.

To execute these excursions, I relied on the people I trusted the most—friends from Shreveport and the New Orleans CORE: Oretha, the Thompson sisters, Jerome, Betty Daniels, George Raymond, and Dotie, who did most of the logistical and organizing work for the rides. We spent two days riding through small towns, simply asking to be served at the bus terminals. If they complied with the ICC, we ate at the counters. If not, we took notes without pushing far enough to get arrested, because CORE didn't have the bail money for all of us. The missions were easy. More importantly, I was able to spend time with my friends. We'd been visiting each other over the few months since I got kicked out of Dillard; either I'd drive down to New Orleans for a few days or they'd come up to Shreveport, but we were always in the thick of work. This felt more like a road trip. Being with the New Orleans crew felt like home, as my actual home felt like fire-bombs and hell. It was a jarring change for all of us as I went from the reluctant rider to field secretary before even Jerome.

"Look at Dave, he got the big britches now," Jerome would say.

"Dave, my sister said that you really proved yourself," Oretha would chime in. "She's ready for a date when these rides are over."

"Really?"

"Hell no!" They'd all laugh at my expense. We were whole again.

We'd all experienced our own personal terrors over the past few months, but it didn't feel real when we were together. Once we all got past fear, the friendships, the shared love during the trauma, not only kept us alive, but some days it was the only thing that got us up in the morning. This was the sentiment across all the organizations and Movements across the country. Black kids and adults found strength and resolve in the comfort of others who shared their experiences. When we were in Montgomery, the SCLC folks told us about how they'd prank each other during rallies and speaking engagements: whenever a speaker was visiting from out of town, they'd get the crowd riled up then promise that the hometown host would be on the front lines if there were any run-ins with police. It was a practical joke we would adopt.

So when Jerome would come to Shreveport to speak, for instance, he'd say things like, "Don't be afraid to stand up to those police. Scream in their faces! Let them know you can take whatever they dish out! You'll be safe because Dave is going to be front and center leading the charge! No one gets arrested without Dave getting arrested!" The crowd would erupt. Then the speaker would be on the first ride out of town, leaving the host (me, in this case) to try to calm the masses.

"You're gonna get me killed!" we'd say. But we didn't actually believe it. Because we were alive. Death hadn't yet pressed its palms against our mouths and held our smiles closed.

Jerome and I loved these back-and-forth shenanigans, putting each other on the edge of danger and laughing about it over a po-boy later. At the end of November, I was in New Orleans to go on a ride into Mississippi. Don drove Jerome, Alice Thompson, Dotie, George Raymond, Tom Valentine, and me to the bus station. Jerome was just supposed to be along for the drive to send us off. For some reason I had it set in my mind that today would be the day I would finally get Jerome in a prank to end all pranks.

I went to the front desk and bought a ticket in Jerome's name, then asked them to call his name over the loudspeaker. He came to the desk, confused.

"Dave, why are they calling me?"

"There's a mix-up, Jerome. For some reason, CORE got you a ticket instead of me."

"The hell? So I'm supposed to—"

"Go, yeah. Sorry, man. I'll tie up loose ends here for you. You're doing this ride." I was holding in laughter.

I'd finally gotten him. Jerome on a bus ride he wasn't supposed to take to a bus station where he might even spend a night in jail. And I'd be there in New Orleans waiting for him with a wide-mouthed smile on my face telling him I'd put his name on the list instead of mine. Jerome was on his way to McComb, Mississippi.

McComb was a house on fire by the time Jerome and the rest showed up. Bob Moses, a Harlemite who ended up in Mississippi as part of SNCC, was registering Black people to vote. Local teenagers Brenda Travis, Hollis Watkins, and Curtis Hayes had staged a sit-in at the Woolworth's in August. A few days later, Travis, Robert Talbert, and Ike Lewis did another sit-in at the McComb bus station and had gotten arrested. When Travis got out of jail in October, she found out she was expelled from Burglund High School. About two hundred students walked out of the school in protest. Moses and Chuck McDew were arrested for contributing to the delinquency of minors. And students had refused to return to school until Travis, who had gotten arrested again as part of the walkout, was released from a juvenile detention facility. McComb was upside down and the white folks there wanted their city back. I didn't exactly know how bad it was in McComb, but I don't think it would have mattered if I had. It was all part of the adventure until it wasn't.

A white mob was waiting for the New Orleans CORE group when they got to the Greyhound station. Jerome, as the observer who would not participate in the actual testing but instead record what happened, went to the ticket booth while the rest went to get served at the lunch counter.

"Hello, ma'am," George said to the waitress behind the counter. "Can I get a cup of coffee?"

She ignored him.

"Ma'am. A cup of coffee, please?"

The terminal operator then walked over to the counter: *Greyhound does not own this restaurant.*

At that moment, one of the white men in the eating area poured a cup of hot coffee on George's head and shattered the cup on the back of his neck. That was the cue for the rest of the mob to join in. George, a slight, athletic kid, jumped across the food counter, dodging the men. The attackers would run over to where he was and he'd jump back on the other side. Again and again. Another group of men grabbed Tom, an even smaller man, and started tossing him to one another, catching him with their knees on the way down. Dotie would say that he looked like a human basketball bouncing on the ground. Jerome gestured for Dotie and Alice to get out of Dodge and run to the waiting area. The mob realized that Jerome was part of the group and ran to where he was, pounding on him and dragging him to the eating area. Fists to ribs. Feet to jaw. Elbows to back. Jerome would have been beaten to death. But George jumped on him, covering his body to absorb some of the blows.

I watched the footage of the beatings on the news and thought I was going to vomit. I'd sent Jerome to die by accident. Soon, I'd send people where death felt certain and learn to feel nothing.

In just a couple of weeks, Jerome was back taking trips from New Orleans to Baton Rouge, organizing as if nothing had happened, despite his busted ear drum and noticeable limp. One night while he was asleep in his room in the Hotel Lincoln, Don and I snuck in and put whipped cream on his hand. We tickled his face to get him to put whipped cream on his face. It was an old prank we liked to pull on each other. This was my way of making things feel normal again. It was how I apologized. When Jerome woke up, whipped cream on his face and hands, he let out a carnal, half-crying scream. Waking up to a wet face sent him to a place darker than we'd allowed ourselves to believe existed. I thought he'd never stop screaming.

Life didn't feel as funny anymore.

• • •

We could have changed Louisiana forever in 1962. But it only took a few weeks for my time in Baton Rouge to be my biggest failure.

Two years earlier, students from Southern University had given us a glimpse of what a Baton Rouge uprising could look like. Thousands took to the streets after police arrested a small group for participating in a sit-in. However, the Movement had stagnated a bit by the fall of 1961, but the New Orleans CORE team was as strong as ever. They had gained notoriety for the Freedom Rides, having trained more than half of all riders who traveled across the country that year. This gave the national office the resources needed to try to spark something again in Baton Rouge. The Southern kids had passion, but they needed people like Jerome and Doris to steady their aim, which they did for most of the fall of 1961, while I was in Shreveport. The students were ready for something big, but we weren't sure exactly what would make the biggest impact while keeping these students safe.

A month or so after I got to Baton Rouge, the Supreme Court gave us the spark we needed. On December 11, 1961, the court ruled in the *Garner v. Louisiana* case, based on the previous student sit-ins, that the state could not use its vague breach of peace laws to stop protesters from sitting at lunch counters. We knew from the Freedom Rides that the stores and local police would ignore the Supreme Court order and refuse us service or find some other reasons to arrest us. This presented us with a perfect opportunity to mobilize the Southern University students.

"That's it!" yelled Jerome, who was still nursing his McComb wounds but pretending he wasn't hurting. "The local restaurant acquiescence is dubious at best. We can run our sit-ins in perpetuity with all those students on those campuses."

"The calendar isn't on our side, baby," said Doris. "We can start the sit-ins, but those students are going home for winter break. We need to do something that'll last."

"Well, we'll just have to stay in jail through Christmas," the words leaving my mouth before they formed in my brain.

This coming from the me who just nine months earlier was too scared to come close to a jail. But this was before the bombs, before the nights on cell floors. Before.

Nine months. That's all it took to turn me into someone else.

• • •

We laid out a plan: A group of us, twenty-three in all, would get arrested for trying to eat at the lunch counters at Kress and Sitman's. The next day, we'd get Southern students to peacefully march to the courthouse, say a prayer in unison, turn around, and head back to campus, where they'd hold a rally. Meanwhile, those of us arrested would stay in jail over the Christmas break so the students would have something tangible to fight for when they returned.

The marches had to be peaceful and without incident. Students couldn't get arrested or kicked out of school. We had to show that we could lead direct action and show the community what we were trying to accomplish. In order to keep the peace, we had to make the rally at the courthouse known to the local police. We needed them to know that we would not engage in any violence. The only way to get the police to trust us was to get the local church leaders, as much a backbone of the Baton Rouge community as they were in Shreveport, to vouch for us. Chief among them was Reverend T. J. Jemison. He'd organized bus boycotts in 1953 in Baton Rouge that would become the blueprint for the famous Montgomery bus boycott a couple of years later. Jemison was respected by students, the community, and law enforcement.

Still, he was old school and many of the older leaders had seen our methods as too radical, inviting police violence and rioting. The clergy were reluctant, understandably, to put their reputations on the line for hundreds of college kids, but they eventually bought in. By vouching for the young protesters, Reverend Jemison was taking a massive risk with the goodwill he'd earned. And we were putting our credibility on the line by asking so much of him. He'd made it clear that if we didn't follow the plan, we would be on our own.

Our initial sit-ins went as planned, and a dozen or so students including Jerome and me were in jail. It was the most excited I'd ever been in a jail. We were on our way to doing to Baton Rouge what we had done to Shreveport. Everything was accounted for. Everything, except for the return of B. Elton Cox.

The national CORE office felt that our march to the courthouse needed a dynamic speaker, which Cox was. We just never knew what he was going to say.

Our jail cell had a window that let us see directly in front of the courthouse, so we could watch it all happen live. We saw the students march, more than two thousand in number, all singing. They stopped short of the courthouse just as we had planned, with the lunch counters a block or so ahead of them. The police were at the ready, guns out, tear-gas canisters at their sides. They weren't planning on using them, but they'd never waste a chance to intimidate Black kids.

Then Cox started speaking. He was in front of the courthouse, the megaphone in his hand pressed closely to his mouth. Then he said something like this:

We will not stop demanding change and we are the people who are going to make sure that change comes. We are going to continue coming to this courthouse until we see equal rights for all people.

"He's revving up, man." Jerome was getting nervous, peering outside. "Just keep calm, Cox."

I couldn't even watch. My head was pressed against the cell wall, eyes down. Just listening. Praying. I could feel the energy changing. I could feel the heat from outside rising.

We at CORE are going to do something special today, brothers and sisters. Y'all hungry? Yeah, y'all are college students so I know you are. Well, we got something for ya. There's a Woolworth's. There's a McCrory's. Kress is right up the street. Take to the lunch counters! And tell 'em the Congress of Racial Equality sent ya!

"Motherfucker!" I ran to the window in time to see carnage. Students were rushing to the restaurants, and as soon as they did, tear-gas canisters started flying through the air like footballs. The tear gas started filling in the jail cell, burning our eyes while we tried to watch. Batons on Black heads. Blood on the streets. Smoke filling a metropolitan downtown. Kids. All of them.

"I t-t-t-t-told you h-h-he'd f-f-f-fuck it up!" I couldn't hear Jerome. I was busy having a riot of my own in the cell. I tossed my mattress on the floor. I started tearing at my shirt. I punched the wall until I thought I broke a knuckle. I was watching everything fall apart. I was watching our hopes go up in a smoke that burns your eyes and stings your chest.

Don, who had come in town to help organize, was standing right by Cox, aghast at what he'd just heard. When the first can of tear gas flew toward him, he kicked it back to the police. An officer next to him saw what he did and shot another canister at Don's chest at point-blank range. Don was doubled over, trying to breathe. He looked up and saw a female protester stumbling away, trying to gain her balance. She ran face first into a parking meter, and was knocked unconscious. When Don tried to get up and help her, his mouth filled up with vomit. Tears, mucus, and puke fell in a pool on the street.

The melee left students laid out in the middle of Baton Rouge, bloodied and pouring water on their eyes. More than two hundred students were arrested. What was supposed to be a relatively un-eventful stay in jail was now on the razor's edge of a full-scale battle. The guards wanted to punish us for as long as we were in jail. They wanted to kill our Movement before it got started.

Cox had been placed in solitary confinement and had an ankle injury from a gas canister hitting it. Ronnie Moore, one of the most prominent of the Southern leaders, was in jail with us, and when he asked the guards to check on Cox, one yelled out loud enough for all of us to hear: *I hope that motherfucker dies in there!*

A few days later, Ronnie started to notice blood in his saliva, from either the tear gas or a beating during the riot. He tried three times to see a doctor. On the third attempt, a guard instead grabbed him by his collar and slapped him to the floor. A few hours later, in another cell, Jerome tried to ask a guard about his property receipt. The guard struck him in the throat.

When I heard what happened to Jerome and Ronnie, I started yelling at the guards for answers, refusing to stop until I had some-one explain to me why two of the people with me were nursing injuries they didn't have when they got to jail. After a couple of hours of yelling, a guard finally opened the cell door.

He didn't have any answers for me. Only a leather glove around my neck, and one pulling on the back of my shirt. He dragged me out of my cell and down the hallway, the toes of my shoes the only thing touching the ground. *You want answers, nigger?*

He opened a door to darkness. He tossed me in.

I don't remember solitary confinement. When Ronnie tried to talk to me about it a few years ago, I thought he had me confused with someone else.

Jail defied geographical location. It's hard for me to pinpoint exactly what happened in any given jail, be it Jackson or New Orleans or Shreveport or Baton Rouge. I can't remember where I had to sleep on bare box springs or on floors. I don't remember which jail gave me a black eye or a bruised rib. I just remember those marks existed.

I remember going on a hunger strike and it not working because Hank was eating all the food we refused to eat. That must have been in Parchman. I remember getting an extra slice of bacon one time for a special occasion. Christmas? So maybe that was Baton Rouge. I remember inmates in every city telling us that we were heroes. I remember Jerome always reading. I remember singing all night to piss the guards off. But that could have been anywhere.

I remember looking into the eyes of men who would never be able to leave. I remember being asked to look out for a cousin Susan or an Uncle Jimmy or an ex-girlfriend Ruby when I got out, so I could relay a message. I remember knowing that bail was coming and I'd always be out in a matter of days, and how hard it was to look people in the eyes who were never going to leave, whether they committed crimes or not. I remember wanting to take them with me. I remember not feeling free when I left them behind.

• • •

Southern University closed the campus a week early due to the chaos and didn't open back up until the end of January, to create distance between the catastrophe and the beginning of classes. All the arrested students were kicked out of school. Most had been bailed out by their parents and allowed to go home to regroup and figure out their future.

By the middle of January, Jerome and I and the thirty or so remaining students were finally released on bail. I was ready to restore the city's faith in us and regain our momentum. The first thing I had to do was meet up with Jim McCain.

Jim McCain was a CORE field secretary over the Southern region in the 1950s and '60s who was largely responsible for the organization's rise to prominence. I first met him in those early CORE meetings in New Orleans and was immediately drawn to the way he always had an answer for every conundrum. An architect of the Freedom Rides, Jim was one of the most brilliant people I'd ever known. He saw the direct action of sit-ins and arrests as something the younger kids felt a passion for, but he had a larger plan in mind for systemic change.

"Dave, we don't have anything for you," he said, his eyes softening like he didn't want to say it. "I know what happened is not your fault. I know as well as you do that Cox went rogue out there, but he still represented CORE. That means the game fell apart with your name on the line. The reverends are out. Jemison is out. We can't put our resources behind you. You're on your own for now. I'll do what I can. But you're going to have to figure it out."

"What am I supposed to do?"

"That's for you to answer, Dave. But what's your long-term plan here? What are you students even trying to accomplish? You kids gonna piss your vinegar out in every jail in America for the next fifty years? Eventually you all gonna have to figure out that eating a burger at a lunch counter won't matter until we start owning some lunch counters. You want to change something? We need political and economic power, Dave. You know how this country could look if every negro could vote? I get it . . . the headlines are in the sit-ins. But the power? The power is in the vote."

We'd of course heard about the idea of voter registration from the beginning and had started going door-to-door trying to register people to vote in Baton Rouge, but it wasn't a central component of our work. We knew that disfranchisement of Black folks was a devastating injustice. But we saw direct action as, well, more direct. Maybe we were just young and wanted more immediate returns on our sacrifices. But the more we got arrested, the more we saw dead ends, the more his words weighed on my mind and heart.

But I'd have to couch those considerations for later. I was too busy having to figure out what to do with the kids in Baton Rouge. There were about thirty students who were left in the city with nowhere to go. They were either homeless and relying on Southern for housing or their parents told them they couldn't come back home after going to jail. Jerome would continue going back and forth from New Orleans. So it was just me. Responsible for dozens of college students who'd just had their lives torn apart.

I was twenty-one years old.

We didn't have the community to support us. We couldn't get free food or find places to stay. We were lost kids with a Movement disappearing over the horizon.

• • •

The Black-owned Hotel Lincoln was the preeminent destination for Black elites looking for a place to stay in Baton Rouge. The hotel, built in 1955, would host everyone from B. B. King to Ella Fitzgerald, who'd come to the city to perform. They'd put us up when we needed rooms too. I met Sam Cooke and Aretha Franklin right there in the lobby. They gave CORE workers good prices when we needed lodging but now we needed fifteen double bedrooms and had no money to pay for them. The owners graciously allowed us a floor to ourselves.

So thirty college kids, fresh out of jail, kicked out of school, and without money, lived on one floor of the Hotel Lincoln for three months. Mostly we tried not to starve to death. We'd scrounged up some change for two hot plates to keep in one of the rooms. Thomas Peete, one of the kids I knew from Shreveport who attended Southern and couldn't go back home, would go out and win money playing pinball games and come back with enough for us to buy blue plate specials to share when he hit a lick. Otherwise it was grits, every day, three meals a day, for weeks. If we had extra money, we'd put beans in the grits. If a restaurateur wasn't too disgusted with our presence, they'd give us some ketchup packets to make tomato soup or to use with the grits. To this day, I taste the Hotel Lincoln every time I eat grits.

We tried to keep our Movement alive, but we were mostly just passing the time. I was out every day begging preachers and business owners to give us another chance. But I could never make any headway. We'd promised Reverend Jemison and the rest that we wouldn't get arrested anymore and CORE didn't have any money to bail us out anyway. So we had to abandon our direct action tactics of sit-ins and picketing.

Then I finally met Bob Moses.

Bob was twenty-seven, so he was considered damn near an elder in our eyes. He was unflappable. Calm. Stoic. He was of the same school of thought as Jim McCain, convinced that registering Black people to vote was the next phase of our work.

"And I have something substantial planned, Dennis. Very substantial."

Bob was pouring resources into voter registration in Mississippi in a way that CORE simply was not in Louisiana. SNCC had almost gotten pastor R. L. T. Smith, the first Black Mississippian to run for office since Reconstruction, elected to Congress. I figured that I could work in conjunction with Bob and SNCC and eventually grow CORE's presence in the state.

There was only one CORE field secretary in Mississippi at the time, Tom Gaither, and CORE had no interest in putting another worker there. But Tom reached the end of his deferment and instead of reporting to Fort Jackson for induction into the army, he decided to enroll in graduate school in Atlanta.

By April, most of the kids in the Hotel Lincoln had either gotten back to school, been allowed to return home, or found somewhere else to go with CORE. There was nothing left for me in the city. I immediately asked Jim McCain if I could take Tom's place.

My six months in Baton Rouge are my biggest failure in the Movement. I'd eventually experience more devastation. More death. More terror. But I'd always felt like we were headed toward *something* and making sacrifices for a larger cause. My time in Baton Rouge just felt like treading water. Sixty years later, I still grit my teeth at the lost opportunity. We had the reverends. We had an army. We had a Movement. But it fell apart. And it fell apart on my watch. I have to own that.

But as real as things had gotten, it was only training. I was on my way to Mississippi. I was on my way to war.

IX.
WAR IN MISSISSIPPI

"Looks like my desk is the first tour stop for outsiders, huh? Someone must have told you that I like it when you all come to Mississippi looking for trouble." It was spring 1962. Medgar Evers was standing in his office at the Masonic Temple in West Jackson, a few buildings down from the CORE office we shared with SNCC, the first time I met him. Tom Gaither had given me names of people I needed to get to know if I was going to survive Mississippi and Medgar was at the top of the list.

The son of a sawmill worker and laundress from Decatur, Mississippi, Evers would go on to serve in World War II, fighting in France and Germany before returning to his home state. He would become the NAACP field secretary in 1954, traveling through the state visiting churches and preaching the sermon of voter registration. He'd also spend much of his time investigating killings and missing Black folks, doing what he could for every family who lost someone. The NAACP was the most established organization in Mississippi, but being caught with a membership card was one way Black people got lynched. Members even hid their cards in tin cans in their backyards as an act of survival. "Here's what you need to know about Medgar," Tom told me. "He keeps his membership card in his damn pocket."

"Where you from, kid?" Medgar's warmth and confidence were evident from behind his desk, even though he was trying to give me a hard time. "Actually, you don't have to answer that. I've known about you since the Freedom Rides. I knew y'all were coming back. You never really leave Mississippi."

"I guess that's true, sir. I'm back here because I want to do what I can to get as many Black voters as possible."

"Hm. Well, Mr. Dennis. What if I told you that you outsiders are going to just show up here and get people killed? What if I told you that you and those SNCC kids running around were reckless and the sharecroppers and seamstresses were doing what they could on their own time and are doing it safely? What if I told you we didn't really need you here?"

I started talking before I had formed an answer. "If I go around this state and people tell me that they don't need me or any of my people then I'll knock on this office door again and ask you to drive me to the bus station so I can get on my way back to Louisiana."

Medgar got up from his desk and slowly walked over to me, his navy-blue suit fitting immaculately. He extended his hand and smiled this big smile that felt like a hug. "Well then all I can say is welcome to the real Mississippi. You got time for Smackover's?"

Smackover's would be the place Medgar and I would go for coffee or a plate of soul food and sweet tea. It's where I would get to know the man I'd call my best friend.

"I admire you kids over there in SNCC and CORE, even though y'all all got screws loose." He was fifteen years older than me, so he loved calling us kids. "Sometimes the NAACP won't mix it up on the street level like we need to and you kids just . . . y'all just get your tails beat like it's nothing."

"That's part of it, right? I've never quite learned how to get anything done without taking a beating. But you're the one with the damn NAACP card. You're just as ready to die as any of us."

"That's where we differ. I love us and I want us to be free. But I have a wife and three babies at home. You got kids, Dave?"

"I, uh, do not." I'd forgotten to even consider such a possibility.

"Didn't think so. The Movement will go on without me if it has to. Those babies in my house won't. Trust me, you'll be less willing to fall in front of bullets when you have to kiss a family goodbye every day. If not, you're not doing those kids any good anyway. And I got two guns in that trunk that say that even if I invite danger, danger coming to me is getting a hell of a welcome gift."

Medgar would drive me around Mississippi, introducing me to every person he thought I needed to know. He could talk business with Black lawyers and doctors and to farmers about how the crops were growing, from Indianola to Hattiesburg. All the while, he taught me about Mississippi. People embraced me because Medgar told them to. I would have never survived without him.

Mississippi was a story of Black folks risking their lives for representation in the face of devastation. Mississippi reminded me of what I had learned in Shreveport: The Movement lived in backwoods and shadows, where resisting was the most deadly thing you could do. The misapprehension about the Movement was that CORE, SNCC, and all the activists who descended upon the state saved the people who were being victimized by white supremacy. The opposite is true. It was the Black folks in every crevice of the state who fed us, kept us alive, and set the blueprint for the actions we'd take once we got there. They treated us like we were their children, caring for us and guiding us. We were kids raised by a community that was just trying to survive.

Our organizations brought more resources and national attention to the cause in Mississippi, but we all only accomplished anything thanks to the bravery and brilliance that were already there. We weren't saviors. We were beneficiaries and peers all learning how to get free together. Mississippians showed us the back roads that allowed us to escape deadly pursuits. They kept us in their homes overnight when it was too dark to drive. They showed us how to organize and whom to organize. The Movement didn't come to Mississippi. Mississippi *was* the Movement.

Before any of us stepped foot in the state, hell, before I had even left the plantation in Shreveport, it was Ella Baker who charged through Mississippi and organized Black folks—some of them reluctant to put their lives at risk—to charter and become members of local NAACP chapters. Mrs. Baker went city by city, church by church, persuading communities that they could make a difference. While not every city would immediately start a chapter, everyone would note that Baker's tour through the state was the impetus for locals to even listen to us in subsequent years. If Medgar built the foundation of the Mississippi Movement, Ella Baker drew up its schematics.

I spent my first few months in Mississippi getting to know as many communities as possible to see what CORE could do. My only real experience in Mississippi prior to this was on the jail-cell floors of Parchman and in courtrooms awaiting sentencing. But now I had to make the state my home, a state that had only shown me that it wanted me dead.

The air was different in Mississippi. Louisiana heat was thick, hugging your body like a wet blanket and swallowing you whole.

Mississippi heat came from the top down, bearing down on your shoulders and your scalp. The dirt roads would kick up so much dust that every night I felt like I had a coat of debris over my body. Some days I feel like I'm still showering it off. And every day there was someone to remind you that there was a long road ahead and you were lucky to be alive. My home base was Jackson, the state capital, but I had to move around the small towns— Canton, Meridian, Hattiesburg, the Delta—because that's where so much of the work was.

I'd travel those towns and learn that there was no one segment of Black Mississippians resisting. Every group, from the business-people and landowners to the teachers and the middle class to the low-wage workers, fought in their own way, however they could. I'd meet Amzie Moore, the postal worker and service-station owner who'd fought for voting rights since the 1950s. There was Dr. Aaron Henry, the Clarksdale pharmacist who was the state president of the NAACP, who welcomed SNCC and CORE to the state with open arms. R. L. T. Smith had run for Congress by then. Mrs. Lenon Woods housed us in her properties in Hattiesburg. Vernon Dahmer, also in Hattiesburg, was a farmer and landowner who presided over the Forrest County NAACP. E. W. Steptoe owned a farm in Amite County where he would advise, front money, and help organize voters. What's remarkable about many of these heroes is that Black landowners were al-lowed to vote with little impediment from angry whites. Their numbers were so few that white folks didn't mind their relatively nonessential impact on any election. These men and women only incurred wrath when they tried to get others, namely the share-croppers, to vote. They dedicated their lives so the rest of their people could vote, knowing that doing so put their families at risk, their businesses in jeopardy, and their houses in the Klan databases as targets for firebombs. Their homes were known to every racist in every town. As were the jobs they held and the schools their children attended. There was no cover. And yet they persisted, doing what they could.

Middle-class Black folks, mostly made up of teachers, get a lot of flak because so many of them were reluctant to involve themselves publicly with the Movement. But they were typically the biggest earners for extended families who depended on them for survival. Any outward involvement resulted in being blackballed from working. Still, many donated in private and others, like Victoria Gray from Palmers Crossing, ended up investing wholly into the Movement.

Meanwhile, the sharecroppers, lumber workers, and low-wage earners gathered in secret. Though most of the land was owned by white people, it was the Black sharecroppers who cultivated it. Many of them lacked access to schooling as children and couldn't read or do much math, so they would get screwed out of the money they were owed for their work. Black families would do enough work to justify being paid hundreds of dollars a month in wages but end up with just a few dollars in payouts, if anything at all. Often, the white landowners would provide sharecroppers with basic essentials they couldn't afford on their wages and hold it against them as debt. As a result, the workers ended up spending many of their years slaving to pay off fabricated loans. If the sharecroppers moved wrong, they'd lose everything. And nobody would miss them if they happened to disappear.

There was one person who stood as tall as anyone else even though she had nothing to her name but fight, a voice, and a light. That person was Fannie Lou Hamer.

I'd heard about Mrs. Hamer soon after I got to Mississippi. She and seventeen other Black people who had been attending voter registration meetings at local churches eventually hopped on a bus—rented by Amzie Moore—in their hometown of Ruleville and rode to nearby Indianola to register to vote. They stared down armed guards and police officers and walked into the courthouse. Mrs. Hamer, the youngest of twenty children, who could read and write, passed the literacy test but was denied her registration when she failed to interpret the sixteenth section of the Mississippi Constitution. This was a typically impossible question to answer, right along with another popular query: "How many bubbles are on a bar of soap?" Wrong answer, no voter registration.

When the group was on its way back to Ruleville, police stopped the driver and fined him thirty dollars for having a bus that was too yellow. As police interrogated the driver, fear took over the riders, worried that they were going to be harassed, jailed, or worse. Then they heard Mrs. Hamer singing her salvation song, "This Little Light of Mine," which would become her trademark when her voice was needed to pull us out of the worst of our despair. Her voice alone calmed the panic as the bus cautiously made its way back to Ruleville.

By the time she arrived back at the Marlow plantation where she and her husband lived, she'd already have a warning waiting on her: Stop trying to register to vote or you will lose your home and job.

"I didn't go down there to register for you, I went down there to register for myself," she told W. D. Marlow, the man who owned the land she worked and lived on. "And I ain't gonna stop trying to vote." Marlow told her he had no choice but to fire her and asked her to leave. Immediately. For the right to vote, Mrs. Hamer had risked—and lost—it all. She showed up to the next SNCC meeting, undeterred, to tell her story to a captivated gathering.

Mrs. Hamer was a product of everything Mississippi could do to Black folks, especially Black women. She walked with a limp because she suffered from polio when she was six. She had to drop out of school at twelve to sharecrop and help support her family. In 1961, she went to the hospital for minor surgery and had been given a hysterectomy against her will. The process had become so commonplace in the state that it would be referred to as a "Mississippi appendectomy." The final straw was being removed from her land and livelihood because she wanted to vote. Yet Mrs. Hamer was more than what this state could inflict on her. She was the embodiment of what was possible. She was the spirit that anchored us and the voice we needed. And one day that voice would shake the country.

My heart was still in voter registration but there was so much more work to be done. White folks in Mississippi had dismantled Black representation that the state saw in Reconstruction, decimating the Black voting populace, adding poll taxes and literacy tests to the cocktail of voter suppression. By the 1960s, Mississippi only had two thousand Black voters, down from almost two hundred thousand during Reconstruction.

There was also unbearable poverty in rural Mississippi, and ransacked, bare-bones schools where kids had no chance at learning. How could we imagine a world where Black people could register to vote if they couldn't even feed their families? The more ambitious I was about helping the people in Mississippi, the more I learned just how much of an uphill battle I was facing. I was the only CORE person in the entire state, and it was clear that there would be limited resources coming my way from the national office. At one point they even suggested moving me out of the state and abandoning Mississippi altogether. Without being able to guarantee help from CORE, I knew my only way to have

a stronghold in Mississippi was to align myself with the organizations already in the state, namely Bob Moses and SNCC, and the
NAACP.

• • •

When the Freedom Riders got arrested back in 1961, Medgar,
the NAACP president Dr. Aaron Henry, and Carsie Hall, one
of the few Black lawyers in Mississippi, created an organization
called the Council of Federated Organizations (COFO) to nego-
tiate our release from jail and pressure Governor Ross Barnett
into a meeting. The organization mostly lay dormant after that.

A few months later, in February 1962, before I got to Jackson,
Tom Gaither, Bob, Medgar, Ella Baker, Amzie Moore, Henry, and
other members from the SCLC, NAACP, SNCC, and CORE,
revived COFO during a meeting in Clarksdale. Their goal was
to create a united front in a statewide plan to get Black people
registered to vote. The Kennedy family had put together a Voter
Education Project (VEP) to fund voter registration efforts across
the country. On August 29, all the full-time civil rights workers in
the state (minus Medgar, who was tending to some other matter)
met in Clarksdale to finalize the reformation of COFO and the
agreement with VEP. Everyone agreed to form a committee to be
in charge of voter registration work. Bob was named director of
that committee, and I was named assistant project director. The
meeting would become a monumental moment for the Movement in Mississippi. I should have been thinking about that. But I
wasn't. I could only think about one of the SNCC volunteers who
attended the meeting: Mattie Bivins.

Mattie was the daughter of NAACP member and organizer
D. K. Bivins, who worked under Vernon Dahmer. Earlier in the
year, Hollis Watkins, the twenty-year-old SNCC field secretary
who threw himself at voter registration, had introduced Mattie

to Bob while recruiting organizers. Soon, Mattie, who had just dropped out of Tougaloo College in Jackson, would volunteer with SNCC and follow Bob to the ends of the earth. She came to the meeting in Clarksdale with her cousin Dorie Ladner, who had formed an NAACP Youth Council in Hattiesburg with her sister, Joyce. I couldn't stop staring at Mattie during the whole COFO meeting. She had these deep brown eyes under hammocks of eyelashes that lay on her flawless honey-brown skin. She rarely spoke in the meeting, but when she did, she had a passion that betrayed the relaxation on her face.

After the meeting, we were all supposed to caravan an hour or so away to Cleveland, Mississippi, to Amzie Moore's house for the night, before heading to Jackson once the sun was out and it was safe. Somehow, Mattie and Dorie ended up in the car with me, my chance to get to know this woman who nestled herself into the soft parts of my stomach. The chance would soon evaporate into the humid night air.

The meeting ended at 12:30 a.m., thirty minutes after a city ordinance said it was okay for Black people to be outside in Clarksdale. Police had been staking out our meeting in nearby buildings, so they knew when to wait outside for us to adjourn. The police let me drive a few blocks away before I got pulled over—the first time for me in Mississippi.

It all started simple enough. *License and registration. Step out of the car, please.* Then the questions.

"Where you from, boy?"

"Jackson."

"Are you heading there now?"

"Yes."

"Excuse me?" He got closer to my face.

"Yes, I'm heading to Jackson."

Boy, do you know how to say 'yassuh'?"

"I'm . . . not sure why that's necessary. "

"I know you heard me. Now repeat after me, when I ask you a question. 'Yassuh.' Say it slow with that drawl like you boys do. Really drag it out for me."

"I can't just say 'yes' or 'no'?"

"Come take a walk with me. We gonna go to my car and have a talk."

"Why?"

He put his hand on his gun. "Because I fucking said so."

I got out of my car despite Mattie's and Dorie's quiet appeals for me to stay. I slowly walked to his car and got in the passenger side, my eyes never leaving his.

"Now, I want you to understand something, you damn moon cricket. I'm a police officer and I can feed my family and you are some race-baiter who gets off on going to jail. You're nothing to me. So you are going to address me as 'yassuh.' That get through to your simple nigger brain?"

"I understand that . . . but 'yassuh' is how we were supposed to talk to slave masters, right? And they were rather despicable people who also lost a war and became poor whites who couldn't feed their families."

"Now you watch it."

"I don't mean no offense. I'm just saying you certainly don't want me to associate you with them, right? So maybe I can stick to 'yes' or 'no' as that is probably more respectful. No?"

He reached for his nightstick. "I will knock every single tooth down your fucking throat and make you dig for them with your bare hands, you worthless monkey."

We did this back-and-forth for an hour. Me in the car. Him calling me every slur he could think of, his nightstick inching closer to my face every time I simply said "yes." Until he gave up. Too cowardly to even beat my ass.

"Well, it looks like I have to charge you with something. Failure to yield the right-of-way always seems to work. You're going to jail tonight."

"Well, can I at least give my friends the keys?"

I walked to my car and passed someone the keys and explained to them what happened and kept them calm. "This crazy ass white man been asking me to call him 'suh' for an hour." No one laughed. "Y'all just follow me to the precinct and make sure that's where they take me, then head to Amzie's for the night. Don't worry, I'm gonna get a good night's sleep on those nice box springs tonight." I think I wanted to appear brave for Mattie, too. The only person I was looking at.

I sat in a cell all night, staring at the ceiling. It was the happiest I'd been in jail. Because I'd met Mattie Bivins, the woman who would become my wife.

• • •

A few days after my arrest, I was back in Jackson in the CORE office by myself at the end of the day when two state troopers came in.

Dave Dennis. You need to come with us.

"Can I refuse?"

They didn't say anything, but I knew I didn't have a choice. The officers drove me a few miles north to downtown Jackson, but not to the courthouse. Instead, they took me to the governor's mansion. "Well, they're bringing back public hangings," I thought, making myself laugh in the car. The two men walked me up winding stairs, through corridors, and into an office. I knew what was coming. Tom Gaither had told me about this. Medgar did too.

It was my interview with Governor Ross Barnett. The governor, of course, had been responsible for sending us to Parchman prison when the Freedom Rides came to Jackson, allowing the guards to take our toothbrushes, mattresses, and food. In 1959, he'd told *Time* magazine that *the Negro is different because God made him different to punish him, his forehead slants back. His nose is different. His lips are different, and his color is sure different.* This was who I was about to be alone with.

After a few minutes sitting by myself in an office, Barnett came in, his dress shirt, suspenders, and neck fat flopping along with each step. Barnett looked like every stereotypical image of a racist white man from Mississippi. He walked toward me and shook my hand. Then he went to his side of a long table, a Confederate flag on the wall to my right.

"I saw your arrest in Clarksdale in the *Clarion-Ledger* the other day and looked you up, Dennis. I couldn't help but notice that you say you're from Shreveport."

"Yes."

"My job is to know the ins and outs of my great state of Mississippi, so correct me if I'm wrong, though I don't think I am. There's no Shreveport, Mississippi, is there?"

"No, there is not. I'm from Louisiana."

"Louisiana! What a lovely state, Dennis. Now, Shreveport being in Louisiana and you being from Shreveport and now being in Mississippi would make you an outsider, isn't that right?"

"Well, Mississippi and Louisiana are both in America, right?"

"Ah, I see how yer gonna play it. Now, here's where I am failing to understand things. You outsiders like to come to my state and rile people up and tell the nigras here that they aren't being treated fairly. You want to convince them that they need to demand more. But I treat my nigras here well. They have their jobs. They have their homes. They're content. They only start demanding things when you people from Louisiana and Atlanta and hell, who knows where probably some Communist country or something, come down here and start feeding them lies about some race problem."

There was something in his tone that I haven't been able to shake in sixty years. The directness of his voice. The way he looked me square in the eyes when he talked. He seemed . . . earnest. He wasn't trying to manipulate me or lie to me. He sincerely didn't understand why I was in town or what Black folks in Mississippi were dissatisfied with. It was like he was genuinely searching for an answer.

"See, nigras and white people need to be separated. It's good for everyone. I love nigras. Where I grew up, some of my best friends were nigras, but we all decided that we should be separated. Inter-uh—what's the word they use now, uh, intermingling—as they say—the races is bad for everyone. The will of the people is to stay separate—white and nigra alike agree on that—and my job is to enforce that will."

"Sir, I'm here to get Black folks equal rights in this state."

"Eq—?! What rights are you losing? You can do everything a white man in this state can do."

"I'm talking about the right to vote."

"Black people *can* vote! It's in the laws of this land. Are you sure they even care about voting? Why don't they just vote?"

"I have lists of hundreds of thousands of Black people from Greenville to Hattiesburg who are eligible to vote but have to take literacy tests and answer questions about the Constitution to register."

"If they valued education then why can't they take the tests?"

"Governor, do you know the sixteenth section of the Missis-sippi Constitution? How about how many bubbles there are on a bar of soap?"

At that moment a Black maid walked in the office to pour Barnett a cup of coffee. She kept her head down every moment she was in that room with us, only nodding her head when he of-fered a "Thanks, darlin'" to send her on her way. His eyes lingered on her two seconds too long.

"I'm sorry, but that's what I don't understand, Mr. Barnett. You can preach to me about not mixing races, but you have a Black woman coming in here to pour your coffee? We can clean your houses. Cook the food your family eats. Our women can put their bosom in your babies' mouths. We mix all the time, Mr. Barnett. Just only the way you want us to mix. Look at me. I have gray eyes, light skin, and kinky hair. Someone in my family did a lot of mixing somewhere from sixteen hundred and something to now, and I guarantee it was some white person and I guarantee the Black per-son wasn't too keen on mixing at the time that happened."

He sat back in his chair, taking in what I was saying. Really absorbing my words. His hands folded over each other and resting on his stomach. Just letting out a soft grunt. It was consistent with what Medgar and Tom had told me. If I didn't know better, or if he didn't say "nigra" every other word, I'd think I was talking to someone interested in making the state a better place for Black people. Like I was changing his mind.

A month later, Governor Ross Barnett incited a riot to pre-vent James Meredith from integrating the University of Mis-sissippi campus.

• • •

We were gaining momentum in Hattiesburg registering people to vote, organizing community service projects and job fairs. This meant I'd need to spend a lot more time in the city. Thankfully, Mrs. Lenon Woods owned a guesthouse on Mobile Street, the Black business sector, which she would let us use as COFO head-quarters and a place to stay while we were in town. The hotel took up two buildings on the street and was much like the Hotel Lincoln in Baton Rouge, with one exception: Mrs. Woods's business was also a place for sex workers to spend time with clients. Locals—oftentimes white men—would come to the hotel with women of their choice or provided by the hotel—oftentimes Black women—and spend the night before going off to their business meetings, jobs, or wives. We made a point of not asking about the businesses run by Black folks who helped fund us and gave us a place to stay.

Going to Hattiesburg felt like a vacation, and I wanted to make sure I was taking every assignment that landed me there, in no small part because I'd be in the same office as Mattie, laughing at her dry humor while she entertained my wild ideas. We'd flirt, cut knowing looks, and become more attracted to each other by the day, but we fell in love doing the work. She'd see my passion for the cause through my eyes and I'd get lost in her words as she filled in logistical blanks, asked the right questions, and made sure every-one got home safely. This was courtship during the Movement: the love we found while working, planning, and getting arrested.

The increased COFO presence in Hattiesburg didn't go un-noticed among the white people, namely the Klan and the police. One night at Mrs. Woods's place, I heard arguing coming from the lobby. I looked out my window and saw three white men at the door. I didn't want anyone in the hotel to get hurt on my behalf, so I quickly packed an overnight bag and walked toward the commotion. When I got there, I saw Mrs. Woods staring them down. I was ready to give myself up, but Mrs. Woods shooed me away from the sight of the men. I obeyed and stayed where I was.

Now, ma'am! We aren't going to ask you again! Either Mr. Dennis comes out or we come in!

"Oh, is that right?" She put her finger right up to their faces. "Chuck, you really want to do that?"

And why wouldn't I? We just wanna talk to him.

"Talk? Well, let's talk to me. You want to have a conversation about how this ain't the first time you been here? You gonna tell all your little cross-burnin' friends about the darker cravings in your life? Should I call up Ebony? Or is it Agnes? And you, Jimmy, you gonna tell your wife about the trips you take here? Or y'all gonna turn around and tell ya lil friends you couldn't find any negro agitators in this here building?"

The men looked at each other. Then at Mrs. Woods. It was like when you raise your voice at your mother and she snaps you back to life. Mrs. Woods had power over these men. I'd never seen anything like it. *You're right. We must be mistaken. But we can't guarantee we won't be back.*

She closed the door and put a rocking chair against it. When she sat down, a woman handed her a bag. Mrs. Woods unzipped the bag and pulled out a shotgun.

"Mrs. Woods, I'm sorry for causing this fuss and I don't want any harm to—"

"I know what you gonna say." She interrupted. "And I'm gonna say this. You try to leave this establishment tonight and them white folks gonna kill you. Actually, they not. Because I'm gonna put a cap in your lil red ass first." Then she cocked the gun. "So what I'm gonna do is sit right here and sing my songs with this here gun in my lap until the sun comes up. Ain't nobody coming in or leaving Mrs. Woods's place tonight. You hear me?"

"And one more thang," Mrs. Woods said, leaning forward. "You need to stop pussyfooting around and ask that Bivins girl out on a proper date or something before these white folks finally string yo ass up somewhere."

• • •

Mattie Bivins was the only woman in my world and I wanted her to know it.

"Boy, if you don't go on somewhere!"

"I'm serious. We should go out sometime. Somewhere outside this office."

"The first night I met you, you went out into a cop car. Then just the other day you were gonna go out there with them officers until Mrs. Woods had to damn near kill you haself. So how I know you gonna live for a second date."

"I'll live as long as you want me to if I can be with you." I didn't think she'd roll her eyes as hard as she did.

"Uh-uh. Don't put that on me. I got a whole state of Black folks I'm trying to help, I don't need you dumping that all on my back. If we gonna do this you gotta wanna live to wanna live. If you gonna make me the reason or if you just gonna flat out die then leave me out of it. I got too much work to do."

"Okay, okay. I promise." It was the first time I lied to her.

Mattie and my time working together melded into a relationship before we even knew it or could put a name to it. We just were. Together. Soon, she became my everything. Mattie was the siren that called me to safety when I was driving around Mississippi. When I wanted to just pull over to the side of the road from exhaustion, the promise of seeing her again kept me driving. She made prison floors feel like feather beds if I daydreamed about her, and the Freedom House beds feel like nails when I agonized over missing her. I wanted a better future for Black folks and I wanted the present to be all about us. I was making twenty-five dollars a week with CORE, and she was planning to return to

Tougaloo College to get her degree, so I couldn't treat her to anything nice. I could just be present, making sure she knew where my heart was. By November, I was ready to marry her.

Thanksgiving 1962, I went to State Line, Mississippi, with Mattie for a church celebration with the plan of letting her father know my intentions. Asking for a daughter's hand in marriage was unimpeachable code in the South, especially for church folks. My plan was simple enough: go to the church celebration, show my enthusiasm for the Bible, and ask for her hand right after. That way he'd know he was giving his daughter away to a man who loved Jesus. It's hard to say no to a boy who loves him some God.

But those plans fell apart Sunday morning. Mr. Bivins was up and waiting for me. He had a shotgun in his hand. "Dave, we goin' shooting!"

"But . . . I thought you didn't go shooting on Sundays."

"You didn't let me finish. One of my other guys has a bottle of moonshine for us, too. The day just lined up beautifully!"

"On a Sunday? What happened to no drinking? No shooting? We're gonna miss church!"

"We'll be fine, boy. And if we're not, I'll blame you!"

My would-be father-in-law. A gun. Alcohol. I wanted to tell him about how his daughter was the most special woman in the world. How she made me want to have a future. How everything felt worth it when I made it to Hattiesburg and saw her. How I wouldn't know what the world would look like for Black folks, but I would fight for her to have the best life imaginable. Instead, we drank in the middle of nowhere in State Line, Mississippi. And shot at buzzards. And drank some more. And all that came out was, "Mr. Bivins . . . I want to marry Mattie."

And all that came out of his mouth was, "If you pass me another shot of that moonshine you can have her momma, too!"

A few hours or minutes or who knows how long later we headed back to the house. Stumbling down the road, arm in arm, hiccupping and burping with each step. My shoulders leaned on his and his on mine and this is how we stayed upright. Mattie and her mother were standing on the front porch, both sets of arms crossed. I could see their clenched jaws from down the street.

"Hey baby, ready for church?" D. K. said.

"We sure are," she shot back.

"Well, *hic*, let's go. You got my good Bible?"

"I don't got nothing for you, D. K. I got my Bible. I got Mattie's Bible. You not going in that church smelling like sin and gunpowder. That piss better be out of yo' system by the time we get back."

We walked to the door to go inside the house, but the door was locked. D. K. put his hands in his pockets but couldn't find any keys. "Bu—"

"Don't even start to ask. You can sit out on my poach and sleep it off."

So we lay on the porch and slept while the women went off to church. I looked at Mattie, who refused to face me. But I noticed a small tear forming in her eye.

Two weeks later, I woke up next to Mattie one morning in Jackson and couldn't wait any longer.

"So . . . how about we get married today?"

"Stop playing with me. Don't you gotta go to Ruleville today?"

"Mattie."

"Well, it's about damn time, Mr. Dave Dennis."

We said our vows in her aunt Alice Ruth's living room in Jackson with neither of our parents aware of what we were doing. We were Mr. and Mrs. Dennis. Married in the middle of a volcano.

Hot tumult waiting to reach the sky.

LETTER 2

Dad,

This is the part where we break and tear the things that have been fixed in place. Because we can't go forward without doing this. Here we go.

I think things started to change for us on your sixtieth birthday. Do you remember that birthday? i was fourteen, a couple of years removed from the divorce, when my cries and screams that I didn't want to hurt like this anymore lined our hallways and when I finally saw my family as collateral from your war; the night I wondered how you could fight for strangers while the people you said you loved the most fell apart. For your birthday, we went to our favorite restaurant, Cock of the Walk, where you'd mash their cornbread into a pot of greens and talk about how a great-grandfather who died more than a decade before I was born would do the same and eat the mix with his hands. We'd always make sure we sat by a window so we could look at the ducks floating in the tiny ripples of moon-gleamed water along the reservoir. A reservoir named after Ross Barnett.

I don't think I told you how much I enjoyed those dinners. I used to love talking about basketball, wrestling, and boring you about the comics I was reading. But your sixtieth birthday was different.

That night you mostly sat silently. I tried to read your furrowed brow as I swirled my straw in a celebratory nonalcoholic strawberry daiquiri. I watched you stare out into the black of the reservoir, your fork nudging around the tiny mound of greens on your plate.

Do you remember what you eventually said? "I'm not supposed to be here."

I laughed, wanting to break the sullenness in your voice. "Hey, Dad," I said, "you're not that old, man!"

You didn't laugh. You just kept looking out onto the reservoir, past me. It took me a minute to recognize in your tone of voice something I couldn't quite name, but it sounded like guilt scraping up against shame. I followed your eyes and saw that you weren't really talking to me. You just kept staring. Repeating yourself. "I'm. Not. Supposed. To. Be. Here."

Over the next hour you told me the stories, some of which I'd heard but not with the pain you were feeling that night. With unrelenting detail, I heard about the times Death grabbed your collar, pulled you close enough to feel its icy breath, and released you back to the fire. That you should have died in Philadelphia—and the parts of you that did—and the best friend you wished you'd saved. The gun pointed at your temple. The DOA posters. The escapes from jail. The men and women who died in your stead. The ones who couldn't escape the inevitable pull of a Mississippi abyss. The bones that were probably recovered when the Ross Barnett Reservoir was built. You're talking beyond me, over the starlit horizon to ghosts, waiting for them to speak back. They never do.

And then you just . . . end.

"I guess I'm not supposed to be here either, then?" It's the only response I could muster.

Then you turned your eyes away from the window and you looked at me. Up and down like I'd appeared out of thin air. Like you were seeing me for the first time.

"Huh," you finally said. "I guess I never thought about it like that."

Some months later we were on one of our road trips. This time, to Meridian or McComb or Hattiesburg. I was a teenager, and as teenagers are prone to do, I wasn't quite paying attention to what was going on, instead buried in headphones or a snake game on a flip phone. The different trips were starting to run together. Freedom Rider reunions, Freedom Summer, Medgar memorials, someone's funeral. The details wouldn't matter so much. I just looked forward to the time—the pit stops for ribs and Krystal burgers; the sadness over Saints losses and the things unsaid. Being father and son.

This time, though, you wanted to talk.

"You know, I got married to Mattie when I was twenty-two? We'd only been dating for a few months. Yeah, I just . . . that's crazy, right? Twenty-two?" I think I felt you turn to look at me, looking for a reaction. I was digging through a to-go box of ribs. "That's just seven years from now for you. That was probably too young to be getting married."

I didn't really know where this was going.

"I guess, back then we just didn't think we were going to live too long, you see. Marriage is supposed to be a lifetime commitment, right? What is a lifetime commitment when you think your life is only gonna last a few more months? How do you even think about a future when you're in the middle of all that shit? I don't know . . . I was lonely and young and . . . I don't know."

I think you were apologizing for our relationship not with excuses but explanations. I could feel you stretching yourself to say everything. When I realized what was happening, I finally looked up at you. You had tears holding on to the edges of your eyes. I just stared at them, waiting. I saw you.

I saw one man. Not the two men I'd kept separate in my head for so long. Dave Dennis, the activist I wanted to be, and Dad, the man I was scared to become. I saw one man, tangled in agony from one version of himself that knots itself up in the other. I saw the life of Dave Dennis bleeding into the way Dad and husband failed so many people. Mattie. My mother. My sisters. Me. Yourself. The ripple in the pond and the rocks thrown at Black folks baptized in a lake of American bloodshed.

That drive was the beginning of my finding language for the pain. You were never mean to me. Never had a temper with me. You never hurt me out of malice or intention. I didn't even grow up wondering if you loved me. All the pain came from your inability to find something that was either lost or never inside of you. I wanted more and deserved more as your son. And I blamed you for not knowing how to give me the whatever it was that was taken from you. There was just a barricade there that I couldn't break or understand as a child. One that softened once you started to understand for yourself what you were going through. It just took so long.

It breaks my heart to write these words to you because I know they're only a fragment of how you've tormented yourself. I also know you want these words to be more damning. "I'm going to be the villain of my own story," you keep saying. But you don't say it as though you're worried. You say it as though you would welcome the carnage. Like this is going to be warranted punishment for surviving and living a life you don't feel like you deserved to have.

But this is how we face parts of us that have been so neglected that they've stiffened to the point of breaking. And by facing those dusty, cobwebbed corners of ourselves, we can make space for something new.

You always say that you went through a "period of insanity" after 1964, where you just floated from one life event to another. The fearlessness you felt after deciding to go on the Freedom Rides created the hero who barged into Shreveport headfirst without any security or friends knowing where you were. That same disregard for your life that made you drive through Neshoba County alone at night is the same recklessness that allowed you to tear through families like a hurricane through a house of cards.

Mattie felt the brunt of that mania while trying to hold on to you and your family, including a daughter, Erika. In those years, you treated your life like you were shell-shocked that you still had one to live and unsure what to do with the years ahead of you. You were self-admittedly self-destructive, burning down relationships and careers in the same breath. You lived like a dead man, like a ghost thinking he could phase through walls and people as if they couldn't feel what you were doing. There were women, drugs, a daughter, a bitter divorce, a new marriage, stepdaughters, a son, business successes and failings, another marriage ruined, and a trail of sorrow in the wake of your self-discovery. Then the years that followed. The day in college when you told me you'd been married for three months. The family I never knew about. The way Erika tried to comfort me and only had "you'll get used to it" to offer.

I am a product of those years of your running.

I've run from any possibility of repeating your mistakes as fast as I once ran toward whatever I could do to make Dave Dennis proud. I've stayed trapped in painful relationships with anyone manipulative enough to ask me not to abandon them. And when I finally did leave, a final battle-ax would fly through the air in a last-ditch attempt to ensure the most devastation: *You're going to grow up to be just like your father.*

I've worn myself thin trying to be the perfect father and bombarded my wife with reassurance that I'll never leave her. I've canceled out-of-town trips and bawled in airplanes when I've had to leave my family behind for days at a time. I've strived to be a better father for my family's sake but also tried not to let the hauntings win. The white men who fired shots at your back may have missed you, but they hit our lineage. They left bullet holes in the foundation upon which your future families are built. Sometimes I feel like they've won. Sometimes I feel like they keep winning.

Your son

X.
MARVIN, MATTIE, AND MEDGAR

We moved from our CORE office to a COFO office in Jackson that was right next to a cemetery on a street named Lynch. We'd joke that when these white boys finally kill us it'll save everyone time to just move our bodies from the office to the graves. Our little street corner would become a popular hangout for Black teens who would play the dozens, shoot craps, and avoid school. One of those kids was Marvin, a scrawny brown-skinned thirteen-year-old who smirked instead of smiled and who joked instead of cried. He hung out with the gangs, gambled, slap-boxed, and hopped fences when the cops came. But he always came by the COFO office to see us off when we left for the day. It was as if he wanted to make sure we left safe and would be coming back the next morning. He'd stop in for extra food, look after our cars, and call us farmers because we wore overalls every day. He was our COFO kid.

One day I'd had enough, not of him being there but of seeing this kid doing nothing with his days. "Hey, Marvin, you in school?"

"Yessir, Lanier High School class of something or another. What's this year plus four? I don't do the maths good, Missah Dave. This racism just won't stop, Missah Dave. Do something, please!" He had one of those laughs that didn't care if anyone else was laughing.

"Lemme tell you this. If I see you here again during school hours I'm driving you to Lanier myself and making sure you're in class."

The next day, he was there in front of the COFO building. That was it. He was coming with me.

"Come on, Missah Dave! I just got this week off. Mental stress and what not. I'm taking a what you call it sabbatical!"

"Marvin. Now." He got in the car and I drove him a few blocks away to Lanier. "Now go on in there."

"Mister Dave. I gotta tell you something. I'm . . . I'm not enrolled in school. Technically. See, I, uh, never started coming to school."

"Your mother know about this? Does she think you're out there in the street instead of going to school every day?" His hands were clasped, buried between his thighs, and his head was down. The shit-talking, unflappable kid was gone, a child in his place.

"I don't think she much care, man."

"Well, we're gonna find out. Let's go."

"Mister Dave . . . please. Can we—"

I just had to say his name sternly one time and his whole body slumped, resigned. He started directing me to his house, barely mumbling the words "left" and "right" as I drove.

We drove through West Jackson, rumbling over train tracks and potholes so bad you had to slow down to a crawl so your bumper wouldn't fall off. The bigger the pothole, the more dilapidated the house in front of it. Finally we got to Marvin's house. A blue construction that looked more like a shack with towels hanging from spaces that should be windows, cracked pillars, and baseball-size holes in the front screen door. The roof was sunken in on one side with a tree leaning on the other. We walked to the door, already barely holding on to its hinges. Marvin begging with his eyes for us not to go in as he put his hand on the doorknob.

We walked into the smell of stale beer, burned plastic, and something that reminded me of rotted ground beef. His mother was laid out on the couch, the top of her nightgown pulled down to her waist. A man was on his knees on the couch, his pants around his thighs. Standing on the opposite side of the room was another man, his pants unbuttoned, a cigarette dangling from his fingers. Everyone's eyes were red.

I looked at Marvin, wanting to cover his eyes, but he just stood there expressionless.

"I told you no one would care," he whispered.

"Go to your room. Get all your clothes. You're coming with me."

Marvin went down a dark hallway with brown stains on the walls from floor to ceiling.

His mother gathered herself and walked up to me, still halfway out of her gown. She looked down the hall at Marvin. She looked at me.

"You want next, huh?"

"Ma'am. I'm Dave Dennis and I think it's best if—"

"I know who the fuck you are. That boy talk about y'all freedom-fighting-ass niggas all the time, like he want y'all to save him. What you gonna do, huh? You gonna take that boy? Where you gonna take that lil nigga? He ain't good for shit no way and yo' dumb ass gonna be dead fuckin with them white folks and then what's gonna happen."

A line of liquid was dripping from her nose to her mouth. She was spitting it at me as she slurred through her words. "Yeahhhh, I know about you and all them wannabe hero niggas. Y'all ain't saving no motherfucking body! You a dead nigga! How a dead nigga gonna raise my son?"

Marvin came out of the back with a pillowcase that had a small knot tied at the top. It was maybe a quarter filled. "No, Marvin, I said all your clothes. You're coming with me for a while."

"Mister Dave. These all my clothes."

• • •

A lot of the winter of 1962 into 1963 revolved around the Delta.

Black people in the Delta, many of them sharecroppers on white land, relied on government assistance to get them through when cotton season was over. One way was with the help of a federal surplus commodity program, which provided food to more than twenty thousand families in the area; 90 percent of them were Black. To retaliate for the grassroots enthusiasm for Black people registering to vote and to discourage others from registering, the Leflore County Board of Supervisors cut off the food program. The other way Black folks in the Delta made it through to the next cotton season was through food and money loans from the landowners, a policy that also kept these Black workers indebted and sharecropping in perpetuity. But now, the white landowners were refusing to offer those loans, leaving Black families without anything to hold them over through the exceptionally cold winter of 1962. We were looking at an unthinkable crisis.

It was up to COFO to keep these families fed. We'd write SNCC and CORE chapters across the country, begging them to donate food and money. Dick Gregory flew down fourteen thousand pounds of food to deliver. Harry Belafonte, Lena Horne, Lorraine Hansberry, Sidney Poitier, and more were organizing rallies to send money down to the Delta. Families would line up and get groceries at stations we set up, where we'd also encourage them to vote. Though Mrs. Hamer would sometimes go further than encouraging.

"Mrs. Hamer, you can't tell people you won't give them food unless they vote, now."

"No, *you* can't tell them you won't give them food if they can't vote. You got theories and philosophies. But you don't understand what's about to happen to them here. They gon' get this food but they gonna register and they gon' be okay. Ain't nothin' else to talk about."

She was right, and eventually we'd have to use voter registration to ration out the dwindling resources we were giving out.

The food blockade changed the folks in the Delta's relationship with voting and government participation. For the first time, many of them saw the connection between voting and legislation and putting food on their tables. They saw the governmental machinations behind their oppression and they wanted to fight. It would have been easy for them to simply give up, but the people in the Delta, the most discarded and ignored population in America, refused. When white violence pushed, Black folks pushed back harder. White folks burned four Black businesses in the middle of town in an attempt to set the SNCC building ablaze and warned that COFO would not be allowed to make any more food deliveries. The next day, 150 Black folks showed up to the courthouse to register to vote, the most at one time since Reconstruction. Days later, I was supposed to ride with Bob, Jimmy Travis, and Randolph Blackwell back to Jackson after a meeting in Greenville, but ended up riding with someone else. The three men were shot at, two bullets hitting Jimmy in the neck. He barely survived.

COFO then sent just about every worker up to the Delta for reinforcements. A white mob shot up a SNCC car and then fired six shots into the house of Dewey Greene, a local who was one of the most vocal in supporting the Movement, bullets flying into the bedroom where his six children were sleeping. Locals responded by marching to City Hall, where police unleashed their dogs. It was a shift from voter registration to direct action, which only heightened the risk for every Black man, woman, and child in Leflore County, just as the uniquely frigid winter combined with the government cutting off electricity caused people to freeze to death in their homes.

The news of the tragedy and the noise caused by the resistance reached Bobby Kennedy, who ordered his Justice Department to get a restraining order to end the cutting off of supplies and promised to get involved more permanently. But either Mississippi politicians fought back or Kennedy got cold feet or both. Whatever happened, the Kennedy administration and the Justice Department reneged on their promises, leaving all of us in the Delta alone to fend for ourselves against the beatings, gunfire, and government sabotage.

But there was nothing anyone could do to stop the Movement in the Delta. These people who had the most to lose walked on the backs of ancestral resistance and generational oppression and didn't blink. They were under the weight of an economic system built on their subjugation and a national government built on cowardice, yet they dug their feet into the crops and pushed harder. Thousands would continue to register to vote and that gave us the resolve to keep going. If they weren't going to quit, we wouldn't either. All we had to do was keep each other alive.

Mattie and I had been married for about three or four months by the time the food shortage took place. We'd been living on the second floor of the Maple Street apartments, where the city's up-and-coming Black professionals would live. Teachers, club owners, and white-collar workers made this their home. Mattie had gone back to school at Tougaloo after the CORE national office rejected my attempt to put her on the payroll, and I'd spend most of my days on the road in some other city. Sometimes I'd see Mattie first thing in the morning, and I wouldn't see her again until night was casting doubt over whether I'd survived.

When I'd get home, she'd be there welcoming me with a smile and a plate of food—catfish, baked chicken, or pork chops, sweet potatoes, and cornbread. And we'd just talk. Or rather, I'd just talk. Dumping my day onto her as if she were a coatrack. The bodies, the police, the beatings, arrests, and strategies. She'd listen, put her hand on my wrist, and tell me everything would be okay. The plans, the wins, the registered voters, and the dreams for the future. She'd celebrate with me, hold me, push back when I needed it, and be gentle when I couldn't take anymore pushing. Then we'd go into the bedroom and feel each other until the world disappeared.

Mattie would tell me that those first few years of marriage were bliss. She'd say that I was the best husband she could ever imagine. When I was home, I treated her like the only woman who mattered to me, because she was. And I was wholly faithful to her through the 1960s. But sometimes I wonder how she could feel lucky to be my wife back then. All those nights of uncertainty about whether I'd make it home. I didn't ask her how the Movement was hurting her because I didn't even stop to think about how it was eating away at me. I thought she was taking it all in stride. Maybe I was naive. Maybe I was selfish.

I only saw the weight of it all bearing down on Mattie twice. Once, I sent her a telegram from New York when I was attending a CORE meeting. The message simply said: "Poochie, love and miss you very much. Kisses and hugs. Dave." I was trying to be romantic.

When I got home some days later, Mattie was in the kitchen, flour flying in the air from her fried catfish. The light dredge and dipping into the milk and flour turned into pounding, until her bowl of milk crashed to the floor.

"Shit! Shit! Shit! Goddammit, I can't take this! Shit!"

"Mattie, what is going on?"

"Your little New York stunt. What was going through your mind sending me a damn telegram?!"

"I was trying to tell you I missed you. I can't tell you I miss you?"

"You know good and damn well what telegrams are for. Mommas and wives waiting for their soldiers to come home get telegrams. Telegrams go out when people are too scared to call you up and tell you what they don't want to say and you don't want to hear. I thought they were telling me to come identify your dead damn body! I saw the funeral. I saw myself alone and for what? For this country? For Mississippi? I told you I'm not going to be just someone who waits all day for my husband to die."

"Now you know there's nothing that's gonna happen to me." I gingerly grabbed her wrists and tried to spin her around close to me.

"No, Dave. I sit here and I smile and hug and kiss you every morning and . . . do you really have to go every time?"

"What am I supposed to say to that? I'm out there keeping people alive . . ."

"And who's out there making sure you're alive? Who's going to be up at night but me?"

"Nothing is going to happen to me. It can't. I gotta come home to you. I gotta . . . You keep me alive."

"See, didn't I tell you about that? I have to be more than that, Dave. I can't be a lifeline. I'm your wife. I'm a person. I'm out here fighting for freedom too. I'm out here risking my life just as much as anyone else. But nobody is waiting for me when I get home. It's just me and these walls. When you're here, you're here. But I need you here when you're not here."

"How the hell am I supposed to do that?"

"I don't"—she took a deep breath—"I don't know. This can't be our whole lives, can it? What's the end here?"

I just walked over to her and kissed her forehead. We stood there in the kitchen, hugging and loving each other, hoping her questions would just disappear.

I woke up the next morning and drove to the Delta.

Another time I came home from Meridian late to find Mattie sitting on the couch in the living room, crying. There were balloons all around the apartment, a bottle of Johnnie Walker Red, which we could barely afford, and party hats sitting on the kitchen counter. "I told all of our friends they could leave." She slowly stood up and walked to the bedroom, her tears falling to the floor as she walked.

It was my birthday and I should have expected her to throw a party. Our house had become the gathering spot for people in Jackson and we loved hosting. We'd get fresh vegetables gifted to us by local Black farmers, and Mattie would cook a homemade gumbo or calf's liver. Sometimes I'd just show up unannounced with Mateo "Flukie" Suarez or George Raymond, who I'd recruited over from New Orleans CORE to join us in Jackson, or Tougaloo student Anne Moody or the Ladner sisters, and Mattie would just smile, ask them if they were hungry, and take care of everyone.

When I showed up with Marvin for the first time, having made the decision to take him in knowing Mattie would be the person doing most of the raising, she simply gave him a hug, said "Welcome home," and walked him back to his new room. We were just twenty-two years old and were now raising a teenager.

Marvin was a different kid in the house with us. Mattie had a cousin who taught at Lanier who helped get Marvin enrolled, tutored, and as up to speed as possible. He went to school every day and was learning how to read within a few weeks. And he was active in the Movement; Flukie and George would take him around with them for voter registration and canvassing runs.

But Marvin missed his friends and seeing them meant meeting them out on the streets. One night Marvin disappeared. He hadn't gone to school and he hadn't come home all evening. Mattie and I spent the night driving around Jackson looking for him, our hands clasped together to keep them from shaking. Black boys didn't have many places in Mississippi they could go without being one move away from death. We gave up our search and sat in our living room trying not to think about the bullets or ropes or knives or jails or ditches awaiting Black boys who don't come home before sundown. Then at 2:00 a.m., a key jingled in the door and Marvin walked in.

"Sup," he said, a half smirk on his face.

"Where in the goddamn hell were you?!" I felt like I was going to charge at him, his cool raising the bile in my gut. Mattie's grip on my wrist kept me in place.

"I had stuff to do, man. What's it to you?"

Mattie jumped between us, her hand still on my wrist but her neck craned in Marvin's direction. "Marvin, you better get to your room for your own damn good."

I started pacing around the living room, stomping like I wanted to break the wooden floorboards in half. What do I do to a fourteen-year-old kid to keep him alive when it felt like he didn't want that for himself? I didn't have whatever it takes to handle it any differently than I'd been taught to my whole life. So I unfastened my belt and slowly pulled it from my pants loops.

The first lash on Marvin's backside sounded like twigs snapping, and the reverberation made my hands tremble. He was bent over in the bathtub, his hands on the edge of the porcelain, his shirt up exposing his lower back, his sinewy spine staring back at me, his pants low so the top half of his ass was exposed. Marvin didn't make a sound, he just breathed through the sides of his mouth, his cheeks expanding from the air pressure like he was playing an invisible saxophone. That second crack of my belt echoed like a rebuke. I'd drive to McComb or Hattiesburg or wherever the hell and preach nonviolence then beat on a Black boy I loved. Each hit made his breathing harder, more spittle leaving his mouth and landing on the turquoise shower tiles in front of him. The third smack sounded like my feet crunching hopeless and dying sweet potato plants in front of a dust-surrounded shack. Now he was pushing his body toward me, inviting more in spite of himself. The fourth felt like everything I wanted to do to cops who called me nigger and white boys in overalls with dried tobacco on their lips smiling while my son's lifeless feet dangle above. I didn't speak while I hit him.

I left Marvin in the bathtub. He was still bent over, like he was expecting more. My hands were trembling and my right tricep felt like I'd stuck my arm in a hornet's nest, I'd been squeezing the belt so hard. Mattie was waiting for me at the dining-room table. As soon as I sat down, my eyes started filling with tears.

"He wanted to cry and he couldn't even let it out. I didn't even ask him where he was all night."

"I know you didn't want to do it but what else do you want to happen? It's better us than them people out there. You not gonna string him up like they will. This is the best we could do."

"I think . . . I think I'm gonna go back and tell him I'm sorry. I—"

Before I could finish, Marvin walked out to the kitchen, his face still wearing the lashes on his buttocks. His pants pulled up but unbuttoned, his white shirt twisted on his twiglike frame. He was crying.

I opened my mouth to apologize. To tell him that I can't be in my house treating his body like white folks would treat it outside. To tell him that whooping him didn't make me less scared or make him a better boy. I wanted to tell him that I'd never do it again. Before I got to say anything, Marvin looked me in the eye and started talking.

"Mister Dave, I-I just want to thank you." He hugged me. His arms seemed firmer than I'd ever remembered before. "I been whooped before, but ain't nobody ever whoop me for not being home. Ain't nobody ever whoop me because they cared about me before." He squeezed tighter around my neck. "I just want to thank you for caring."

He turned around and walked toward his room, hiding his wincing in the darkness of the hallway. I looked at Mattie, her hands over her cheeks. Her mouth open like she wanted to let out a scream, but nothing came out.

• • •

"Well, Dave, it looks like I'm in between what they call a rock and a hard place." Medgar and I had begun getting together more frequently in the early months of 1963, meeting every few weeks at Smackover's, or when he was particularly stressed, we'd go to a restaurant owned by his friend Cornelius "C" Turner, and order these huge T-bone steaks as a splurge. Tonight was a steak night. "I'm in the middle of this chaos and it's gonna get me killed." He laughed like you laugh when nothing's funny.

The national NAACP saw legal challenges and voter registration as a way to differentiate itself from the work of King and establish its own identity. However, a youth NAACP chapter had taken shape led by Tougaloo students Colia Liddell, a white student named Joan Trumpauer, Betty Poole, Anne Moody, Joyce and Dorie Ladner, the Tougaloo professor John Salter, the school's chaplain Ed King, and students from Lanier High and Brinkley Middle School. They had previously organized a boycott of the State Fair in Jackson that led to all but a handful of Black folks staying away. For Christmas they led a boycott of downtown Jackson merchants, accompanied by picketing. It was the first demonstration in Jackson since the Freedom Rides. The boycotts were still going strong by April.

All the national organizations were opposed to their Mississippi representatives working closely together and were against the idea of COFO. Eventually we would have to appease them by splitting up the state by region, with each organization having its own congressional district. CORE was to handle the fourth congressional district, stretching from Canton to Meridian—the most dangerous and Klan-heavy area of Mississippi. The regional assignments were just cosmetic, as we all had agreed to work seamlessly together. Our respective national offices were concerned with things like visibility, funding, and making sure the country knew who was leading the Movement. They each wanted their own victory parades. They didn't see what we saw: that true unity comes from putting colors to the side and working together so collaboratively that organization names didn't matter. We were only SNCC and CORE by the names on our paychecks. We were COFO by heart.

The more the lines between organizations were muddled, the harder it was for one particular group to take credit. The national NAACP organization was the most vehemently opposed to collaboration, which was in direct opposition to the way the local NAACP members embraced unity. Maybe they felt that as the oldest and most revered organization, they deserved all the recognition for what was happening in the state, free from anyone confusing them with the upstarts at CORE and SNCC. And, of course, the singular recognition would bring funding, resources, and, most important, notoriety.

The NAACP wanted its own Martin Luther King, who had just written his *Letter from Birmingham Jail* and was knee-deep in an uprising in Alabama. King was also months away from his March on Washington. The NAACP saw Jackson as its Birmingham and wanted its national leader Roy Wilkins to be the closest approximation. But it would be Medgar who would be blamed in Jackson if things went left. Which they did.

Medgar was in the middle of two opposing forces and was just trying to keep everyone alive. While he wasn't wholeheartedly invested in direct action, he knew that the students weren't going to take "no" for an answer, so his best option was to try to make their protests as safe as he could, which meant he had to lead them as best he could. But the national NAACP wanted nothing to do with arrests, bail, and beatings. It wanted legal victories and to make sure that the small Black elite in Jackson maintained the ability to vote. So it forbade Medgar from leading any direct action even as he felt obligated to keep the students as safe as possible. He knew that unless the NAACP gave him its blessing to direct pickets, organize the direct action, and train the kids, things would only escalate. And no matter his actual involvement, the white folks of Jackson would see Medgar as the leader of all disruptions and take violent action right to his doorstep.

"You know I don't mind being front and center," he said, his eyes fixed on his near-empty glass. "But this is just reckless. If I'm dying, I should die for something, right?"

He was right. As things got more dangerous in Jackson and tension rose, he'd be the biggest target. He was the most prominent activist in the city, having single-handedly kept the NAACP relevant there for years.

"Dave, I need your help. We're blind out there and I need you to come train these kids. You have to help keep the body count down."

So that's how it came to be that Medgar Evers and I would meet and strategize every couple of weeks through the spring of 1963. This is how we became brothers.

George and Flukie joined me in our spare time in Jackson, training students to protect themselves when they would get beaten and harassed during demonstrations—get in the fetal position on the ground with your hands on your head and your knees to your chest, don't punch back or give any reason to get shot, get your one phone call in jail and use it wisely. We'd been through it all, so we knew what to expect.

During those unofficial meetings I had with Medgar, we'd talk about his frustrations, his worries about the growing target on his back. He talked about Myrlie and his daughter and two sons every time I saw him, pained by being away from them even for the couple of hours we were out. In many ways, Medgar showed me the possibilities of what a father's love could look like, the father I aspired to be, the father who deserved to see his babies grow old.

I don't know how Medgar was able to handle May and early June 1963. The Jackson Movement was going to keep going with or without the NAACP's full help. Students from Brinkley Middle School and Lanier High had staged a mass protest through Jackson. Police arrested hundreds of kids, and instead of putting them in jail, they stuffed them in cages at the Mississippi fairgrounds with barely any food and no toothbrushes for days. Medgar had promised that he would get the kids out of jail if anything happened and forced the NAACP's hand to send $200,000 to bail them out. These young protesters never forgot how they were treated.

Meanwhile, Mississippi white folks pointed to Medgar for everything anyone did in Jackson that they didn't like, especially as he kept making public appearances locally and nationally. Early in the month he spoke out in the *New York Times* against false charges that Bob had firebombed NAACP member Hartman Turnbow's house, not the Klan. Two weeks later Medgar delivered a seventeen-minute televised address called "I Speak as a Native Mississippian," and said things like "whether Jackson and the state choose change or not, the years of change are upon us." It was a rallying cry for the Movement in Jackson, but it also gave the general public—not just the police and politicians—a face for the activist they'd heard about for years, the man who was leading the charge to get Black activist James Meredith registered at Ole Miss and to bring national attention to Emmett Till. There was no turning back.

As Medgar predicted, the city of Jackson responded to the protests with militarized violence, and he was the prized oppositional trophy. Mayor Allen Thompson deputized nearly a thousand white men, a group made up mostly of Klan members and the most violent racists in the city. Two hundred of them walked down Capitol Street in downtown Jackson arresting and assaulting any Black person they laid eyes on, whether they were protesting or not. Medgar charged back with more than two thousand strong behind him leading a demonstration through the city. That night, while Medgar was out at a meeting, a small firebomb detonated in his home. Myrlie had to extinguish it alone while their children slept through it all.

"You ever let your wife see all of this on you, Dave?" We were back at Smackover's. Medgar looked weary. Bags under his eyes, and it looked like holding his head up was tiring out every bone in his body. His shoulders looked like they were draped over a clothesline. I wanted to hold him.

"What do you mean?"

"This . . . this extra skin of pain that's under our real skin, you know? You ever let her see it? Does she ever see you?"

I didn't answer. I just let out a sigh and took another sip of sweet tea, hoping this moment would pass. "Medgar, you're gonna be fine, man."

"I cried to Myrlie last night. I broke down. She's putting out Molotovs in her living room and breathing life into a man who doesn't have it in him anymore. I tried to tell her about the calls and them telling me I had a bounty on my head. I had been trying to protect her from all that, but, but that's my wife. When I was close to getting the words out, I just . . . I cried. And she saw me. And she held me. And she cried. And it felt so good and so scary and so final. I don't know how many more of these nights we have left.

"I got my kids doing damn military training. Stuff I learned back in the war. They're babies and they know not to sit by windows, how to listen for the dogs to know if there's an intruder. How to duck under their beds if there's gunfire or where to go if they hear an explosion.

"The other night, I . . ." His voice was cracking a bit, but he swallowed it down with his water. He'd barely touched his food. "I heard something in the house, and I jumped out of bed and grabbed my shotgun in one move. I snuck through my house and saw a light on in front, so I crept along. I popped out to the light ready to shoot whoever was in my house." He started folding a paper napkin into no shape in particular. "It was my son, man. He was just up and using the commode. And I had my gun ready for him. What the hell are we even doing?"

I was out of comfort for him. I was watching a man in quicksand knowing what was coming and wanting to fight against it, but the harder he fought the closer the end would come.

"I fought the Nazis, Dave. I was in Germany fighting for this country. I saw Negroes and white boys alike out there dying. Their whole legs and arms blown off like it was nothing. I spent nights wondering when it would end or when I was next. It was hell, all right. But I knew that if I survived long enough, I could leave either when the war was over or when I was discharged. At least there was a finish line there. But now? Here? With these bombs and these Nazis? You don't get discharged from this war. I can't leave Jackson. Everywhere in this blasted country is Jackson."

"We have your back. We're not going to let anything hap—"

"You know they're tracking my car, like they do all of ours. But they're not even trying to hide it anymore. They're running me off the road every day now. They don't even stop to try to do anything to me. They want me scared." His hand was so tight on the glass I thought he'd shatter it. "I'm just trying to get home to my family, man."

"You know I'll take that car off your hands if you don't like it." That got him to at least smile a bit.

"Oh, I bet you would. You still gotta get outside to crank yours up, right?!"

"Hey, my car is nice! It's vintage. Leather seats so if they run you into a ditch, you'll at least be comfortable."

"How about this, roadrunner. You switch cars with me for a day and we'll see how long you survive."

It was silly. A lot of us would trade cars all the time for no reason whatsoever, but not with someone who was in this much danger. I don't really know why we agreed to it. Medgar was going half crazy, and I was just trying to make him feel better. So we walked out of Smackover's and got into each other's cars. I'd be Medgar Evers for a few days.

• • •

I was in Medgar's car driving down a narrow dirt, one-lane road in Madison County, right outside of Canton. Those back roads felt like nighttime even when the sun was out. The wind still as if it's afraid a sudden gust will make hanging bodies sway. Trees, unmoving for fear they'd draw a robed white man's attention and get chopped down for crosses.

I came to the end of the dirt road and a pickup truck was waiting for me, blocking my path. White men stood on both sides of the road, lined up like a processional to my funeral. I should have rammed the truck and kept driving. For the life of me, I don't know why I didn't.

Get out the car, boy.

This was the end that was promised me from the moment I took the bus from Montgomery to Jackson. I got out of the car and looked at wide eyes.

Oh, this not Medgar, it's that CORE nigger! You'll have to do, boy. See all those trees around you? Those trees, they provide a whole lotta shade. And a whole lotta cover. And you see that dirt under those trees, boy? Here's what you don't know about that dirt. It's easy to dig up a hole as big as we want as quiet as possible. You get to pick what hole you gonna sleep in, nigger.

I looked around at all his buddies and the bedeviled smiles on their faces. Beads of sweat on their foreheads and pools of perspiration under their arms. These men didn't deserve to see me scared. I took a deep breath. I held it and waited for a release that never came.

Right then, I heard the thundering of a truck behind me. I turned around and saw a flatbed truck. There were about six Black men and women standing and sitting on the bed in the back. The driver leaned his head out of his window. "Excuse me, suhs. All of us just tryinna pass by if ya don't mind and y'all can keep on carryin' on with whatcha doin'."

The white man stood silent. Everybody was silent. I could only hear my heart beat and the life hum of the truck.

"How bat y'all just move y'all's vehicles out the way right quick? Really . . . it's just a second of ya time, suh, we gotta get back before it starts to get dark."

The white boy whispered to me. *Get your ass in that car and move out their way and not an inch further.*

To this day I don't know what possessed that white man to let me back in Medgar's car. He was going to have to catch me again if he wanted to lynch me. I nodded to the man like I was going to obey. I slowly got in my car as the white man got in his. I looked out of the rearview mirror to my unlikely saviors in that flatbed truck, nodded, and stomped on the gas. As soon as I did, the Black truck pulled up behind me, creating a barricade between me and the mob, then slowed down so that nobody could follow me. I sped off and drove straight home to Jackson, away from a landmark on a back road where one Black man was almost left for dead.

• • •

I caught up with Medgar that night at a meeting.

"Hey, Medgar, take these damn keys. They caused me enough trouble."

"Who're you talking to? They ran me off the blasted road while I was driving your car!"

It was our biggest laugh in months.

I saw him again four days later at yet another meeting. All anyone could talk about was what would happen in a matter of hours: President Kennedy was set to deliver a speech promising the passage of some sort of Civil Rights bill by the time he ended his term as president.

"Say, Dave, why don't you and Mattie come out with me to watch Kennedy tonight. Let's pretend these white people are going to do right by us for a change."

The truth was, I was exhausted. Mattie and I had invited Dorie and Joyce Ladner and Annie Moody over to wind down for the night, but even that felt like something I didn't want to do. I just wanted peace.

"Hell no! Someone's gonna get killed riding around with you." We laughed and allowed ourselves, if just for a second, to be carefree.

The next thing I remember is Mattie's scream when I hung up the phone and told her that Medgar was dead. A white man had gunned him down in his own damn driveway, shooting him in the back, the bullet tearing apart his insides and flying out of his chest. The news hit everyone in the house like shrapnel. I didn't move, but everything that made up my insides sank. I just thought about Medgar crawling to his family, wanting to tell them everything was okay, to show them he made it home like he said he would, but he bled to death right before he got to the door.

I blink and Mattie and I are in our bed, our legs tangled together, our arms holding each other like we were afraid the other person was just going to float away. Our faces so close to each other that it felt like we exchanged one breath between us all night.

XI.
A WEEKEND IN JACKSON

There's a desire to romanticize the way our heroes acted in their last days, as if there were some Zen-like peace that came with the inevitability of their demises. Malcolm, Martin, and Medgar all talked about death right before they were killed, but it wasn't because they'd accepted what was coming. It was because white America had gotten close enough to them to reveal its true self right before pulling the trigger. Medgar Evers didn't give his life to the Movement. His life was taken. Stripped away while he was trying to save his family from the country that looked him in the eye as it loaded its pistol, unlike the actual killer, who hid behind bushes and shot him in the back.

The bullet tearing through Medgar's flesh changed the Movement forever. The country couldn't deny the truth of what happened to him, using the word "assassination" for the first time to describe a killing of a Black activist. For all of us, it changed the way we looked at danger. Death was always possible, but some deaths we'd have time to prepare for. A wrong turn or saying the wrong thing or a bomb going off or whistling at a white woman. That's what death looked like for us. The act of voter registration and dismantling the American power structure elicited a different kind of terror. We were going to change the country and that meant we were going to face coordinated, organized, directed murder. A sniper rifle in our front yards just feet away from our children. That was a different type of dying altogether. Assassination. The word leaves gunpowder on your lips.

In the 1950s, Mississippi formed a government entity called the Sovereignty Commission with the goal of ending the pursuit of integration by stopping direct action and Black voter registration. Essentially the state's own CIA, the commission was behind widespread misinformation efforts and the private funding of groups opposed to integration, including the Klan. They helped the legal defense for Medgar's assassin. The Sovereignty Commission was a daily nemesis in our lives, as it also routinely employed spies to attend our meetings and follow us around. Many of these spies were Black people who were either bribed or had jail time hanging over their heads. All we could do was go about our regular business and hope for the best.

And now there were assassinations. Whatever sense of adventure we were feeling disappeared with Medgar. We weren't fighting against racists and cops. We were fighting the entire government. This is something we always knew, but the way they killed Medgar was a ringing in our ears that kept us from sleeping for the rest of our lives.

For me, losing Medgar ripped my soul apart. The last words I said to him—"Someone's gonna get killed riding around with you"—bounce off my walls at night and welcome me when I wake up, sweat trickling down my chest. Medgar was the best of us. Why Medgar?

Why him and not me?

• • •

Life after Medgar was killed felt like a series of things we did between tragedies. And it started the very next morning, before I even had time to mourn.

John Salter and the student activists had already gotten riled up enough to start marching, so I had to try to make sure they could do it as safely as possible. Two hundred or so of us set out from Medgar's office at the Masonic Temple. The march didn't last long, as the police and the deputized Klansmen tossed dozens of students in paddy wagons and had them locked up at the Mississippi State Fairgrounds—the same tactic they used during the direct action initiatives earlier in the month. The underage students would not be freed unless they named me as someone who manipulated them into protesting and getting arrested so that police could charge me with childhood endangerment. But I didn't have time to worry about that because I got another call: Mrs. Hamer was in trouble.

Three days earlier, Mrs. Hamer and ten other activists were on a bus trip back to Greenwood from an SCLC training in South Carolina. They would catch a bus, stop at a lunch counter or restroom to test out their compliance with the federal laws prohibiting segregation, and be off to the next stop. As they continued their journey, they noticed their white bus driver becoming increasingly frustrated. Mrs. Hamer just continued leading the rest of the group in song, maybe in part to needle him. When they got to Columbus, Mississippi, the group went to a lunch counter and noticed the police gathered around and their bus driver on a longer-than-usual break. By the time Mrs. Hamer's group got to their next stop, Winona, it was clear he'd made a call to the police.

Five of the riders, June Johnson, Annell Ponder, Euvester Simpson, Rosemary Freeman, and James West, got out to use the restroom and grab a bite at the lunch counter. The police were ready, and the riders were arrested. Mrs. Hamer saw the arrests from the bus and got out, demanding answers. The police intercepted her, tossed her in the police car like a bag of laundry, and kicked her in the ribs. The jailhouse in Winona, Mississippi, would become a torture chamber for those who were forced inside.

First was June Johnson.

Lil nigger you in the NAACP? June could have said no. She looked the cop in his bloodshot eyes and said yes. He punched her in the cheek. She fell to the floor, covering her head. He started kicking her sides and yelling, *Who runs the NAACP?*

In the midst of the beating, she just repeated "the people." The sheriff, the chief of police, a state trooper, and another cop began beating her, stomping her, and tearing her clothes. They cracked her head with a blackjack, leaving her bloodied and in the fetal position. She never gave them the answers they wanted. June Johnson was fifteen years old.

Annell Ponder, an SCLC field supervisor, was a Georgia native and graduate from Clark College. The officers locked her in the booking room and beat her with blackjacks and nightsticks and said they'd keep beating her until she said "Yes, sir." She, too, never capitulated.

The police had tossed West, the lone male of the group, in a cell with other incarcerated men. The cops then handed them belts and blackjacks and told them to beat on West. While the men whipped his shirt into tatters and his back into a terrain of welts, the police officers went to their desks and returned with shots of corn liquor as a reward for the violence. The screams from nearby cells and interrogation rooms offered a sound track to Mrs. Hamer's future.

The officers dragged Mrs. Hamer into a cell where two incarcerated Black men were waiting for her. They reeked of alcohol, as the guards had been giving them moonshine for hours without telling them why.

"What am I supposed to do with this?" one of the incarcerated men asked when a cop handed him a blackjack.

Boy, if you don't whip her, you know what we'll do to you.

The imprisoned man then told Mrs. Hamer to get on a cot, where he lashed her until his arms gave out. The flesh welting on her back with every hit. That booming voice that awakened the spirit in so many of us now a scream of terror behind cell doors. It was the second imprisoned man's turn. By now, his face was wet from tears and snot and slobber.

"I-I can't do this. Please don't make me do this."

Mrs. Hamer, her dress pulled up, exposing her back and buttocks, blood soaking the sheets below her, looked back and told the man, "Now go on 'head and do what you gotta do because they gonna do you worse than you do me if you don't."

The man started sobbing, whipping her as he wept. Apologizing through tears and the thud of leather and flesh. But his crying didn't pause his swings. "They beat me anywhere you can see skin," she'd say. Black men beating. White men laughing and watching, toasting their brutality. Mrs. Hamer wailing.

When Mrs. Hamer was finally allowed back into her cell, Euvester, all of seventeen at the time, was left to care for her. Through the night, Mrs. Hamer would develop a fever as her blood pressure spiked. Euvester, wetting a towel, wiped Mrs Hamer's forehead, the welts on her back, and her hands, which had turned purple from trying to shield herself from the brutality.

"E-vester," Mrs. Hamer whispered through gritted teeth. "Let's just . . . let's just sing my favorite song."

The teenager started singing "This Little Light of Mine."

"No, no. Not that one. This one. Walk with me lord. Walk with me lord. While I'm on this tedious journey. I want Jesus to walk with me."

• • •

The whole weekend was spent trying to find Mrs. Hamer and the others and get them to safety. Hollis called every precinct in Mississippi threatening them with false claims that the FBI were looking for the missing. Lawrence Guyot, a SNCC field secretary from Pass Christian, Mississippi, figured out they were in Winona. When he got to the jail demanding answers, he was arrested. While still handcuffed, the police pounced. More billy clubs. More blackjacks. More swelling and blood, this time coming out of Guyot's mouth. They dragged him to a cell.

The call about the jailing sent every worker in the country into a frenzy. I spent hours calling whoever I could trying to find out what was going on. Thankfully, I got word that Andrew Young and the SCLC had secured bail money, so they drove down from Atlanta to get everyone out of jail. The first thing Mrs. Hamer heard when she got out of jail was that Medgar was dead.

Police had brutalized activists in Winona. Deputized Klan members arrested children in Jackson and threw them in cages. And Medgar was assassinated. All in one weekend in Mississippi.

I'm just now remembering what happened next. A couple of days later, I was in Ruleville. We were trying to find care for Mrs. Hamer. I listened to those teenage girls crying as they relived the way those grown men beat them. I felt a rage that I hadn't felt before. Then I saw Mrs. Hamer.

She looked like she was wearing a mask too small for her face. Her cheeks and forehead were swollen beyond recognition, and she could barely open her eyes. I remember her trying to smile and her face barely moving. "It's not the physical pain," she tried to say through cracked, bloody lips. "They made me lift my skirt for those boys, Dave. That's the worst part. They made me lift my skirt for those boys."

We were able to get Mrs. Hamer to a doctor in New York to take care of her, but I'll never get over her face. For the first time through all of this—bombings, burning crosses—I felt a desire for revenge. I wanted those white men dead. I wanted to walk to Winona and kill them all in their sleep. I wanted to bring their bodies to Mrs. Hamer and Annell and Euvester and tell them that I had done this for them. I wanted those white bodies to be the balm for their wounds.

I returned to Jackson, to a city that felt like I felt. The Black community loved Medgar and they wanted the same revenge I wanted. But I had to betray my own instincts and keep as many people alive as I could. It would all come to a head at Medgar's funeral.

I didn't want to go to the funeral. I didn't want to see the pomp and circumstance. I didn't want to hear the NAACP pretend they had been there for him. I didn't want to hear King inaccurately call him nonviolent. I didn't want to hear about his sacrifice. I didn't want to believe he was dead. Instead, I roamed around Farish Street in the heart of Jackson's Black business district, where the funeral would be held, and walked by an alley where some young Black men were gathered. Medgar had previously introduced me to the crew. They called themselves the "Corner Boys" and thought of themselves as community protectors, always keeping an eye out for when white folks were driving down Farish Street. They were generally peaceful but today I noticed the handguns in their pockets and the shotguns they weren't even trying to hide.

"Fellas, what exactly do you all have planned today? Trust me you don't want to do it."

"Dave, why you not at that funeral? Don't y'all got a mass sacrifice or some shit to do for freedom?"

"Y'all know as good as me that Medgar wasn't a pacifist. But you go out there and shoot those white folks once and they're going to shoot you twice. Please, can we jus—"

"Your way gets niggas killed. How about you do what you do best and don't do shit and let us do what we shoulda done and what woulda kept Medgar alive. We dyin' anyway."

We were arguing but saying the same thing. We just wanted the hurt to go away.

I kept walking around Farish Street, peeking through alleyways between the buildings lining the street. Scattered about were men standing by the windows, guns in their hands, like they were ready to rain down on anyone who dared to bother the funeral. I kept walking south toward downtown. There, over the horizon, hidden from plain sight, I saw the horsemen of the Black apocalypse. Not just four, but dozens. Some were police officers, but the rest were the deputized Klansmen. They were dressed for a massacre. Riot gear. Automatic rifles. Grenades. Some were on horseback. Others holding back dogs foaming at the mouth. They were waiting for the march to come their way. Violent or not, it wouldn't matter. Those Klansmen were going to have the green light to kill as many Black people as possible.

I started back to as many alleyways and corners as I could to talk to the men who were waiting with their knives and guns. I kept begging them not to do anything, for their own good. I had to stop them from running into that armada of white rage without telling them what was waiting for them. I didn't want them to take the possible war as a challenge. When I looked back on to Farish Street, an increasingly agitated mass of Black marchers was heading straight toward the white militia.

The police arrested the first few marchers, Dorie Ladner among them. But they weren't going to stop there. A few of the white militia took to Farish Street, batons swinging with abandon. The Black folks weren't having it. They started tossing bottles and swinging any objects they could, fighting back. Their righteous rage as their guide. This is what the police wanted. They were going to have the massacre they'd hoped for. The only thing to stop it was a single white man with a megaphone.

John Doar was a Republican lawyer from Wisconsin who worked his way up to the Justice Department and stayed there under Kennedy, making it his personal crusade to find justice for Black folks. He'd put his life on the line to bail Bob out of jail in McComb and gave him permission to call the Justice Department anytime he was arrested. When Black people disappeared, it was Doar whose fingernails were filled with dirt from digging up bodies. He was there to make sure James Meredith got to Ole Miss. And it was his presence that halted the white militia's march, as the police knew he was a government official and didn't want the federal government on their backs over their unjust violence.

But most of the protesters on Farish Street didn't know that. They just saw a white man who looked like an FBI agent. "Please! Just listen to me! This is an unsafe situation! Please turn around!" He kept yelling into the megaphone.

As I approached Doar, I saw a Black man running toward him from the sidewalk to his left, out of his line of vision. He had a brick in his hand, raised above his head. I sprinted and got between the man and John.

"Dave?" said the man with the brick. "The hell you doing?"

"He's with the Movement, brother. You're making a mistake." Behind him, another man had put down a shotgun he had aimed at Doar. "Jesus, thank God, Dave," said Doar. He handed me his megaphone. "You gotta say something and help me stop this from going any further."

I grabbed the megaphone and begged everyone to stop their march. To deescalate, calm down and to go home, even though I wanted to join them and burn everything down. It's what this damn city deserved. But we had to survive to fight. The kids listened to me because Medgar had brought me in to train them. The rest of the people, rage-filled locals who loved Medgar, listened to me because they'd seen me with him and knew he would have vouched for me if he was there.

Medgar was still saving lives from a grave he hadn't yet been buried in.

XII.

MISSING

One night years later, sometime in the mid-1990s, Bob and I were sitting across from each other at an Italian restaurant down County Line Road in Jackson. As we talked through plans for the Algebra Project work that week, finding our rhythm like we'd done four decades earlier, an elderly couple came up to our table. The woman, her knuckles pulling at the skin between her fingers as she gripped her cane, her gray hair in a knot behind her head. The man, all veins and blood vessels, had a gait of someone thirty years younger.

"Excuse me, Bob Moses? Dave Dennis?"

We'd been back in Jackson together for a few years now after our decades away and had gotten used to older locals coming up to us, remembering us from various church meetings or speeches or Freedom School classes. Maybe we had helped them register to vote or brought bail money to their jail. Maybe we handed their parents food during the winter. Maybe their families hosted us for fish and yams one night. Usually there would be some recognition, some tickle in the back of my mind as to who I was talking to. But this couple looked like people I had never known well enough to forget. Still, Bob and I, almost by muscle memory, stood up, hugged the woman, shook the man's hand, and waited for their story.

"Dave, you don't remember us, do you?"

"No, ma'am, I'm sorry, I don't."

I'd spent the decades removed from the Movement, hiding from interviewers, recognition, friendships. The only conversations I'd have about Medgar or anyone else I lost would be with other veterans who felt what we felt, and with myself at night, when the slight wind whispering against my window shot me out of bed. I didn't realize, though, that my mind—my subconscious— was hiding things from me too. As she talked, I started feeling the lump swell in my throat.

"Dave, I can't believe it. You really don't remember us smuggling you in our trunk when they wanted to kill you?"

• • •

Nineteen sixty-three. The COFO office was transforming into a nightmare of silence and chaos as alarms started going off in my head. Mattie had gone missing. A few hours earlier, I'd asked her to observe a protest downtown. Students were still raucous with direct action after Medgar's death. We tried to make sure they were as safe as possible, so we always had someone present to record who got arrested, beaten, or both. We'd usually reserved that job for a white ally because they could blend in with the mobs and were less likely to be arrested with the protesters. For some reason, whoever we had for this mission backed out. "All I gotta do is go watch, right? You know I ain't trying to go to jail," she said, half joking, half warning.

"I promise, baby."

Mattie was supposed to check in a few hours later, but she missed her time. I gave her ten more minutes before the panic started to set in. I ran out of the COFO office, jumped in a car, and drove home. She wasn't answering the door and I couldn't get in because she had my keys; asleep maybe? Lord, please let her just be asleep. I ran outside and climbed up the fire escape to our apartment on the second floor. If any police saw me, they'd think I was breaking in, and then I'd go missing. But I had to find my wife. I opened the window and walked into an emptiness that stalled my breathing. I ran down the hallway to our bedroom. She wasn't there, but I pulled the covers back anyway. By now, it had been half an hour. There's never a good ending to someone missing a call for that long. I got out of the apartment and sped to Carsie Hall's office. He was the lawyer in charge of handling bail for this particular situation. By the time I got to his office, an hour had passed. I had stopped hoping.

"Okay, so we got the students who were arrested covered for bail and they're going to get out later tonight. Dave? You okay?"

"Mattie is missing." I was swallowing the words as I spoke them to keep from sobbing in his office right then and there.

Carsie started laughing.

"Man, Mattie is in jail with the rest of the kids."

"But she was just lookout!" I'd taken my first breath in an hour.

That night, I picked Mattie up from jail and kissed her harder than I'd ever kissed her before.

"Well?"

"Well what?" We were in the car now. Everything felt slippery.

"Well how in the world did you get arrested?"

"Everything was going fine. I was minding my business, taking notes, and then the cops came like we knew they would and put everyone up in a paddy wagon, and I'm looking around and I'm the only negro out there, surrounded by Klan-ly-ass white people. So I went where I would be safe. Around more Black people. I got in the crowd of Black kids and got arrested too. Made sure the cops threw me in that car and everything."

"You . . . asked to get arrested?"

"Yeah! Hell, the best place for me would be with some witnesses, and all the witnesses were going to jail, so that's where I went!"

This would be one of those stories that we laughed about. Eventually. But that night, hours removed from being sure my wife would be dead, I couldn't find the muscles in my face to part my lips.

Since Medgar died, Mattie and I slept in bed with our arms wrapped around each other as if the sun would pull us apart forever. On this night, though, I buried my forehead into her neck, kissing her collarbone and breathing my fear onto her skin.

"I thought you were gone. I thought I'd lost you. A whole hour. An hour, Mattie. You know how long that is? I was panicking. Mattie. I thought I'd lost you. I wouldn't know what to do with myself. God. Mattie. I thought that was it. I was losing my mind."

As I was talking, I felt her body going limp. Her arms weren't squeezing like they usually do. She was just there. It felt worse than her pulling away.

"You understand now?" she finally said. "That hour you felt today? I feel it every night while you're gone. Your nightmare is my Monday. You see me now?"

I closed my eyes. She closed hers. And that's how we fell asleep.

• • •

A few days later I was in the trunk of a car. When the kids got arrested in the protest after Medgar was killed and the police would only let them go if they named me as the person who directed them to disobey the law, I suddenly had a slew of charges that I couldn't shake. Usually CORE lawyers could quickly plead down a felony or two into a misdemeanor and a fine, or a weekend in jail. But there were dozens of charges and significant jail time this time, so CORE would need weeks to harangue lawyers and offer a plea that would let me avoid jail. In the meantime, there was a warrant out for me: dead or alive. I had to get out of town.

I don't know how I ended up in the trunk of this old couple's car, which smelled like mints and my grandmother's perfume. I don't know what made them want to risk their lives for me. I just know they had volunteered to smuggle me out of the state to meet Ronnie Moore at the Mississippi-Louisiana border so he could drive me to the city of Plaquemine, right outside of New Orleans.

Plaquemine was minutes away from the Mississippi border and was just as volatile a small town as Hattiesburg or Greenville. Ronnie, who had taken over my position as field secretary for CORE in Louisiana, was leading voter registration efforts across the state. Local leaders Dr. Bertrand Tyson, W. W. Harleaux, and Spiver Gordon were among twelve Black candidates running for various Democratic primary positions in the area. Hundreds of Black people in Plaquemine had registered to vote. So naturally the town was under fire. The Klan wanted to quell the Movement with as much violence as possible. This is where I was going for salvation.

I was staying in some family's house when I heard the blasts. They sounded too loud to be gunshots but too small to be bombs. I was in my room, ducking and staying away from windows, the walls reverberating with every bang. The teenage daughter of the couple who owned the house came into the room, crouched down herself.

"Mister Dave, what are you doing?"

"What the hell is going on?!"

"Here, put this over your head." She handed me a damp towel that covered my head and upper back, wetting my shirt. Then she grabbed my head and pushed it to the ground. "Now just wait and don't take any deep breaths."

I sat there crouched for what felt like hours while the tiny cannons shook the walls from outside. With each crash, I felt my nostrils burn and my eyes water. I dry heaved until my ribs felt like they'd explode from my sides. Then, suddenly it was over.

"You can get up now, Mister Dave," the girl said, still unfazed. "They gone for the night."

"What in the world just happened?"

"They ain't tell you, Mister Dave? That's the sheriff and them. They come 'round here every Saturday night since Mr. Moore an' 'em started raising a fuss. They ride their horses firing tear gas into our houses. Sometimes they run up in someone house and take 'em to jail. But mostly they just shoot them canisters at us every Saturday. It get smoky in here. But you get used to it and them towels over your head make it not burn too bad. If you okay, Mister Dave, I'm gonna go back and finish my homework."

The next day, I walked over to the CORE office in Plaquemine, waiting on Ronnie Moore to get there.

"Say, man. I need you to do something for me." I didn't even give him a chance to take off his hat.

"I need you to smuggle me back to Mississippi."

"You drunk?! You know white people don't just stop wanting to kill you after a couple of days? Where in the hell are you going to go?"

"Take me to C. O. Chinn's house."

• • •

Back in early 1963, a few months before we lost Medgar, I drove to Canton for a voter registration drive run by George and Flukie, who were turning the city into one of our strongholds. I saw C. O. Chinn sitting outside our headquarters on a truck bed. He had a sawed-off a shotgun on his lap and a pistol in his waist.

"Excuse me, Mr. Chinn?" He stood up, taller than I thought he'd be. He was built like a washing machine and looked like a gunslinger.

"I appreciate you coming out to our meetings and all. I-I-we value as many people coming to get registered to vote as possible. And—"

"I'm not registering to vote." He looked me in my eye. "These your people?" he finally said.

"Yes. These are our people."

"No. That's where ya wrong. Them negroes in Indianola and Meridian your people. But see, Canton? These my people. You come here to my city and you talking to my people. And what I do is protect my people. So you best believe I'm gonna have this gun and any other weapon I see fit at all times. Now if you'll excuse me, suh, I'd like to return to sitting outside and enjoying this beautiful day."

There were three types of Black people white folks treated with any modicum of decency back then. You could be a "good nigger" who said "yassuh" every chance you got and cozied up to as many white people as possible while reliably selling out every Black person you could. My stepfather, for instance, was a "good nigger" until he wasn't. "Land-owning niggers" held power by virtue of their capital. They voted, owned businesses, and operated like respected members of society as long as they stayed out of the business of uplifting any other Black people. Or you could be a "crazy nigger" who didn't give a good goddamn what any white person said or did. This type of "nigger" was too fearless to be considered sane, so white folks either stayed away or stayed on their good side. C. O. Chinn was both a "crazy nigger" and a "land-owning nigger."

He established himself as "crazy" when he was in his early twenties. C. O. had decided he wasn't going to work for any white people, so a white man decided to test that resolve by telling C. O.'s mother that he could either work for a white person or leave the county. C. O. Chinn showed up at the white man's house with a pistol drawn and one warning: "Stay the fuck out of Chinn family business."

Chinn was a "land-owning nigger" because he had a handful of businesses in Canton that varied in legitimacy. He had a 152-acre farm and ran a club called Desire. He also bootlegged liquor and had other businesses we don't talk about in mixed company. C. O. was the most powerful Black man in Canton, and his sworn enemy was the most powerful white man in Canton, Sheriff Billy Noble.

The two men grew up together on a nearby plantation; C. O.'s grandmother worked for Billy Noble's family. Some say C. O. and Billy Noble played together growing up. Some say they just had an understanding that grew into respect. But Black boys and white boys don't grow up to be friends. Instead, they established a working relationship. Billy Noble, like many sheriffs back then, was wealthy partly because Chinn gave him a cut of the businesses so he could run unimpeded no matter what laws he broke.

Their uneasy treaty would only get more tenuous when the Movement arrived. Chinn immediately took to George especially before warming up to the rest of us. He believed in what we were doing and wanted to protect us however he could. But his protection and involvement in getting Black people registered to vote was an insult to Billy Noble. Now white folks needed Billy Noble to start cracking down on C. O.'s businesses, performing raids, sanctioning him, and taking his liquor.

One day, C. O. was fed up. His two sons walked in their house and saw their dad loading up his pistols. "Y'all go find Billy Noble and tell him to meet me so we can settle this once and for all." The boys drove around pretending to look for Billy Noble, only to return home hours later, after C. O. had cooled down.

That's how it was with them. Some days it felt like they were seconds away from a shoot-out. Some days it felt like they'd just been out drinking with each other and couldn't let anyone know it. Billy Noble was cruel and said "nigger" like it kept his teeth white, but it was as if he were performing his terror for the white folks watching him. He'd beat up on Black folks and let his officers tear into us, but there was a line he wouldn't cross. He was violent but we never thought he would kill us. That is what safety felt like.

A few months after I met C. O., I was in court for a bond hearing for some volunteer who'd been arrested in the area. In walked C. O., his pistol on his hip as always. I thought we were all going to get strung up right there. The judge looked at C. O. and said, "Now you know you can't come in here with that weapon, boy."

C. O. put his hands on his hips, teasing, like he was going to touch his gun. He didn't look at the judge. Instead, he looked right at Billy Noble. "If that son of a bitch right there is gonna have his gun in here, I'm gonna have mine."

The judge, almost chuckling at the two men and sounding more like a parent than a law enforcer, simply said, "Can y'all two just put y'all guns on my desk until this hearing is over? Can y'all just be good for once? Lawd!" Everyone was entertained by the two men and their rivalry. They kept order by threatening chaos. Nobody messed with C. O. Chinn or Billy Noble except for C. O. Chinn and Billy Noble.

So when I needed one place in the whole world to go where I knew I'd be protected, it would be with C. O. Chinn. I spent weeks in one of his houses while CORE settled up my warrants. I watched the March on Washington in C. O.'s living room. Mattie and Marvin would even come visit sometimes to bring me food and spend time together. Everyone in Canton knew I had a warrant for my arrest, but nobody dared ask C. O. about it. Some days, C. O. would sit on his rocker out front with that shotgun on his lap, just to make sure everyone knew that I was protected. C. O. Chinn, the crazy nigger of Canton. The gun-toting protector. The Black-ass superhero. The third person to stand at his doorstep and keep death outside. The man made sure I was alive when Mississippi wanted me dead.

• • •

Marvin was at the March on Washington. He rode a bus from Jackson to D.C. with his buddy Gene Young, who had also been adopted as a kid of the Movement. Gene could recite King's speeches verbatim and sound just like him. He'd go on the road with COFO raising money, as people would beg him to speak. Marvin had a passion for direct action and organizing, even getting arrested during Medgar's Movement a few months earlier. We saw Marvin's future so clearly. We saw the next generation of people who would carry our batons.

Sometimes dreaming feels like such a bother.

I blink and I'm at the train station in Jackson, Marvin soaking my shirt as he screams out his tears. It's the end of 1964 and his mother has been dead for months. Marvin had family in Chicago who got word of how much money he would be due from inheritance or government aid or something and they wanted to adopt him. Mattie and I spent tear-filled weeks trying to figure out how to fight this in court, but Carsie Hall made it clear there was no path to our keeping our child. Marvin's family had every legal right to take him in, plus any white judge who we'd try to make our case to would relish the opportunity to take a child away from two known civil rights workers who were in and out of jail. Our family never stood a chance.

"Please don't make me go! Please! I'm doing so good! Miss Mattie?! Mister Dave?! I thought you was a freedom fighter! Why you not fighting for me?!" I squeezed his shoulders, pushing him away and holding on as tight as possible. Mattie was caressing Marvin's arm with one hand and gripping my arm with her other, her nails digging into my flesh. I'd dumped this child on her lap without asking her first, watched her love this son, and now I was sending him away. She just kept telling Marvin she loved him. Her lips quivered with each syllable. I could feel her heart breaking through double-timed breaths. I couldn't look at her or try to imagine the pain she was feeling. But I knew one thing: she'd carry this loss forever.

Marvin was our son. He was the completion of our family. He was our tomorrow. And he was begging us to love him harder. I finally pried him away. He couldn't lift his head.

"Hey, look at me. Nothing is too heavy for your head. You keep it high. You always—"

He just kept looking at the ground. "I don't wanna. I just." And he walked away, boarding his train.

We never saw Marvin again.

XIII.
VOTE

Allard K. Lowenstein was a Jewish white guy from New Jersey equipped with a heavy Yankee accent and a law degree from Yale. Al had a talent for organizing students, having spent much of 1959 in what is now Namibia, collecting information and testimonials he'd use to try to dismantle apartheid. In 1968, he would be a chief organizer for students opposing Vietnam, a campaign that is largely credited with Lyndon B. Johnson not seeking reelection. Al came to Mississippi in 1963 to add a spark to another movement. He knew all about political processes and saw a way to improve upon our voter registration efforts. He presented an idea of going further than registering Black people to vote and engaging in a full-on challenge to the validity of the Mississippi Democratic Party and the so-called democratic process in the state as a whole. This endeavor would require documenting all the ways the state denied eligible voters their rights, while we would also run our own parallel party, the Mississippi Freedom Democratic Party, and hold our own elections and register people to vote without the state's oppressive Jim Crow barriers of paying poll taxes or taking literacy tests.

This process would require Black residents to show up to all 1,884 Democratic precinct meetings and get denied entry. We would then collect affidavits from as many of these people who tried to register to vote as possible, to prove that the current state of democracy in Mississippi excluded Black people. Then we'd go to the Democratic National Convention in Atlantic City in the summer of 1964 with those affidavits and with lists of the people we had registered for our own elections, in an effort to make a case for why our voter roll should pick the state's nominee. We'd show that our party was a true democracy, delegitimizing the regular Democratic Party in Mississippi and having ours take its place. We'd rewrite the rules of democracy in Mississippi and, thus, this country.

Bob Moses, who loved big ideas and felt a kinship to his Ivy League peer, immediately embraced the concept. If we could create our own voting blocs and delegates at this convention, it would send a ripple effect across America. If we could empower Black representation in Mississippi, we could do it anywhere. It was ambitious, revolutionary, and as transformative a task as we'd ever take on.

The biggest logistical hurdle was we didn't have the manpower needed to register thousands of Black folks and run political campaigns for our candidates. We'd been holding mock elections—"freedom registrations" and "freedom votes"—across the state to get the locals excited about the political process as well as to show that Black people were interested in voting, but we were stretched thin. COFO only had a couple of dozen members in the state. We needed hundreds.

Lowenstein knew where he could get the help we needed. He wanted to recruit college students across the country, mostly white, to come to the state en masse to volunteer. This plan would represent the biggest, impassioned debate we'd ever have in the Movement and the turning point for everything. There were infinite angles of contention, even within groups that agreed with one another. The discussions raged through the winter of 1963 and 1964 in meetings from Greenville to Canton, McComb to Jackson.

"There ain't no way in hell we need a bunch of white boys and white girls turning up in Mississippi and taking this thang over!" Hollis would argue. "They gon' come here, raise up some hell, then go home. Then what? Who the white folks here gon' be mad at? Who gon' catch them beatings? Who gon' be hanging from them trees you see outside? Mr. Jim and Miss Jane on they farms out in Canton."

Charlie Cobb, a brilliant strategist and former Howard University student who'd joined us in 1962, looked at the long game. He and some others felt like those white kids were going to come here and shift our Movement into something white people wanted to hear. He felt like the gentrification of our Movement would dilute our hard-won progress.

Mrs. Hamer, who had been in favor of having students come because she was of the mind that more help would never be a bad thing, cornered Charlie after a meeting. Her finger millimeters from his face, her hand on her hip, and fire at her throat, she said, "Outsiders, huh? So y'all the only outsiders who can come here? Remember, y'all was outsiders too, sir!" Charlie didn't really have many more objections after that.

"Bob, you either a genius or a fool," Stokely Carmichael would say with his charismatic nonchalance. "If this thing goes right, it goes right. But if it's wrong, it's gonna get people killed."

This is how meetings would go for months.

I was torn. I was wary of white college kids coming to Mississippi and treating this like a summer vacation, mixing with the local Blacks so they could snap pictures and tell their friends, only to leave the locals more vulnerable when school started. But we needed help and we needed the country to see what was going on in Mississippi. We'd started talking about these kids representing the "children of the Constitution," as the document was clearly written for their forebears. Now it was the white kids' turn to ensure that the Constitution was actually the freedom-based document the country claimed it to be. In October 1963, I wrote a five-page manifesto called "Mississippi: A Pregnant State in Need of an Abortion." I wanted the 1964 summer to change the world, and maybe it was worth it for some white kids to come in and help. Deep down, though, I think we all had another, more cynical reason for why it would be a good idea for white kids to put their feet to the mud. One I think nobody wanted to admit to themselves let alone say out loud.

Our last meeting about bringing white kids to Mississippi came on January 31, 1964, in Hattiesburg. We had been arguing about this issue for months without reaching a consensus. So we took a vote. As we tallied, Bob got an urgent phone call and ran out of the office, leaving me to chair the final decision.

While Bob was gone, the vote to invite white students to Mississippi failed.

"So . . . now we have to figure out how to make this year work with the folks we have working for us."

For the next few hours, we mapped out a summer of voter registration with the workers we had and tallied how many votes we'd need to truly challenge the Democratic Party. Then Bob came back.

He walked in, head down as he dragged his feet to the front of the room. He was sniffling, his voice trembling as he spoke a sentence that changed the course of the Movement forever: "I just came back from Liberty. Louis Allen is dead."

• • •

When Bob Moses got to Mississippi four years earlier, in 1960, he learned the same lesson I learned in Shreveport and Jackson: the Movement predated our involvement in it. Ella Baker in particular had taken a liking to Bob and sent him to the Deep South to recruit students to come to a SNCC conference in Atlanta. It was during that trip that Bob met Amzie Moore, a World War II veteran raised on a plantation in Cleveland, Mississippi, who was the first Black person to own a service station in Bolivar County. Moore helped found the Regional Council of Negro Leadership in 1951 and became the president of the local NAACP. Moore knew the ins and outs of roads too dark for Black people in Mississippi. He showed Bob ways to organize and who to know. In the process, Moore became a father figure for Bob.

Amzie was just as much a genius and strategist as Bob, who was just a few years removed from getting his MA in philosophy at Harvard. In fact, it was at that SNCC conference that Amzie and Ella first mentioned the idea of voter registration to the activist students who were focused on direct action such as sit-ins, just as we were in New Orleans and across the South. As Amzie and Ella saw it, the sit-ins were only helping one class of Black Americans. "Most of us here are too poor to go eat at a lunch counter anyway," Amzie said.

Bob would return to Mississippi in 1961, where Amzie introduced him to a network of Black fighters—activist descendants of the same networks that Black folks once used to escape slavery a century earlier. That group included E. W. Steptoe, who let Bob live on his farm in Amite County, and C. C. Bryant, who lived in McComb, both of whom were interested in having Bob lead the voter registration charge in the state.

Empowered by Amzie, Ella, Steptoe, and C. C., Bob continued to hold voter registration classes across the state. It didn't take long before he was a marked man. Bob was introduced to Steptoe's childhood friend Herbert Lee, a founding member of the Amite County NAACP. Herbert would drive Bob around, helping him encourage people to register to vote. Soon word spread that Herbert had been aiding the troublemaker.

One afternoon in September 1961, Herbert found himself on one of those Mississippi dirt roads of no return, followed by E. H. Hurst, a state legislator and avowed racist. Hurst pulled up next to Lee and jumped out of his car, a .38 revolver in his hand. The two men were childhood neighbors, who sometimes played tag together. They grew up to have a polite relationship; Hurst, who now lived on land he rented from Steptoe, even helped Lee get a loan at one point. But Lee's willingness to help Black people vote ruined that. Hurst shot Herbert Lee in his left temple; Herbert fell face first, his head pressed against the dust and rocks on the ground.

There were twelve witnesses to the murder, mostly Black members of the community, who were too scared to collect Lee's body. White people wanted his body to be a warning to every Black person who wanted to vote. So Herbert Lee lay facedown in Mississippi mud for hours, rotting in the sun, a threat to anyone who dared to hope for an honorable American future.

At Herbert's funeral, his wife, Prince Melson Lee, gathered their nine children, wiping their tears and holding them tight. Then she locked eyes with Bob, her jaw muscles protruding. "You!" she yelled, her mouth quivering as she tried to get the words out. "You killed him! You killed him!"

Prince's screams played in Bob's head for the rest of his life. Screams that would have been the biggest tragedy of Bob's time in the Movement; screams that only warned of what was to come.

Bob searched for justice for Herbert with the same tenacity he was fighting to get Black people registered to vote. With the help of John Doar, Bob got word that someone who witnessed the murder was willing to step forward. His name was Louis Allen, a World War II veteran and owner of a timber business in Liberty. Originally, police coerced Allen into going along with Hurst's story that Lee brandished a tire iron and the murder was actually in self-defense. Allen couldn't live with that lie, so he had Bob and Doar arrange for a meeting with the Justice Department to tell the truth: Lee had his hands up when he was killed. When the Justice Department refused to offer him protection, Allen recanted. It was too late. The police and the Klan heard that Allen had flirted with telling the truth. He was now a target. *The* target.

Soon white people stopped supporting his business. They cut his line of credit. They arrested him for bad checks and false domestic violence charges, and threatened to send him to jail for three years for trespassing. One night, a deputy broke his jaw with a flashlight in front of his children. Louis Allen wanted to flee for Milwaukee, but he had to stay in Liberty to work off accrued debts and to take care of his ailing mother. By 1964, though, the years of abuse became too much to bear, and Lee prepared his escape. He got his affairs in order, including a recommendation to drive a bulldozer in Milwaukee. Louis Allen had found freedom and was on his way north.

But those dreams of freedom are as fleeting as gun smoke. Word had gotten out that Allen was leaving town, and that sealed his fate. He was gunned down as he was packing up to leave for Milwaukee. His son found him with half his face blown off.

Another death. Another funeral. Bob and I, supposed to be leading everyone but too pained to see our own paths to freedom. Bob still hearing Herbert's wife every morning. Me replaying the night Medgar was killed like a ballad on repeat. The fog of murder clouding our path to freedom. Again and again. Louis Allen's death planted Bob's feet deeper into the ground, making him immovable from his stance that we needed to have our Freedom Summer plan.

"Now, I know we have been voting," Bob kept on, his voice trembling. "I know we have been debating. I know the COFO way. But we need the participation from as many people in this country as possible. I can't have any more Louis Allens and Herbert Lees. They're just going to keep going unnoticed unless we bring attention to what's going on here. We're *doing* this. We . . . we just are."

Hollis, through his own anger at the news, stayed headstrong. "Now Bob, we just as hurt as you are. But you can't just—"

"Bob is right." My voice was beginning to crack now, too. "We can't just let our people get killed like this. We have to take a re-vote." That callous, cynical reason I had for white kids to come was at my throat, where I held it: maybe when this country sees white people get beaten then maybe everyone will see what we're going through here. If this is what it's come to, then this is what it's come to. Some of them have to face what we face. Some of these white kids might have to be Louis Allen for things to change.

The second vote came in support of going forward with the Freedom Summer and inviting white students. Some of the shift came from people thinking as I had about who America needed to see suffer. Some revisited the urgency of the summer and what was at stake. Some felt like they owed it to Bob, especially after seeing the pain he was enduring. Some of the change came because it was clear that Bob and I weren't taking no for an answer. The two of us pushed harder than we'd ever pushed and turned the meeting into something less than democratic. We damaged the trust other members had in us, but we were doing what we thought was right.

This is how Freedom Summer was born: not with a grand speech or a magical treatise. Not with scholarly journals or political savvy. It was Black folks in a room in the state that wanted us dead. It was with the ghosts of our friends on our shoulders and communities of the bravest people we'd ever know strengthening us with their belief in change and the power of their own efforts at organizing. A handful of Black folks trying to do what was best for the store owners and sharecroppers and pastors from Greenville to Meridian, Hattiesburg to Jackson. We'd felt handcuffs, batons, slurs, and the deep loss of friends we'd never see again. We were fueled by our pain but driven by a refusal to fold. We didn't know if we would win, but we knew the world would change.

I argue with myself every day over whether we should have had those white students come. I can't find the precise calculus to determine whether the damage outweighed the progress. But I do know one thing: I miscalculated the depth of cruelty that comes with racism. I went into the summer of 1964 thinking that white people seeing their own beaten or killed would elicit the type of sympathy that would appeal to their humanity.

I was dead wrong.

XIV.
JAMES, MICKEY, AND ANDREW

Two weeks before our Freedom Summer meeting in Hattiesburg, the CORE folks in New York let me know they'd be sending help in the form of a couple of workers they said were relentless in their organizing and who would be an asset to Mississippi. I was cautiously optimistic, but even that optimism faded when I saw a Volkswagen with a flower on the dashboard pull up to the COFO building. A thin woman in a long, flowered dress and sandals stepped out of the passenger side. Then a man with a goatee, blue jean overalls, and a button-up shirt underneath stepped out of the driver's side.

They were both white.

That was the first time I met Mickey and Rita Schwerner.

Mickey was a social worker out of New York who had seen the inequalities Black and brown kids faced firsthand. Same for Rita, who was a public-school teacher in Queens. Then he got mixed up with CORE, started volunteering, ended up on the payroll, and was valued enough to be sent to the most dangerous state in the fight. As a big, pale sore thumb.

What the hell am I supposed to do with this?

"Mr. Dennis, I'm Mickey and this is my wife a-and we are just over the moon that we can come here and help. We . . . we are just so inspired by what you all are doing in Mississippi. Just tell us where to go and we are all yours."

I looked them up and down. I don't even know if I shook Mickey's hand. "Sure." I immediately went into the office to call Jim McCain and find out if this was some sort of a damned joke.

"They're solid, Dave," he tried to assure me. "I swear. They're going get their hands dirty with you and get things moving. You wanted help, right?"

"Jim, I don't care how well they work. You send me two white kids to be out here by themselves? From New York? What do they know about Mississippi? They're gonna get themselves killed. Hell, they're gonna get some of us killed."

"Isn't this what you all want? A bunch of Mickeys and Ritas running around?"

"Yes, Jim. A *bunch*. Not two. Two hundred brings attention. Two disappear without anyone knowing."

Rita and Mickey felt like more responsibility. Like two burdens I had to keep from becoming dead bodies. I wasn't concerned with how much work they could or couldn't do. So I put them with George and Flukie, who'd become two of the most important workers in the state. They were putting together community centers and engaging locals in Canton, Meridian, and all across the fourth district.

"What the hell are we supposed to do with these white people?!" George asked.

"George, you're the only person who can get them out of trouble when it gets thick."

"So we're babysitters?"

"To freedom, brother."

I tried to keep Rita and Mickey out of sight and out of mind for as long as possible. The less I knew about them the better. Not hearing any news meant they hadn't gotten themselves or anybody else killed. A few weeks later, George called me with a report.

"Dave, why haven't you come down to Meridian yet? It's been weeks." George and Flukie had assigned the Schwerners to Meridian because Canton was too dangerous. And apparently the couple was transforming it.

"Look, I'm just busy with all this stuff we have going on out here. I know that you guys have it under control."

"I don't want to overstep or presume," George said. "But you can't be scared to get to know new people even if you think you'll lose 'em. Now these white folks done came down here to Meridian and done some shit. You gotta come see what they doing. This could be big. I'm sorry, but . . . you gotta get over yourself."

George was just too damn wise even when I didn't want him to be. He was right. I didn't want any new friends who were going to die, especially white people who were going to show up with some flowers on their cars. But if they were doing work and getting Meridian on track, I had to go see them.

When I got to Meridian, I saw a town that was beyond my dreams. Rita and Mickey had used a building donated to them by a local businessman and turned it into a community center. Flukie and George had built a similar one in Canton, but this was bigger—a manifestation of our imaginings of what we wanted that summer. They had their friends from up north and around the country donate thousands of books. The center had voter registration classes, a Ping-Pong table for teens, arts and crafts, literacy courses, and job training, and they were raising money for pianos.

When I got there, they had dozens of Black kids waiting in line for a jacket giveaway. It was beautiful. Rita and Mickey had come to Meridian and set a new bar for what we could accomplish in a Mississippi town. But they didn't do it alone.

They were guided by James Chaney.

James Chaney was a Meridian native and son of Ben, a plasterer, and Fannie Lee, a domestic servant. He joined CORE a few months before the Schwerners got there, hanging out under Flukie's tutelage. James was a skinny kid, only twenty when he started, but he dove after every task like he was trying to catch a rabbit. He was fearless, having been suspended from school for refusing to take off an NAACP button. In public, James was quiet, but get him one-on-one and he was wisecracking and almost hyperactive when talking about the Movement. He was the Schwerners' lifeline.

Initially, Mickey and Rita were able to quietly learn about Meridian and stay away from the Klan, death threats, and arrests. Again, I underestimated them. But once their community center was up and running that was over. They started getting phone calls through the night, white folks threatening to beat Mickey and kill Rita. It took a while, but they'd gotten the targets on their backs that I had been expecting. Through it all, they'd built something transformative.

"Not all of us hippies are so bad," Mickey said when I first walked into to the community center. "I know you were skeptical when we got here. We get it. But we are about this work and we're not going anywhere. This isn't a hobby for us. We're here for the long haul."

As he talked, Black folks would walk by and say, "Hey, Goatee!" It was the nickname the Klan had given him when they were lobbing their threats, and the Black community used it too. He'd in turn call them by their first names or nicknames and ask them about their kids' grades, their businesses, their girlfriends. He wasn't just visiting. He was part of the city.

"No hard feelings, Dave. But if you think this is something, wait until you see what we're going to do in Neshoba County."

Neshoba County was just an hour north of Meridian but an entirely different world. The city was run by overlord Sheriff Lawrence Rainey, a lumbering football player of a man who carried his racism on his broad shoulders. His power came from his role as sheriff as much as his position as the leader of the Klan. White folks knew they could kill in Neshoba with impunity and a blessing from Rainey. Neshoba was terrifying.

"Wait, no. Y'all not going to Neshoba. Please tell me you're not going to Neshoba County."

That's when James walked out of the center, a wide grin on his face. "I told y'all he'd flip out."

Rita could sense my anxiety and how close I was to shutting everything down: "Well, as you know, Dave, lots of people come here from Neshoba on the weekends to shop and they've been dropping their kids off at our Freedom School. And, well, they were interested in us starting one there. Flukie's already been and you know I'm not going so . . ."

"Yeah, I know Flukie's crazy ass has been, but he's been here a while. He knows how to blend in and survive. Mickey, come on, man. You gotta know how dangerous—"

"Dave, ya gotta relax." James was still smiling. "Flukie set everything up with Reverend Collier out there. He drives down the street from the church, flashes his headlights, and they meet and he comes back. They're waitin' on us now to do what we doin' here. And I can handle the safety. I'm doin' the drivin', Mick out there getting folks registered, and we are back in Meridian before Rainey and them white robes know what's hittin' em. And

Rita stays here so they won't be trying to kill me for having a white woman in the car. We got it figgered."

No. Not the fire. Not headfirst into a grave.

James kept on, his eyes wider than the highway. "Yeah, we got a voter registration meeting today. Right there at the church. We're going to have a whole setup there in no time."

"You just can't go into Neshoba County. You're not going to make it."

"You just have to see what we're planning," Mickey said, beaming. "We can handle it. Especially with Chaney behind the wheel."

"Okay" I was pressing my forefinger and thumb into the bridge of my nose. "If you're set on going, then I'm coming with you. I can't let you go by yourselves."

It only took an hour to get there, and the smooth ride betrayed what would come next.

"Okay, we're here. Dave? You ready?" We were in Philadelphia, the biggest city in Neshoba County. The epicenter of hate. James gripped the steering wheel.

Mickey leaned up to James. "Maybe we can take it a little slow with him, no? We got precious cargo!"

"Nah," James said while cutting his eyes at me. "Dave gon' get the real deal."

James slammed his foot on the gas, the tires kicking up dust behind us. He never let up, through backroads, church parking lots, behind grocery stores, the car hitting corners on two wheels, disappearing behind shade trees, bouncing along wooded pathways, driving like he was going to run headfirst into a tree then turning at the last second. My nails were digging into my seat. The whole time, Mickey was calmly explaining his plan, but all I heard was my intestines crashing into my inner ears. It went like this for an hour straight, and even with the chaos, we never caught the eye of any police cars, any curious white men, or any state troopers. We were phantoms because James had learned those roads so well. The dusty pathways were his plasma, the roots were his veins. And he made it his work to protect us and protect Mickey.

As soon as James made it to the church, his foot eased off the gas. I lifted my nails from my the seat. And we were at Mt. Zion Church. Dennis, Chaney, and Schwerner.

I could never get over how beautiful riding through Mississippi can be. When the sun is out, the trees are still, the magnolia flowers are kissing the sky, and the cotton has its hands lifted to the heavens. The whole state can feel like God taking a deep breath. I detest the fact that I spent so many days on those roads with my eyes locked on rearview mirrors and plotting ways to get off without being cornered. Instead of seeing the land as a piece of heaven, I saw it as a pit stop to the afterlife. Low-hanging tree limbs made me wonder which Black foliage would weigh them down and dark infinities made me wonder where I'd eventually find my burial plot.

But I remember that drive with James and Mickey. James in the front singing Freedom Songs. Mickey in the back seat singing along, talking about their plans for registering voters in Neshoba County and their dreams for the Meridian community center. A perfect spring day, so the windows were down and Mississippi was at our noses. For that moment, our futures seemed possible. Revolution was at the next exit. Laughter was at the tips of our tongues. I wish I'd known this would be the last time I'd feel close to serenity on a Mississippi road.

• • •

Our next weeks were all about Freedom Summer. Charlie Cobb had come up with the idea that we could use some of the incoming college students to teach in Freedom Schools—educational centers for local kids across the state, who could get tutored in reading and math. The rest would come and get Black people registered to vote while preparing our case for the Democratic National Convention just a couple of months away. I was also helping run campaigns for local elections for people like Mrs. Hamer, Victoria Gray, James Houston, and John E. Cameron, while trying to secure room and board for the volunteers. I was going to Canton to help George and Flukie; Meridian to help Mickey, Rita, and James; the Delta with Mrs. Hamer; Hattiesburg with Mrs. Gray. I had to find ways to make sure hundreds of these kids could stay alive.

Meanwhile James was driving Mickey around Neshoba County in the shadows. Rita was staying behind in Meridian handling calls and communicating if Mickey ran into trouble, which was happening more often as he became more well known. As the Black community embraced him, he became the Klan's worst enemy. Mickey represented absolute betrayal: a white man defying white supremacy. His being Jewish also represented a proximity to marginalized people that made him fodder for more hate. By the spring, the Klan had put out a bounty on "Goatee." Rita would be up every night Mickey and James were in Neshoba, wondering if her husband was going to make it home. They were just so dedicated, even coming to Jackson every time we had an event. James and Mickey became brothers. And they became my friends, especially Mickey.

COFO set up a training center in Oxford, Ohio, where members would help the incoming volunteers learn how to get people registered to vote, teach in the Freedom Schools, and navigate the communities. Mickey, Rita, and James were part of the group that went to Oxford to help in the training. Before they headed off, I went to Meridian to see them. I wanted to hang out with my friends.

"I gotta tell you something." Mickey had told me he needed to talk when I got to town. When I saw him, he looked like his body had been fighting itself and nobody was winning. I'd never seen him so stressed.

I didn't know what was coming.

"I . . . I think I'm Black."

"Mickey, what they hell you talking about?" I couldn't stop laughing.

"Before coming here, I just didn't know how evil white people were and what we did to everyone here. I've been here in these houses and seen so many Black people without electricity and kids who can't read and don't have any food. And . . . it's not their fault. It's all white people's fault. And the Black people are here and they're all fighters and they are living in spite of it all and . . . I just can't come from the people who do this to other people. I can't be like them. Can I?"

I was baffled, but I just let him keep talking.

"And Black people are just so beautiful, Dave. They're resilient and they are still dancing and partying and they even still smile. Despite everything."

"All you can do is the best you can, Mick. You can't undo what's happened, but you can use your power to make a difference."

"But what if it's not enough. How do I know if we're gonna win?"

"That's what we're doing this summer. You have to use the stuff all those white kids have that keeps them ahead and make some changes here. That's what you can do. But, Mick, you're just gonna have to be stuck at white." I was trying to keep my chuckle light. He didn't join in.

"I mean, I identify with the Black people here and their fight more than with these racists. Why can't I just *be* Black? Hell, they want to kill Chaney *and* me, right?"

"Well, that's true. But they're gonna make you remember one thing no matter what: that you're white and he's not. Somehow. That's what they do. They never let anybody forget it."

• • •

In the middle of June, as night fell on the Longdale community off Highway 16 in Neshoba County, a few members of the Mt. Zion United Methodist Church were leaving the house of worship after a weekly planning meeting. The church was going to be the site of our Freedom School for the summer. As the clergy left, they approached a roadblock, where Klan members with baseball bats and crowbars were waiting for them. One man broke Georgia Rush's collarbone with the butt of a gun. Another dragged Rush's son out of his car and started beating him, his blood forming pools on the red clay under him. More men stomped Bud Cole while his wife tried to escape, screaming and praying that he'd survive. When the mob was done with them, they emptied their gasoline containers at the foot of the church and set it on fire.

This was a terrorist attack on a Black church in America. But it was more. It was a military-grade tactic to smoke out innocent men and get them killed. It was planned with precision and executed like a war mission. They wanted to burn the church, yes, but that was just the first phase of their plan. The Neshoba County Klan—police, businessmen, and politicians among them—wanted to sniff out Mickey and Chaney and bring them to the area for an execution.

Mickey already had the bounty on his head, and they wanted him dead. I knew this. Mickey knew this. Rita knew this. It didn't matter. Neshoba was his area and he investigated the church burning. Mickey and James had to show their faces and let the community know that it wasn't being abandoned when the violence came. That's just what we did. We went into places where we knew death was waiting and we found our way out. It was protocol. We didn't think about the danger until days, months, decades later. If we made it out alive. When I called Mickey to tell him about the burning, he didn't hesitate. He immediately started packing. He grabbed James and they were on their way to Mississippi.

The plan was for Mickey, James, and Flukie to head down to Jackson to pick me up, and we'd all head to Meridian for the night, then on to Philadelphia the next day. But Flukie had to cancel to tend to trainings in Oxford. However, James and Mickey still had a third person with them when they came to the COFO office to get me.

Andrew Goodman came from New York, a middle child of three boys from the Upper West Side of Manhattan. He'd applied to join the Freedom Summer in April and had made his way to Oxford for the training. He wasn't like most of the other white kids who came to Oxford. He wasn't treating the summer like a missionary trip or vacation. He was earnest in his desire to make actual change. He was fearless. Mickey, Rita, and James took to him immediately and saw someone who could handle Meridian and maybe eventually the volatility of Neshoba. Mickey and James thought that their trip to Mississippi would be a good, short test for Andy, to give him a taste of the area he'd be handling when Freedom Summer started.

So the three men drove south.

We were heading into Father's Day weekend, and the lack of sleep and the stress were breaking my body down. I'd been diagnosed with bronchitis and was falling apart. I'd planned to

go home to Shreveport to spend time with family and heal up—
"Come get some home remedies," my mother and grandmother
said—but I'd decided to change plans and ride with Mickey,
James, and Andy. I felt like I needed to go with them. Mickey and
James had other ideas when they saw me.

"Whoa, Dave, you sound horrible, and quite frankly, you look
like shit," Mickey said when they showed up. "You sure you don't
want to just stay home?"

"No, I'm fine. I'm fine. Seriously. I'm coming. There's something about this that . . ."

"Yeah. I know what they want out of this. I know what that
church burning was all about. But we got James. They're not
going to catch us."

"I can't let you all go alone. I need to be there with you. I've
already canceled my plans. I'm coming with you."

Mickey put his hand on my shoulder. He locked his eyes on
mine.

"Dave. Go home."

The thing about dying is never having to live with the guilt.
The thing about living is the guilt never dies.

The three men headed on to Meridian without me. The plan
was for them to leave Andy there, because he wasn't ready for
Neshoba County yet. I'm not sure how he ended up going to
investigate Mt. Zion with the other two. One story has it that
Andy stood in front of Mickey's blue station wagon and refused
to move until they let him ride with them. While they were on
their way to Philadelphia, I was on my way to Shreveport. When I
got there, Mom and my grandmother had all kinds of hot toddies
and oils and medicine in mason jars for me. I slept all day.

Mom woke me up because I'd gotten a call. It was 6:00 p.m.
The voice on the other end of the phone, one I don't remember,

told me that James, Mickey, and Andy had not made their four o'clock call to check in. They just wanted to let me know and would keep me updated through the night. They said not to worry, that they probably got arrested and would be out by the morning. I hung up the phone and buried my head in my hands. Coughing, shaking, and too angry to cry, I knew.

"Sonny?" my mother asked.

"We just lost three of our people."

LETTER 3

Dad,

I remember when I first sat across from you with an audio recorder between us. You had a glass of Crown in your hand and I was squeezing a water bottle. I was asking you about Goodman, Chaney, and Schwerner. I wanted to know what you thought you would have done differently. Where the guilt came from. What you were feeling that very next day. Then you put your glass down, and calmly said, "How long are these interviews, goddammit?" Then you laughed and walked away. Then we played cards and didn't do another interview for the rest of the weekend.

But I knew I had to keep pushing. Even when I could see how it was hurting you. I hope you'll understand.

For example: When we went to New Orleans to talk to CORE veterans to see if they could jog your memories, you made sure we scheduled some time to go to Bogalusa, the nearby mill town on the Mississippi-Louisiana border. "You can't tell this story without talking about the Deacons for Defense and Justice," an armed militia composed of rural Black workers who protected each other and any Movement person who came to their city. You'd set us up for a meeting with Barbara Hicks-Collins, daughter of Bob and Valeria, who organized the Deacons. You'd told me about how they even protected you when you started working with them in 1965, after you returned to Louisiana from Mississippi.

But on the morning we were supposed to go to Bogalusa, you had an upset stomach and stayed behind. So I drove there alone and met Barbara, who was dressed in all black and wearing white tennis shoes. I hopped in her Ford Explorer so she could take me to some landmarks of the Deacons' history. After some time, she said, "A few years ago, we were at a memorial ceremony in Mississippi for my father and your dad was there. He stood up and talked about the Deacons and started getting choked up. Right then, my mother leaned over and whispered to me. 'Dave just still never got over it. That poor man.'"

We finally made it to the house she grew up in, a historical landmark sign on the front honoring Bob Hicks and the Deacons for Defense and Justice. Inside, the house is stripped down to its baseboards and is a skeleton of what it once was—a headquarters for an armed resistance Movement that transformed Louisiana. Barbara walked me to the living room, where Sheriff Claxton Knight once told her father that if he was going to continue housing two white members of CORE, a white mob would come burn down the Hicks home. Barbara pointed to a corner of the living room, where phone wires were hanging from the wall. That's where she and her mother made frantic calls to as many Black men in Bogalusa as they could, asking them to come help before the mob made it to the house. Their instructions were simple: "Bring a gun. Call two more men and tell them to do the same." By the time the white mob showed up, dozens of Black men were waiting for them in the Hicks front yard. The mob turned around and went home. Barbara explained to me that this was the night the Bogalusa chapter of the Deacons for Defense was formed. Ironically, it was February 21, 1965, the day that Malcolm X was assassinated in Manhattan.

Barbara drove me to more landmarks for the next couple of hours: where the Klan shot the first Black deputies in the parish, killing one and leaving the other blind in one eye, where the Deacons housed James Farmer to keep him safe when he came to town. And, finally, to Cassidy Park.

The park, as you know, Dad, is the site of "Bloody Wednesday" in May 1965. CORE had directed the Bogalusa Deacons to try to desegregate the whites-only park. Black families, led by Bob Hicks and Sam Barnes, showed up thinking that the presence of women and children would stop the night from getting violent. That dream ended when a mob of white folks started beating mothers and children with belts and bats. Police joined in, swinging billy clubs and letting attack dogs brutalize as many Black people as they could. They even stuck one man in a cage with a police dog.

Barbara kept driving around the park, stopping to point out the patch of grassy land where a police dog bit her brother. "It was the worst day we had here. It was like a massacre. No one gotta die for it to be a massacre, you know."

Our last stop was at her mother's house. When we got there, her mother did that thing your friends do where they look at me and think I'm actually you, Dad. Their brains tell them it's impossible for Dave from the 1960s to look the same now as then, but their eyes still see it. I'm used to it by now.

I hugged her and she walked me to her living room to show me the guns she used to scare off a car full of Klansmen who tried to come to her house when she was alone, ironing her kids' clothes. Then I apologized that you couldn't make it.

"Oh, I didn't think he was gonna come back to Bogalusa. He probably feels guilty," Mrs. Hicks said. "For what happened."

"For what happened? What happened when?" I asked.

"Your father. It wasn't his fault. He didn't know it would turn out like that. We don't blame him. But he took it so hard, it was such a terror. That night. It wasn't his fault."

"I'm sorry . . . I don't think I follow."

"Cassidy Park, baby. He sent us there to desegregate it. That was his call."

I know you're reading this and laughing. Because when I tried to tell you what Mrs. Hicks said, you said that calling for the people in Bogalusa to go to Cassidy Park was one of those memories that got closed away forever, and you still don't remember doing it but "it sounds like something I would have done." You also swore your stomachache came from something you ate or whatever. I believe you on both accounts.

I've come to understand that your history is as much about what you don't remember as it is about what you can recall with precise certainty. The gaps and the clarity, the stories you cry about and what you laugh about, all imperfectly positioned to carry the narrative strands of your life. But you know that our bodies tell the stories our minds can't. And it's hard to ignore the stories your body has been telling while I try to pick locks in your memory.

I've watched you turn red hot like a carpet burn when I ask you about Medgar. I've watched you struggle to hold your head up when we walked into his office and you looked around with tears in your eyes and said, "I can still feel his spirit here. He just wanted to come to wor—" before your voice broke and you walked away. I'd asked you if you really wanted to go back to that office. Tried to tell you we didn't have to. Then, for the first time, I saw the younger Dave Dennis you described in Shreveport. The one who went headfirst into the fire with little regard for his own life and what would happen next. Your determination to do this, to continue your work, shook me. But even that deep well within yourself has limits.

Erika called me some weeks after Bogalusa. She'd just spent Christmas with you and she was worried. She can tell this all is weighing on you. Something about labored breathing and your hands shaking and just an agitation that's different than before. "Is there any way you can get his stories without actually pushing him so hard? He's almost eighty," she asked.

"I'll figure out a way to lay off him a bit," I lied. Then when I see you I'm back to performing surgery with a switchblade, knowing you feel every cut. I know you want to embrace the gashes like you've been waiting for them; like you deserve them. To make amends for however you think I feel about you. Or amends for your friends who you think still resent you from the grave for not dying with them. I want to stop. But I can't. I need to know what's inside. I need us to see it no matter how much we hate what it takes. So we kept pushing and digging and hurting and hugging and trying.

Until some months later when it all just stopped. And you went away, hiding from the questions and the discovery. Leaving me alone.

"Please don't do this to me," I thought. "I need you to answer my questions, read my pages, and make sure I'm doing the right thing. I can't do this without you. But you've gone silent and I'm a kid again waiting for your promises to come true. I swore I'd never put myself in a position to need you, but I believed in this too much not to at least try. My dad is letting me down. I thought I'd stopped being angry with you."

I emailed those words to you without realizing what Dave Dennis was going through. I should have. It was the summer of 2020. The summer of reckoning. The summer of George Floyd and Breonna Taylor and Rayshard Brooks and the largest protest in American history. I was tearing myself apart trying to cover as much of the American terror as possible, traveling to Brunswick, Georgia, to get the story of Ahmaud Arbery and chronicling every police killing because I felt like it was my responsibility to save these lives that had already been taken from us. I was burning out, breaking down, and falling apart. My body was failing me as well. And, on top of it all, I was hurting as your son. But I didn't see where you were hurting. Until I demanded to know where the hell you were disappearing off to. Then you finally called me.

"I'm seeing how they died now, Davy. George Floyd cried for his damn momma. I can't stop hearing him screaming. He was scared. I watched him die. For the first time I watched what it was like for white folks to kill us slowly. I watched that whole damn video and I don't know why. But now it's on my skin. I can't peel it away. It's in my spirit and it won't shake free.

"I hadn't even considered if Medgar or James screamed for their mommas. Now I can't stop wondering if they did. I can't stop hearing them.

"I couldn't ever hide away the thought of Medgar bleeding out on his driveway while he dragged himself to his door to see his wife one more time. Thirty damn feet. Ten yards. A bullet through his back to his heart and he refused to let terror and blood and gravity stop him from trying to kiss his family goodbye. I've been awake for decades thinking about every one of those last footsteps. Now I can't unsee his last fight because of what I saw happen to George. Did Medgar want to scream for Myrlie? Was he afraid he'd scare his children? I saw that living come out of George and I'm seeing it come out of Medgar on his porch a few inches away from his family.

"You know they killed Mickey and Andy first, right? Shot them dead in front of James. What was he thinking about, watching them get killed and knowing they were lucky? I think about them beating

him, breaking every bone in his body. How he must have screamed.
I've imagined his last thoughts. His last screams. His last prayers.
But now . . . I hear him screaming for his momma, but it's George's
voice in my head instead. My mind doesn't even care to tell the
difference.

"You think he begged?

"George is now James is now Medgar is now all of them. The un-
breathing. The all-screaming.

"I can't stop hearing and seeing it all again for the first time.
Memories aren't memories anymore when they keep happening in
real time. I just . . . I can't look at these pages right now. I can't go
back. I'm already there. I never left."

I'm sorry, Dad. I should have seen what this was doing to you. I
knew this would hurt. That's what this work does. But I didn't think
it would be like this. What this country did and is doing, again, is
keeping this distance between us. Making you retreat into darkness
from a son who wants to love and honor you.

Eventually you came back, reluctantly. Fearfully, I think. I swore
I wouldn't let you down again. You're fighting so hard for this, and I
see how you've been fighting for me this whole time in your own way.
But my sister's words stay with me.

I try to cut our conversations short, right when it feels like the
tidal wave of memories will crush the dams in your skull. That's when
we stop. But not a moment before.

When I'm done torturing you, I hug you each time. I thank you.
You apologize for the holes. You use the phrase "post-traumatic
stress disorder" and how a therapist said you were showing similar
signs of trauma as someone who had come home from war. You
talk about the decades you spent learning to sleep again because
any creak in a wooden floorboard woke you up like you were still
in a Freedom House thinking some Klan member or cop had found

his way in. I note the irony of the word "post" in that phrase when we live in a country that has never stopped terrorizing. I tell you that you're doing great, and this is one of the bravest things you've ever done; facing all this again when hiding for however many years are left would be so easy. I think this is good for us. But it doesn't feel like it. I keep telling myself there's a line. And that there are stories and memories and confessions and crosses I won't demand that you tell. Nails I won't let you hammer into your palms. I promised I'd take care of you while we did this work and suddenly I'm the one making pledges I'm not sure I'm able to fulfill, no matter how much I assure myself I can.

I don't know exactly what you felt sending people you loved off to die for their hopes of freedom. I wonder if it felt like this.

XV.
SEARCH

I should have died twice in Philadelphia, Mississippi.

In a matter of hours, the news was spreading across the country that three men had gone missing. The kids in Oxford had heard and were increasingly afraid to come to Mississippi. Bob was blunt with them and with those who had already arrived: we can't guarantee your safety. The picture of what happened was starting to take form, like concrete drying, but the truth was somewhere encased below. The three men had been arrested that afternoon and disappeared sometime that night.

"The slaying of a Negro in Mississippi is not news," Rita told reporters, who were swarming around her to get her story, enamored by the white woman who'd lost her brave husband in Mississippi. But she rejected that privilege and the narrative of the lost white boys. She centered James in every conversation, even while grieving her husband. "It is only because my husband and Andrew Goodman were white that the national alarm has been sounded." And she was right; FBI agents and journalists were pouring into Mississippi, hot on the trail of the disappearance.

Meanwhile, in less than a week, we were going to have thousands of students come in for Freedom Summer in addition to the three hundred we'd already lodged across the state. So, with endless fires to put out and me being the main extinguisher—most of the veteran workers were still up in Oxford training volunteers—I knew I'd have to keep a cool head. I couldn't leave for Mississippi that night and be away from the phones for the four pivotal hours it would take to get to Jackson, so I spent the night at my mother's coordinating with Doar for a search and talking to families before heading back. My mother knew I had to go back too. It was killing her.

That morning, I sat in silence near the entrance of her kitchen, having made a tiny space for myself amid the newspapers and various hairdresser catalogs she kept scattered around. She stood with her back to me, hovering over the stove with her head down. I watched her shoulders rise and fall as she kneaded dough for her famous drip-drop biscuits—tiny pockets of wonder, always filling the kitchen with the smell of reunions, birthdays, and safety. Today, my mother was trying to hum church songs to herself, but I could hear her voice wavering underneath her harmonies. I watched her cook, grappling for the words to tell her I was going back to the heart of it all. But no words were coming to me.

"I packed you a bag of drip-drop biscuits and some chicken for your trip," she said, without lifting her head from the stove. I could tell even from the back of her head that she was fighting. I sat staring at her, taking in her familiar shape.

"But I let that first batch of biscuits sit a lil too long. They might be kinda hard," she continued. "If you stay until these are done I—"

"Mom. I have to—"

"I know!" She pounded her fist into the dough. "I begged for you to get out of Shreveport. I thought I was saving your life. But this?" She shook her head. "It wasn't supposed to be like this, Sonny."

I drank a glass of milk and grabbed the bag of food on my way to the door.

I stopped, put my hands on mom's shoulders, and gave her a kiss on the cheek. I gave her shoulders a squeeze and lingered for a beat while she put one hand over mine. She tapped my hand twice and I let go. I didn't tell her goodbye. She didn't say it either; we were both thinking the same thing. This was likely to be the last time she'd see me alive. I walked out of my mother's house and drove to Jackson.

The first thing I did there was drive to the COFO building. I spent the next day trying to keep everything together while others in the office manned the WATS lines, the private phone line we used to check in or for locals to call if they ran into trouble voting. I spent my first day back in Jackson picking up calls in case anyone had threats of violence to report, jotting down relevant details, and securing stays for the kids coming to Mississippi. I tried desperately to put Philadelphia out of my mind. There was just too much work to do to think about my friends, I told myself. But then the three men would come right back at me: I knew, deep down, I'd sent them to their deaths.

One thing I couldn't get over was a tactical error I had made. We wanted to make sure we sent as many seasoned workers as we could up to Oxford to train, leaving just a few of us back in Mississippi who actually knew the ins and outs of survival. I'd left young workers in charge of the WATS lines in Meridian and Jackson. They didn't understand how seriously we had to take punctuality. If someone had to check in at 4:00 p.m., they checked in at 4:00 p.m. We'd even pull people out of the field if they took too long to check in, because they would have drained resources and put people in danger by having us form search parties in volatile areas. Mickey and James were the most punctual of all. They'd never be a minute late to check in. The person on the WATS line in Meridian waited an hour to call the person in Jackson, who waited an hour to call me. They should have called me at 4:05. By the time they called, it was too late. That's how I knew the boys were gone.

But nothing weighed heavier than me not being in that damn car in Neshoba with them. I kept thinking about Mickey and James telling me to go home and take care of my cough. Why did I let them talk me out of going?

Doubt had started to creep in, and I was wondering if I let them talk me out of going because deep down I was too scared to go. Was I a coward? I went back over the last few days in my head. I mean, I'd felt well enough to drive to Shreveport and then back to Jackson two days later. So how sick was I, really? I let three kids overrule me; I'd backed away, when I should have stepped forward. I had let them throw their lives away and said not a goddamned word. Only a coward would do that. Slowly, the notion that I could be scared became a prospect more terrifying than any other I'd known before. It came over me with a terrible power.

The rest of the summer loomed ahead of me. If I was too scared to ride with those three men into Philadelphia, then how the hell could I keep anyone safe in Mississippi? The thought started in the corner of my mind, a tear that grew wider with each distress call that came into our phone lines. Finally, the ringing anxiety became louder than any WATS device in the building. All the voices of people around me looking for guidance started to become mute. All I could hear was the voice in my head whispering cruelly: *You're too scared to go to Philadelphia, you're too scared.* Then the voice was yelling. *You're only alive because you were too scared.*

I knew then that I couldn't be consumed by these thoughts. So, on my second night back in Jackson, I got up from my desk in the COFO building, grabbed a set of keys, hopped in one of the COFO-designated cars, and drove. To Philadelphia, Mississippi. In Neshoba County. Where a part of me died with those men.

It's impossible to relay the level of recklessness it took for me to make that trip. I used a marked COFO vehicle, so any cop who stopped me would have known I was in the Movement. I didn't tell anyone I was making the drive. We had no system in place to check on my whereabouts or for me to confirm that I was safe. And I drove alone into the heart of the same Klan country that had just taken three lives, with no justice in sight.

My solo trip wasn't some death wish—at least I don't think it was. I just needed to know that I was still willing to die for my beliefs. That kind of conviction had become part of my identity. So I drove down 16 West in dimly lit back roads with my radio off singing—no, screaming—Freedom Songs to myself. The car slipped under black trees in the dark, moss-covered ditches and creaky overpasses. The same roads James drove us through months earlier. I could only wonder if the boys were buried nearby.

To distract myself, I spent part of the drive running through the logistics of the summer. Where would the kids stay in Atlantic City for the Democratic National Convention, did we have enough places for them to stay in Jackson, do we have enough people manning the WATS lines? Those problems were easy to work out in my head. But I had questions that night that I still haven't been able to answer.

The day before I decided to make my trip to Philadelphia, the FBI had alerted us to the fact that James, Mickey, and Andrew had been arrested and sent to Neshoba County Jail before being released with the disappearance occurring some time after. What I couldn't make sense of were all the scenarios that played in my head of what happened next. The logical conclusion would be that the sheriff or the Klan followed the three men from the jail-house and pulled them over. But every Black person and activist knows that standard protocol when being followed by police was to keep driving until you can pull over in a public place. Even if that results in a high-speed chase. Better to get arrested for a more serious crime in front of witnesses in the nearby bigger city of Meridian than to be pulled over on a Mississippi back road where trees cover graveyards. James and Mickey especially knew this rule, yet they stopped? Why the hell did they stop?

For six decades now, I've been reassured by friends, family, and other veterans in the trenches that there was nothing I could have done to keep those men alive. This is the sensible argument. But in the parts of my mind darker than those Philadelphia roads I drove through, I still feel like I could have saved them. Maybe all they needed was a veteran directing them to keep going, keep pushing, until they had the salvation of others' eyes on them. I could have made the difference. I should have given myself the chance to try.

Nothing happened to me that night in Philadelphia, despite how risky it was for me to return to the scene of the crime with zero lifeline or safety net. No one spotted me. I didn't run into any police or Klansmen. Regardless, before I got home, I resolved not to tell Mattie what foolish gambles I'd taken. I put my keys on the kitchen counter and kissed her on the forehead as I climbed into bed. I told her I'd had a long day, and then I lay there, staring at the ceiling until the sun came up, alone in bed with my wife.

• • •

Mississippi had descended into a war zone that summer. It was burning, and in that dark fire, the drive through Philadelphia became my first eulogy for James, Andrew, and Mickey. But there was too much work to do; besides, I couldn't offer much help with any attempts to recover their bodies. The Black locals who were raised in Philadelphia and knew those woods like the backs of their hands had insisted that we stay away. They were accustomed to such gruesome searches and knew where to look.

We'd get calls about bodies being found in ditches and lakes all across Neshoba County. We'd learn that the bodies weren't the ones anyone was looking for and someone would inevitably let out a "thank God it's not *them*." Eventually that relief would fade. They were finding *bodies*. All during the search for Mickey, James, and Andrew, locals and police kept finding bodies of Black people that were missing hands, heads, feet. Unidentifiable, forgotten Black people who had families that never stopped looking for them. More than a dozen bloated, waterlogged bodies that we never would have found if not for the fact that two white kids were now missing too.

I spent the next month diving into crises to distract myself from the missing men.

Our challenge to the Mississippi Democratic Party at the DNC meant running our own precinct meetings on farms and sharecropper land across the state. We had to run county and district conventions. We would have to run a state convention as well. We were forming a grassroots democracy in Mississippi. In enemy territory where opposition forces walked among us.

Then the rest of the Freedom Summer volunteers arrived.

Despite the training they received in Ohio, the workers were still mostly naive white kids who didn't fully understand what they were getting into. Every day there was a new call about violence. White girl Freedom Summer volunteers in Natchez riding around on the back of a pickup truck driven by Black men, putting bull's-eyes on everyone's back. A white kid from Connecticut talking back to a cop in Meridian and getting tossed in jail. A white couple in Canton getting beat up by Klansmen for wandering alone too late at night. I'll never forget one group of about four volunteers I had to get out of Mississippi after they'd spent a night in a Yazoo jail—the police would come into their cells with revolvers and play Russian roulette with the kids every hour on the hour until the sun came up. The group was so shell-shocked, we had to send them home to recover.

The volunteer presence also made life more dangerous for locals who were getting fired, beaten, and punished if anyone found out they were housing any of the Freedom Summer kids. Meanwhile, the Black community treated the volunteers like they'd treated us for years—like extended family. They took the kids in, fed them, protected them, and kept them alive.

In the meantime, my job had shifted. I wasn't just a community organizer anymore; I was a war general. And when you're a war general, you have to stop thinking about people as individual human beings. After the three men went missing, I felt a shift inside me. I left Philadelphia forcing myself to understand that every person I sent on assignment wasn't likely to make it back. They had to be dead to me before I sent them away. It's hard to explain just how cold that makes a man. How people with whom I shared meals and laughs suddenly appeared to me as kindling for an endless fire of violence and sacrifice. I had to bury my conscience in Philadelphia. Nobody knew where those three bodies were, and I didn't know where my soul was either.

I didn't realize how emotionally detached I'd gotten until I got a call to meet three workers at the tiny café adjoining the COFO building. They'd just returned to Jackson after a trip to Natchez. When I saw them, their eyes were darting around the room, their hands shaking so much that the meat was falling out of their sandwiches as they tried to force their meals down their throats.

"D-Dave," one of them was saying. "We were in Natchez getting affidavits from the Brown family. They tried to vote and got turned away . . . so . . . we were parked outside of their house. A-and we were about to go in. We were just sitting in the car getting our files together. Then some white boys . . . they started shooting. Either they got word we were in town or they saw our car or . . ."

"Yeah," another one chimed in. "The car, it's right outside. You can see the bullet holes. R-right there."

They were terrified. And I'm sure they wanted some re-assurances from me, words of encouragement and affirmation. They wanted to know they were safe and, most importantly, that they'd done a good job. I didn't have those words for them. Instead, I listened to their story silently and didn't speak until after they finished.

"So, did you get the affidavits?" I asked.

". . . Dave . . . We . . ."

I reached in my pocket, never taking my eyes off the men, pulled out another set of keys, and tossed them on the table.

"There's another car for you outside. Go back to Natchez. We need those affidavits."

I got up and went back to work without saying another word to them.

I wasn't myself anymore. I was losing my humanity and I may have been losing my mind. I didn't know how to get either of them back. Or even if I wanted to.

One night around 10:00 or 11:00 p.m., I had left the COFO building and walked to my car a few feet away from the front door. After I got in, another vehicle with two white men in it pulled around the corner and stopped parallel to my car, our windows lined up perfectly. One white man in the car pointed a shotgun at me. I could see straight through the barrel.

Die, nigger.

There's the old saying that your life flashes before your eyes in these moments. I'd spent the last three years wondering what I'd do when the wrong racist got his hands on me. How would I prepare myself to meet my death? Would I pray? Would I think of my grandparents? Mattie? How would I make my final, defiant stand in the movement? From the moment I decided to join the Freedom Rides in 1961, I played this over in my head every day. And now that I had the cold metal of a shotgun aimed at my temple, I laughed.

Wildly. Uncontrollably. Mouth agape. A hearty, sincere laugh from the belly of my soul—a laugh like I was at home in Shreveport with my family, telling jokes. I still don't know why I laughed. I do know that the sound of it—the deep shock of that laugh bursting out of me—unsettled the man who wanted to kill me. He paused with his finger on the trigger. And while he hesitated, one of the women who had been working the WATS phone walked out of the COFO building. As soon as she saw the gunman she turned around and screamed back into the building, "They're about to kill Dave!"

Her yelling startled the two white men, so the driver pulled off. I got out of the car, calmly walked into the COFO office, and shrugged off what had just happened. "I'm good, everyone," I said as the few people left in the office started to crowd around me. I couldn't let them see me rattled even as I felt my guts readjusting.

"Ain't nothing to worry about, y'all. We scared them white boys off for the night. I just need to wash my hands real quick and I'll be back on the road." Everyone prepared to leave as I headed to the back of the building, directly to the bathroom.

I scrambled to get my pants off in just enough time not to shit in them.

• • •

I eventually made it back to Philadelphia with more COFO members to the site of what used to be Mt. Zion Church. We were trying to let the city know we were with them still and reignite any momentum we could for voter registration and the Freedom School. It was the first time I'd shown my face since the church burning.

I was catching up with people when I heard the shuffling of feet approaching me. It was an elderly Black woman I'd met at the church a few times when I'd gone to meetings. She was almost running to me, her arms extended and her eyes wide. She put her wrinkled hands on my face. Then on my shoulders. Her lips were quivering.

"Ma'am, is everything okay?"

"Dave? Is this you? How?!"

"Yes, I'm sorry, I'm not sure I understand."

"How are you alive? I thought we lost you!" She hugged me like she wanted to squeeze all of my air away. She put her head on my chest, her eyes tightly closed, and I could feel her lip quivering against my chest. "This whole time . . . praise Jesus . . . all these days . . . I thought you were in the car with those boys. I thought you'd been dead this whole time."

XVI.
EVEN IN HARLEM

The New York City CORE chapters were going to hold a rally in July to bring more attention to the search for James, Andy, and Mickey, who had been missing for a month. They wanted me to lead the rally. I agreed to go but the more I thought about it, the more uncomfortable I felt. They wanted me to inspire hope, promote peace, and uplift the community. I had none of those sentiments to offer and didn't want to pretend.

But I did need to make a trip north to Atlantic City to secure our hotel for the Democratic National Convention. COFO workers Jean Wheeler and Mary Lovelace had worked magic to get a Black business owner to let us use his hotel to house all the volunteers and delegates during the event. I would make one more pass through the property to make sure rooms were assigned and we had enough space, and while I was there, I would decide if I wanted to participate in the New York protests. It was a peaceful break from Mississippi. But peace always finds just enough space to slip through clasped fingers.

On July 16, while I was still in Atlantic City, a group of Black teenagers in New York City had been hanging out in front of a building in the predominantly white working-class Yorkville section of Manhattan. The building's superintendent grew annoyed by their presence, so he'd sprayed the youngsters with a water hose, allegedly calling them niggers while doing it. James Powell, a fifteen-year-old, saw the commotion and followed the super into the building to confront him about his treatment of the Black boys. According to witnesses, Powell was only in the building for a couple of minutes.

When the teen came out, he ran into white NYPD Lieutenant Thomas Gilligan, a seventeen-year NYPD veteran who was posted nearby. What happened next remains under dispute. Gilligan, a six-foot-tall former U.S. military officer, says he ran toward the building after hearing glass breaking. He says he yelled out, "I'm a police lieutenant. Come out and drop it," then fired a warning shot after seeing Powell lift a knife and charge. He contends that he dodged another attack from Powell before shooting two more times. The second bullet hit Powell in the right forearm before traveling into a main artery above the heart. The final shot hit him in the abdomen before exiting his back.

Eyewitnesses have a different story. They say that Powell came out of the building unarmed and laughing. They say that when Gilligan pointed his gun, Powell lifted his arm to defend himself. A knife was later found about eight feet away from Powell's body, and one of his friends, Cliff Harris, would testify that Powell had a knife before going into the building after the building owner. Also, Gilligan had a history of disarming violent attackers, which led the public to wonder why he didn't disarm a fifteen-year-old if he did in fact have a knife on him.

Powell died on the scene.

The killing of Powell was all over the news, and Black New Yorkers were ready to fight for answers. CORE wanted to shift the rally for the three missing men to now include a call for justice for Powell. But they also wanted to remind everyone to stay nonviolent. I knew CORE was going to ask me to keep preaching the sermon of peace and I just didn't think I could muster those words. It felt dishonest.

I'd decided to just leave from Atlantic City and go back to Jackson to get us through the rest of the summer. But first, I had to cancel plans with my friend David Baldwin, whom I met through his brother, James.

I first met James Baldwin in 1961. By that time, he had become infatuated with CORE and wanted to help. He'd done some speaking engagements and donated some of his earnings—upwards of $10,000 per appearance after 1953's *Go Tell It on the Mountain* made him a prized voice—but he'd have me tag along as an opening speaker. Most of these trips were in New York. My purse was much less, but I had my checks sent directly to the CORE office and it helped local chapters. It was during these trips that I really got to spend time with him.

James would also travel to Mississippi to work on his play *Blues for Mister Charlie*, based on the 1955 trial of Roy Bryant and his half brother J. W. Milam, who murdered Emmett Till. At that time, Baldwin hadn't written any fiction set in the South, though he'd begun to focus his reporting there, the beginning sparks of *The Fire Next Time*. To add realism to his play, he wanted to spend some time in Louisiana and Mississippi. He'd spend nights at Dooky Chase's and Oretha's house, quietly stirring his glass of whisky with his straw. He'd sit with his legs crossed, absorbing the way the locals talked. Jerome, who had done far more in helping with *Blues for Mister Charlie* and was even credited as an adviser, introduced me to James as someone who could add insight into Southern culture and how we felt about the white people we came in contact with every day. Sometimes he'd have Jerome and me read lines to each other to see if it sounded natural.

Baldwin, of course, was a master orator. But I noticed he only spoke around us when he felt it absolutely necessary. Otherwise, he just listened, his eyes sharply focused on the people in the room. He'd nod, let out a soft bellow of understanding, and occasionally jot down notes. He was the proverbial fly on the wall, constantly thinking and breathing in the Movement. If you observed him closely, you could see how he listened with a deep passion, leaning in and nodding intensely as we talked. It was that quiet enthusiasm that let us know he cared about what we were trying to achieve.

The thing about James was that he drank like a fish, but never got drunk. He just got more honest, more biting, and seemingly more intelligent. Often, I'd watch him at our speaking engagements, surrounded by white intellectuals who wanted to test just how smart the well-spoken Negro really was. He'd sit around with these rich white folks who kept pouring him his whisky. And inevitably, at some point, one would try to have a philosophical sparring contest with him. James's response was typically laconic. He'd put his drink down, and his voice would lower and slow down at once, reverting to a measured, calm cadence. "Well, my dear . . . ," he'd start, before whipping the argument of his would-be contender. If he wanted to, he could leave any man red-faced and embarrassed.

It was during one of these New York trips that I met David Baldwin, and we became good friends. He knew how to captivate audiences and become the life of any room, just like his brother. But whereas James was all wit, David was all charisma. David was

an actor and he seemed to know everyone in New York, schmooz-
ing his way to the center of attention. Whether it made the
situation more or less volatile didn't concern him as much as
the sense of drama he could add.

Needless to say, David was a good time, and I tried to make
sure I hung out with him whenever I could. So I'd called him
when CORE invited me to New York so I could stay with him
instead of at the YMCA, where I'd sometimes spend the night
when I came to town. Now, I was just giving him the courtesy of
letting him know those plans had changed.

"C'mon, brotha, you can't do me like that! I got liquor and
things for us to get into, my man."

"I just can't come out there. I don't want to be in the middle
of all of that. There's too much going on in Mississippi I gotta get
back to."

"Look, how about this. You come to New York and you don't
have to do any of that ra-ra freedom fightin' when you up here
with me. We can just hang out incognito-like, you know?"

"How the hell am I gonna do that?"

"Just trust me. Drinks, food, and hanging out. CORE won't
even know you're here, my man."

• • •

We spent most of my first day in New York at David's apartment
on 110th Street and Fifth Avenue, catching up, drinking, and, beneath the pleasantries, playing an unspoken tug-of-war. Despite
my heart's desire to enjoy spending time away, my mind would
wander to Jackson. In turn, David would notice and try to pull me
back to distractions.

"Nothing is going to happen to those white boys who killed
them," I remember him telling me. "You know that already. So
you might as well drink!"

By this time, it had been three months since *Blues for Mister Charlie* debuted at the ANTA Playhouse in April. David, who was acting in the play, saw it as one of James's crowning achievements for the way he was able to give a voice to the voiceless Southern Black folks terrorized by racial violence. But it was the song that came from the play—a titular track by Bobby Sharp that had those church pianos and a voice that sounded like every ounce of agony we'd ever felt. The track had been reverberating in jukeboxes from Chicago to Harlem.

"Man, I gotta hear that track. They don't play it in the South like they do up here." I was starting to feel the liquor at this point.

"Dave, you gotta hear it out here around *these* Black folks," he said, beaming. "This is really our generation's 'Strange Fruit.' You gonna go back to Mississippi a new man when you hear that song in Harlem."

By the time we looked up, it was dark. We needed to grab something to eat, so we headed toward 125th Street, the part of Harlem I loved because it reminded me of the smaller Black communities in the South that felt the safest in between the moments the police, racists, and whoever else would come bother us. Where we could feel like we were at a family reunion even when we walked down the street. As we kept walking, we kept hearing more commotion than usual. Then we finally saw it: great plumes of smoke billowing over the horizon. Police sirens were wailing blocks away, and far off, glass was breaking. We were in the middle of what would be known as the Harlem Riots.

Earlier that night, the Downtown, East River, and South Jamaica CORE chapters held the rally they'd originally wanted me to attend on the corner of 125th and Seventh. During the rally, one high school student from the Bronx CORE chapter stood on a chair and yelled out, "This shooting of James Powell was murder!" She was followed by a twenty-minute speech from Fountain Spring Baptist Church's Reverend Nelson C. Dukes, with James Lawson by his side. They then organized the rest of the group of protesters to march to the 28th Precinct.

The NYPD responded by rounding up, beating, and arresting as many Black folks as they could, agitating and inciting as much chaos as possible. A police line had already formed, and protesters started tossing bottles at them. Black folks took to rooftops, tearing apart loose pieces of mortar and bricks and throwing them at police. Harlem wouldn't know peace again for days.

When we left David's apartment, I was hungry and meditative. But now, facing the outside world, I was speechless. This didn't look like the New York we thought we knew. This was the world I was trying to escape. So we walked. In the direction of the smoke and sirens.

My plans to remain under the radar had vanished, so I asked David to walk me down to the Harlem CORE office on West 125th Street to see if I could help.

The first thing we saw as we approached the building was a cop car that had been set on fire. CORE members—a mix of Black and white—had formed a bucket brigade, passing water from cups, vases, and bottles from inside the building to the car to put out the fire. "Of all the damn things they could be doing right now," I thought to myself. We made our way upstairs to see if anyone needed any immediate help, but it didn't take long for me to realize that we needed to get away from the building. These people were just as lost and confused as the rest of the world.

"David, we gotta get out of here, man. They're going to get us killed in he—David?"

He was already halfway out of the second-story window and climbing up a fire escape.

It was a pastime for Black kids growing up in Harlem to hang out on rooftops and back alleys, and David knew those as well as he knew the name of every socialite he ran into at a club on a given night. We jumped from rooftop to rooftop, climbing up and down fire escapes and through back alleyways. I was a country boy who was more used to running barefoot in cotton fields than on loose rocks and concrete beneath my shoes.

As we made our way, we saw Black faces that ranged from angry to scared to sad and broken, the same faces I saw in Mississippi— Black people desperate for answers and solutions, trapped in a cycle of violence not of their doing. And we saw so many beaten, bloodied Black people, all across Harlem. Groaning, writhing in agony that came from being at the wrong end of police nightsticks. At one point, we saw police hosing off the side of a brick building with the water flowing red into the sewer. And around us, we saw windows, unwashed, coated with grime and blood. It felt almost too much to bear, being that close to their faces and their screams. And just when I thought my knees might buckle, David and I would shimmy back up the fire escapes, observing again from above. That day in Harlem I thought, if this is what God sees when he looks down, then what possible faith can he have in this world?

It was there, somewhere between heaven and Harlem's hell, that I found out there was no break from the Movement. The Movement simply wouldn't pause—not for anything, nor anyone. I couldn't escape it; it would always find me. None of us could escape it.

"Okay," David finally said while we were resting on a rooftop, breaking me from my spell. "Ready for some Wells?"

• • •

Ann and Joseph T. Wells opened the Wells Supper Club in Harlem in 1938, in a tiny haven with room for only five stools. Soon, it was a staple for Black jazz musicians either local or popping into town for a gig. After their acts at other clubs, these performers would come in looking for something to eat, usually at that 3:00 a.m. sweet spot, some hours too late for dinner and too early for breakfast. Struggling to figure out what to serve at this hour, Joseph Wells came up with the idea of frying leftover chicken for his patrons and pairing it with cheap breakfast fare, namely waffles. The dish became so popular that soon enough Wells, on Seventh Avenue between 132nd and 133rd Streets, became a regular stop for Black Harlemites. This was the impetus for America's chicken and waffle craze. By 1964, Wells was a 250-seat must-visit for Black folks. Sammy Davis was a frequent diner there, and it's where Nat King Cole held his wedding reception.

Hanging out in Wells felt like being in a Black galaxy away from the outside world. But on this night, my biggest obstacle was surviving the walk there.

Somewhere along the way, we found ourselves in the middle of what looked like an old-fashioned standoff. In front of us were NYPD officers; behind us, Black Harlemites, bricks and glass bottles in their hands. Just as we saw the two groups fixing to charge at each other, I pulled David into a phone booth.

"Dave," he said to me.

"Yeah?"

"I don't think hiding in a glass phone booth is a good idea."

"Good point." We jumped out and ran for cover, ducking away in the shadows until we could resume our quest. This would be one of the only things we laughed about that night.

When we finally arrived at Wells, smooth-talking David had no trouble getting a table, even though the place was buzzing from the chaos hitting the neighborhood. We were sitting swallowing our waffles and chicken and talking about what we had seen over the last few hours.

Suddenly, two white female cops came scrambling in the restaurant, their eyes wide and darting around the room. A white male cop followed them in, letting them know he would stay with them in the restaurant and wait for a police car to come and pull them out of what they saw as danger. At this point, the conversations in Wells turned to murmurs. Everyone's eyes and ears were focused on the officers. The uneasiness building. Then a Black teenage boy stormed in. Everyone in the restaurant could see that he had blood splattered on his shirt. He walked right up to the cops.

"Why are you here?! What are you doing here?"

One of the women, her hands shaking inches away from her nightstick, said, *Look, kid, we're just trying to help you all. We're out here to protect you.*

The kid looked her square in the eye. And without raising his voice, he asked, "You're here to protect me? Then why did you shoot my brother?"

At this moment all the Black men in the restaurant began to stand up one by one. No words were spoken. It was dead silent, but suddenly the air was beginning to drain out of the room. My pulse quickened. We watched the officers watching us, surveying the volatile situation they were in. Sometimes stillness is just as scary as movement when you know that every single person is a split second away from acting on their most basic, emotionally raw instincts. The entire country was in that restaurant. Goodman, Chaney, and Schwerner. Powell. Vietnam. Emmett Till. Each person in that room had a personal story of death and persecution, and all our ghosts were in attendance, our pain ready to be unleashed. A room full of silently detonating warheads.

David took his napkin out of his lap and slowly placed it on the table and stood up. Without saying a word, he walked to a tiny jukebox at the corner of the restaurant. He put a nickel in. And pressed play on "Blues for Mister Charlie."

• • •

It was the way the song cried. The way the piano wept. That song was the fire that sparked the powder keg forming in Wells. The male cop walked to the jukebox and smashed it with his nightstick. The rest of us were yelling at the cops, indecipherable screams. Half wanting to know if what the boy said was true, the other half not needing confirmation. We were in the middle of our own insurrection inside a tiny chicken and waffle joint while the rest of Harlem was burning.

Joseph Wells, who was respected as a community leader, came out from the kitchen to calm us down. The cops called for backup and got the hell out of that restaurant, leaving us there to hold ourselves together through the denouement of our turmoil.

To this day, I don't know what happened to the boy or his brother.

• • •

That night in Wells felt like the end of the world. All our anger, pain, and confusion had been harnessed in one place, and the power of those emotions couldn't be set loose without more violence. The next day, I was supposed to head back to Jackson, but now I knew I wasn't ready. I was too shaken up and David was insisting that another day in Harlem would be therapeutic, somehow. So, I stayed. I wish I hadn't.

We spent the next day walking again, eating at Wells again, and trying to stay out of trouble. By this time, the Black Harlemites we'd seen had calmed down. In fact, the whole next day, Black folks had pretty much gone back to their lives, minding their business. That was how unstable our world had become: one day, Harlem was burning down, and the next day, the people calmly moved across the city in the same old patterns. They had to; there was food to put on the table. But that didn't matter to the police. At this point, the NYPD was actively antagonizing Black people for simply walking down the street. They'd pull up in their squad cars and trucks whenever they'd see Black folks and demand that they get off the street or get arrested, beating and pepper-spraying as many as they could. The Harlem Riots were called such because of the Black uprising, but as has always been the case, it was the police doing the rioting.

That night David and I were walking when we saw a Black kid with jeans, a T-shirt, and an Afro running out of an alley. He seemed like a kid just playing, even jovial as he ran. We couldn't even get a good look at him. While he was running, he darted right in front of two cops—one white and one Black—manning the corner. With poor timing, the boy was crossing the street away from the cops just as someone on a nearby rooftop tossed a bottle at those officers. The bottle hit the ground and made a loud pop, eerily similar to a gunshot. We were startled—David and I jumped—and everyone on the street stopped to see if someone had started shooting.

Without hesitating, the white cop pulled out his gun and fired. David and I ducked. We covered our heads and ears, faces to the concrete, and when the shots stopped, we got up and checked ourselves to make sure we weren't hit.

"You good?"

"Yeah, I'm good."

Then I heard David. "Oh, God."

He ran down the street to the Black figure crumpled on the ground. It was the boy.

I followed behind David, running toward the boy. A boy. I was screaming in my head. I had no idea how old he was, if he'd be someone I'd end up knowing. But we knew we had to get to him fast. David got there first. By the time I arrived, he was holding the boy's limp head up. Blood dripped from somewhere on the child and started to cover David's hand. In that pool of dark blood, almost black, I could finally see the boy's face. He couldn't have been older than ten. His mouth was agape and for some reason I noticed that he still had some baby teeth.

The police were right behind us. The white cop shoved past me and pointed his gun at David.

Get up, nigger.

David didn't move.

Get up, nigger, or I'm gonna blow your fucking brains out.

David looked up at the officer.

"You just did."

In the cop's eyes, I saw fear—but also adrenaline. I could see that he had no idea what he was doing, and yet he knew exactly what he was doing. He'd shot one Black person and he couldn't control himself anymore.

Hey, calm the hell down. The cop's partner intervened and took him away. Soon an ambulance came and medics worked on the boy. David and I were cast aside and left standing there. We watched the medics gather the boy up and toss his body—his little limbs dangling by his side and his head leaning lifelessly on his shoulder—into the back of an ambulance like a bale of cotton onto the back of a trailer. We didn't move. We couldn't. There was only stillness between us, the world moving around our standing bodies for what felt like hours. Soon, there was nothing left around us. No boy. No police. No medics. It was like he was never there. The only proof we had that he ever existed was dried blood on David's hand. And as soon as David found a leaking fire hydrant, even that proof of life would rinse off onto the street corner and into a gutter.

● ● ●

David and I spent the rest of the night crying. Of all the violence I'd witnessed in the summer of 1964 and all my years in the Movement before that, I hadn't ever seen anyone get shot. Every day America was showing me how ruthless a country it could be, and I was seeing the effects in ways I hadn't imagined when I joined the Movement in 1961.

A refrain surfaced inside me, bubbling forth: They shot that boy. I kept repeating it all night. I'd been visiting Harlem for three years by then and had created an image of the neighborhood in my imagination. This was the Black utopia. The Black heaven unsullied by the scourge of white supremacy. I'd dreamed of turning Jackson into Harlem. I'd envisioned a Shreveport that felt like 125th Street. Sometimes, in the darkness of my own dreams, when crevices of my mind opened enough to allow me to fantasize, I'd drift off into a different world, where I'd pretend that if things got too dangerous, Mattie and I could just leave and head to a place like Harlem. I knew I'd never do it—but the possibility was like a window I knew I could open, some fresh air to help me sleep some nights. But now it was all laid bare: Where the hell could we go? They are shooting boys in Harlem. Harlem! They're killing us in Harlem like they kill us in Neshoba County. I heard Medgar's voice again. *Everywhere in this blasted country is Jackson.*

I knew then that I was trapped. America had caged me. I was locked into a cycle of unrelenting death, and there was nowhere to go to get away from it. From Hattiesburg to Greenville in Mississippi, I'd spent every day watching people get beaten—

only to go to Harlem to watch a child get shot in the street. America wasn't going to stop until it killed us all. They shot that boy. All night. They shot that boy. All the way on the plane ride back to Jackson. They shot that boy. We'd never even find out if he survived.

I didn't sleep much after Harlem, but the work couldn't end. There was too much to do for me to dwell on ghosts. I had to contain my emotions and trauma for the Freedom Summer to work. But tamping my fire wouldn't last long. Because it wouldn't be even two weeks after my return to Mississippi that I'd have to deliver a eulogy.

XVII.

THE EULOGY

They're dead I've known they'd be dead since I got the call they were missing but now I'm in a church and there's a casket with Chaney's body in it or what's left of it after the bones in his shoulders and jaw and ribs and spine were ground to dust. Like a plane crash, a coroner said. A jet engine of white-hot hate melting his body. They shot Mickey and Andy once but rained hellfire on James's body.

Someone from CORE is talking to me about this speech. They're telling me to be peaceful when I walk out to the stage to deliver James's eulogy in this tiny church where he sang and volunteered and registered people to vote and loved and prayed for tomorrow. A sweaty church with women waving paper fans and the type of heat you feel but don't mind because you know God is there. One of those churches, like Mt. Zion in Shreveport, that made us feel free. Not even bombs and fires and dead Black people filling up caskets could stop us from talking to Jesus. The type of church four girls could play in.

These people from CORE are telling me to offer a message of optimism. They're telling me Freedom Summer depends on my speech. If I incite a riot all we've worked for is over.

I don't hear them, I hear the lies from the past six weeks. The lie that after those boys were arrested at 4:00 p.m. they were released from jail at 10:00 p.m. and pulled over again and killed, but I know it's a lie because James didn't stop for police. He would have driven until sunlight. I know that. I remember swerving those roads with him and his big smile and Mickey's sarcasm and the way they teased me and made me their friend when I was too scared to be. Why did they make me love them if they were going to die?

I nod and tell the people from CORE that I'll share a message of hope and nonviolence.

I'm not in this church right now. I'm in a car with Mickey, James, and Andrew. I'm telling them to keep driving so they don't get pulled over the first time. I'm looking out of the car window and showing them a back road they can take to get away. I'm jumping in front of a bullet and giving James enough time to get away. I'm screaming so that people can hear us. I'm saving I'm dying I'm anywhere but here.

Each step I take toward the microphone in front of this church in front of the people I've let down and sentenced their brother or son or nephew or friend to death is a stomp inside my chest. I'm digging. I'm digging a hole large enough to put my anger and covering my agony in dirt as it claws to the surface. Stepping and digging. I'm at the microphone and I'm in the crowd watching myself speak and bury.

I deliver a eulogy for James Chaney.

I'm not here to do the traditional thing most of us do at such a gathering. And that is to tell of what a great person the individual was and some of the great works the person was involved in. I think we all know because he walked these dusty streets of Meridian before I came here. With you and around you. Played with your kids and talked to all of them. And what I want to talk about is really what I really grieve about. I don't grieve for Chaney because I feel that he lived a fuller life than many of us will ever live. I feel that he's got his freedom and we are still fighting for ours.

My fury is clawing faster than I can dig and I'm standing in front of the church with the dirt in between my fingers and watching myself try and fail to be the man of peace they wanted. I don't know how I can save a Freedom Summer and what saving Freedom Summer even means if they'll kill Mickey and Andy and more and not even care about killing Chaney and this won't end.

As I stand here, I not only blame the people who pulled the trigger or did the beating or dug the hole with the shovel. I blame the people in Washington, D.C., and on down in the state of Mississippi for what happened just as much as I blame those who pulled the trigger. Because I feel that a hundred years ago, if the proper thing had been done by the federal government of this particular country and by responsible or irresponsible people across the nation, we wouldn't be here today to mourn the death of a brave young man like James Chaney.

As I stand here a lot of things pass through my mind. I can remember the Emmett Till case, what happened to him, and what happened to the people who killed him. They're walking the streets right now, and the brother of one is a police officer in a place called Ruleville, Mississippi. I remember back down here, right below us here, a man by the name of Mack Parker, and exactly what happened to him and what happened to the people who beat, killed him, and dragged him down the streets and threw him in the river. I know

that those people were caught, but they were never brought to trial.
I can remember back in Birmingham the four young kids who were
bombed in the church and had just gone to services and I know
what has happened to the people who killed them—nothing. Re-
member the little thirteen-year-old kid who was riding a bicycle and
who was shot in the back? And the youth who shot him, a white guy
from Birmingham who got off with three months.

I can remember the Medgar Evers case in Beckwith. The governor
of the state going up and shaking the judge's hand when the jury
said that it could not come to a verdict. I can remember down in the
southwest area where you had six Negroes who'd been killed, and
I can remember the Lees and all the other people who know what
has happened to those who have been killing them. I know what is
happening to the people that are bombing the churches, who've been
bombing the homes, who are doing the beatings around this entire
state and country.

The deaths tumble out of my mouth faster than I could stop
them and I can never stop them. I'm always too late or too sick or
too tired or too incapable and the deaths keep coming. I can't even
collect them in my throat before they spill out onto the church
floor. I see Chaney's twelve-year-old little brother, Ben. His face is
buried in his mother's chest and he's trying to hold his head tall
but the weight of it is too much and I see him strain to look up.
And I see his face and the stream from his nose to his mouth and
from his eyes to his chin. He sucks his bottom lip in with each
breath and he's shaking his head as if his "no" will change reality.
Ben's face is a boy's face, but a place where all the loss converges
for eternity. No matter what comes next I'm always standing in
that church and looking at a boy and seeing James and Medgar
and Trayvon and Black boys in Harlem and Tamir Rice, who was
Ben's age, and the people we'll cry for forever. I see Marvin.

I see the people left behind to cry. I see Medgar's three kids who waited for him to come home and Alton Sterling's son weeping at his press conference and Herbert Lee's children and his wife with her finger in Bob's face and Atatiana Jefferson's nephew and George Floyd's daughter and always Ben's face all of them wiping away tears as I stand before them in this church in 1964 exhausted and without any answers to make it better. Our deaths become a Möbius strip of loss that brings me back to this goddamn eulogy. I'm always delivering this eulogy.

Well, I'm getting sick and tired! I'm sick and tired of going to memorials! I'm sick and tired of going to funerals! I've got a bitter vengeance in my heart tonight! And I'm sick and tired and can't help but feel bitter, you see, deep down inside and I'm not going to stand here and ask anybody here not to be angry tonight.

You see, we're all tired. You see, I know what's gonna happen! I feel it deep in my heart! When they find the people who killed these guys in Neshoba County, you've got to come back to the state of Mississippi and have a jury of their cousins, their aunts, and their uncles. And I know what they're going to say—not guilty. Because no one saw them pull the trigger. I'm tired of that!

We can't take it any longer and be wiped off the face of the earth. I look at the people of gray hair down here, the tiredness in the faces, and I think about the millions of bolls of cotton that you picked, the millions of actions it took to chop it for ten dollars a week, twenty-five dollars a week, or whatever you could get to eat. I watch the people here who go out there and wash dishes and cook for the whites in the community, the same ones who come right out and say, "I can't sit down and eat beside a nigger." I'm tired of that, you see. I'm tired of him talking about how much he hates me and he can't stand for me to go to school with his children and all of that. Yet when he wants someone to babysit for him, he gets my Black mammy to hold that baby! And as long as he can do that, he can sit down beside me, he can watch me go up there and register to vote, he can watch me take some type of public office in this state, and he can sit down as I rule over him just as he's ruled over me for years.

This is our country too. We didn't ask to come here when they brought us over here. I'm sick of hearing over and over again that I should just go back to Africa. Well, I'm ready to go back to Africa, baby, when all the Jews, the Poles, the Russians, the Germans all go back to where they came from too, you see. And they have to remember that they took this land from the Indians. And just as much as it's theirs, it's ours too now. We've got to stand up. The best thing that we can do for Mr. Chaney, for Mickey Schwerner, for Andrew Goodman is stand up and demand our rights. . . . Demand! Say, "Baby, I'm here!"

I'm not standing anymore as much as I'm leaning on a lectern to hold me up. I don't have that thing in me anymore that allows me to smile when police call me *nigger* or compels me to sing Freedom Songs at funerals. I'm burning like this country should. My tears feel cold on my face until they mix with the froth of the inhumanity I feel. This isn't a speech this isn't a eulogy this is a midair grenade. I've been asked for peace but that part of me isn't alive anymore the part of me that cared for peace is buried and the rage holds the shovel.

Don't just look at me and the people here and go back and say that you've been to a nice service, a lot of people came, there were a lot of hot-blasted newsmen around, anything like that. But your work is just beginning. I'm going to tell you deep down in my heart what I feel right now. If you do go back home and sit down and take it, God damn your souls!

Stand up! Your neighbors down there who were too afraid to come to this memorial, take them to another memorial. Make them register to vote and you register to vote too. I doubt if one fourth of this house is registered. Go down there and do it.

Don't bow down anymore! Hold your heads up! We want our freedom now! I don't want to have to go to another memorial. I'm tired of funerals, tired of 'em! We've got to stand up.

I'm tired of funerals.

We've got to stand up.

I'm tired of funerals. We want our freedom now.

Stand up.

LETTER 4

To my children, Oktober and Max,

When I was kid and we moved from Lafayette to Jackson, Mississippi, your Big Pop showed me the Civil Rights documentary *Eyes on the Prize* for the first time I was old enough to remember it. When I think back on it, I imagine he was preparing me for something about Mississippi I wouldn't understand yet. I wonder if he was inspiring me or warning me.

I was too young to understand everything in the movie, but I remember that night I ran to him crying. Squeezing him and bunching up small handfuls of his shirt. I told him I was scared that the white men with hoods were going to come to my room and take me away. He caressed the back of my head and lied again and told me those men didn't do those things anymore.

A couple of years later, when I was eight or so, about your age now, Max, I was home with your Big Pop and the tornado sirens went off. I ran to him, ramming my forehead into his stomach and screaming, "Daddy protect me, Daddy protect me." He told me he would. Like all fathers do. Like I'd do for you two. But he knew better.

"What can I do about a tornado?" he says when he retells that story. "I'm sitting there telling my son everything is gonna be okay and I guess I have to but, hell, if a tornado comes there's nothing I can do to protect him. Something like that is just too big. But what else are you gonna tell your kid?"

Those two memories tell the same story. They're both stories about the inevitable and the futility of trying to stop the natural and unnatural. When your Big Pop was a kid, barely in his twenties, he fought a war he thought had an ending. "I thought we were going to win," he once said. "There was a time in the Movement when I thought that by the time I had kids or grandkids—if I ever had any— that the fight would be over. It took one summer for that idea to go away."

My brain tells me I should know better than to think I can stop the American terror in its tracks before it comes for you. But I still tried to protect you from it. I spent your early lives trying to keep you aware of a Movement that was right outside of our windows. I'd tell you about police sometimes doing bad things or why there were marches or correct you when you'd come home telling me about wars of "northern aggression" or Columbus Day. And of course you knew the broad strokes of your Big Pop's story. But I wanted to make sure I never made you feel part of a Movement before you had the agency to decide for yourselves. I tried to guard you.

That's why I lied to you in early 2017.

It had been three months since Donald Trump became president. Three months since I sat on my couch as my body went from shivers to sweats while I watched the TV show me state after state revealing this country to me for the last time. That night I came to your room while you were sleeping, Max. You were curled into a tiny ball. I scooped you into my arms and lay you on the bed between your mother and me. I hugged you tightly and buried my head into your back and wept: the weight of the night on your shoulders. A grief you never should have had to carry. You just nestled your head into the bend between my bicep and forearm, your thumb in your mouth. Oblivious to the growing sogginess at your shoulder blades. The next morning, Oktober, I explained to you that the man from that recording you heard about grabbing women without their consent had become president instead of a woman. You asked me if we could move to another country and I told you everything would be fine.

America had notarized white terror as being worthy of the most powerful office in the land, corroborating every white supremacist inclination held by everyone who would ever learn to hate us. The shift wasn't as sudden as so many who have faith in America would have us believe. Ferguson, for instance, predated Trump's presidency. So did every story your Big Pop tells you about the Movement. Nevertheless, kids, there was a shift. The openness of the racism and the vitriol to anyone who opposed it was as tangible as any I'd every witnessed. The hatred had seeped into the responses to my work. I'd write about this country and white folks would threaten me. Us. They'd say things about you when I'd write about your intersectionalities. I'd do what I could to stop them, absorb it all in quiet and play with you two like the rage gathering at the corners of my mouth wasn't there. These were the tiny lies I told to protect you.

I told the big lie on the February after Trump became president, though. I'd written an article on the eve of the Super Bowl that declared Tom Brady's act of promoting Trump's MAGA hat for a press conference was more un-American than Colin Kaepernick's act of kneeling during the National Anthem to bring attention to the extrajudicial killing of Black people. The backlash to the article put my name on white supremacist public relations sites, Breitbart, *Fox & Friends*, and anti-Black mascot Tomi Lahren's lips. Within hours I was fielding calls while pretending to be my own secretary and listening to angry white men call me a terrorist.

Two days later, I got a call from Homeland Security.

Some white guy phoned Morehouse, where I was an adjunct professor at the time, saying he was in Tennessee and he and some of his friends were going to grab some shotguns, hop in pickup trucks, come to Atlanta, and shoot up the school. The Homeland Security guy told me to stand by while he got more information. Your mother and I got you two out of school and told you we were going to just hang out for the rest of the day. I took you to Dairy Queen as an apology for something you were oblivious to. Then Homeland Security called back to tell me that the man who called was actually in Massachusetts and just pulling a "harmless prank." Case closed. I looked at you two, vanilla and mint chocolate chip soft serve smudged across your lips and cheeks, and I had to face the reality I was trying to deny: I can't protect you from this. I can't press my hands against gale-force winds to hold it away from our home. You were going to get caught in this no matter what I did. I felt so ashamed for thinking otherwise.

Can you imagine that? Our lives are threatened by white supremacy and I feel a shame that white folks don't even have for themselves. They don't give their kids the talk about how to stop racial violence and keep their Black friends alive or weep over the disgrace of what their generational cruelty has birthed. We have a country full of Civil War reenactments and Confederate statues and altars to slave owners that tell us that white supremacy doesn't come with shame. But there I was, guilt-ridden that I couldn't protect you from all of that. The cruelty is relentless.

There are some days when you feel like being Black in America is just time spent between fury at what white supremacy has done to the people who came before you and fear of how it will destroy those who come next. I spent too many years in this purgatory.

These last few years of seeing Big Pop through his own eyes have given me answers I didn't know I was looking for. Your Big Pop and I have been putting ourselves through something that has bent and cracked our spines for years now to tell his stories. I've spent months wondering why I kept pushing both of us beyond where we thought we'd be, and I didn't know why I kept digging in ditches I was scared to fall into. But I started writing this letter to you and I know why.

Seeing him—really seeing him—and then looking at you, has taught me why we've been pushing so hard here. Why I've been pressing my palms against his temples to squeeze out all the "why" I can. I thought I was doing all this for him and his legacy, to find a way through the morass of hurt to show him that he's my hero. He thought he was doing this for me. But I've come to realize we've done this for something bigger. We've been fighting for you this whole time. We were doing this to get rid of fear. And make room for something else.

I've learned to see you two as more than a history I had to undo, or a future I had to protect you from. Oktober, I remember you walking out of your school to protest gun violence and I've heard the anger in your voice when not just you but someone you know is victimized by racism, homophobia, or transphobia. You have much more empathy and understanding of social issues than I did at your age. Max, when you were six, I was driving us home from school and asked you about Martin Luther King and you said that America was a puzzle and all the pieces were different races and the pieces were on the floor and all he wanted to do was put the puzzle back together. Then you said it was our job to pick up those pieces for him. I turned around and looked at you in your car seat, your eyes never leaving the Scooby-Doo comic book you were reading. I asked you if that's something your teacher said. Or where you got that idea from. You still didn't lift your eyes from those pages. "It just came to my head, silly."

I watched you two and your fervor for the Black Liberation Movement in the wake of George Floyd's death, with a passion and understanding beyond your ages. And for the first time, I didn't see it with fear in my eyes. I had to learn to stop projecting our future by the immenseness of the terror and start looking toward the endlessness of your resolve. I'd been seeing this all wrong. You two are the storm.

Our people can take to the streets out of a refusal to give up when faced with the seemingly unstoppable force of generational terror. So many of us dedicate our lives to the irrational and radical belief that we can change the course of the three-dimensional flow of history. We fight for a new future, but we fight to save our past too. When we say Breonna Taylor's name, we are screaming for George Floyd's daughter, too young to know what happened to her father, and we charge for Mamie Till, so she can know her child wasn't taken in vain. The Movement is a defiance of time itself. And I can't give up on our Movement.

I want these words you hold in your hands to remind you that you'll never be alone. Even after your Big Pop and I are gone. I want you to see that there are and were people just as scared and uncertain as you will be. And all they did was their best. I want you to grow up unburdened by the dichotomy between activist and useless bystander. I want you to see your survival as the work. Your love as the Movement. And your refusal to break as the realization of your dreams.

Live. Be alive. Live.

XVIII.
DEMOCRACY

Deeply buried in the Mississippi Freedom Democratic Party was a belief in America and the idea that following the rule of law would work. Yet by the time James, Mickey, and Andy went missing, I knew better than to expect this country to redeem itself even in the face of irrefutable legal precedent. My faith in America was gone. My faith in my people was all that remained. And three of those people who we counted on completely were women: Mrs. Fannie Lou Hamer, Mrs. Victoria Gray, and Mrs. Annie Devine.

Mrs. Gray was a rarity in Mississippi. She was a middle-class schoolteacher in her late thirties—an elder to us—who was loudly and unapologetically a forerunner in the Movement. Much of the middle class was reluctant to show their faces in any Movement activities. They had a lot to lose—houses and cars and their status as upwardly mobilizing members of society. Many, though, secretly donated what they could. Mrs. Gray didn't share the fears of Black folks in her tax bracket. She was married with three children and still showed up at the very first SNCC meeting in Hattiesburg with Hollis and Curtis Muhammad.

She took to us and was one of the reasons Hattiesburg became so successful. While Mrs. Woods kept us sheltered, Mrs. Gray kept us fed. She organized a phone tree among other middle-class Black folks to get us a hot meal when we were in town. She pushed people to register to vote, refusing to take no for an answer. Eventually she'd become a field secretary for SNCC, running voter registration workshops and tutoring sessions for kids in any church that would have her. She'd become one of the founders of the MFDP and one of the women who encouraged us to drive to Atlantic City.

Mrs. Devine was as crucial to the Canton Movement as George or C. O. While Mr. Chinn was the bulldozer tearing down opposition, Mrs. Devine was the architect ready to create new structures in its place. A former insurance agent who graduated from Tougaloo, she cared deeply about the education of the kids in her city. Eventually she'd quit her job to work with CORE full-time. Mrs. Devine was in her fifties but as energetic as any of us. She was fearless, organized, and one of the kindest women you'd ever meet. That kindness got as much done as C. O.'s aggression.

These three warm, kind, loving women put COFO, Mississippi, and the entirety of American democracy on their shoulders and would not budge unless this country transformed into something different. And we'd be damned if we let them down.

• • •

I'd found my rhythm as a behind-the-scenes organizer through 1964 and was happy continuing that role in Atlantic City, even as my eulogy for James had made headlines across the country and helped bring national attention to the violence we were facing. As our sixty-eight delegates took to the convention center, Mattie and I were outside picketing with volunteers and making sure they were taken care of. This is where I felt at home.

Inside, the Democratic Party's 108-member credentials committee was hearing testimonies from the MFDP. Dr. King spoke on our behalf, delivering one of his unmistakably passionate pleas for our voices to be heard. But it was the locals whose voices rang out the loudest. Hartman Turnbow, a farmer from Holmes County who would become one of our most vocal leaders, told the story of how his house was firebombed when Klan members found out he'd tried to vote. A bombing that Bob was charged with committing when he was seen investigating Turnbow's house the next day.

Mrs. Hamer would go last. She'd always go last. She was the anchor.

Lyndon B. Johnson was a cowardly, desperate man whose ego made him determined to win an election to prove he deserved to be president and not just Kennedy's replacement. He was worried about the MFDP because acquiescing to a bunch of Black folks from Mississippi would alienate his Southern base, which he needed to win. He couldn't allow us to get those seats and he couldn't allow the country to see that we deserved them. Mrs. Hamer's voice, her story, her courage, her singular unbreakable entity terrified Johnson and the white power structure as soon as she opened her mouth. He rushed to cut her speech off from being broadcast live, but he should have known that trying to stop her was futile. So even though Johnson aired a bogus press conference to interrupt the live broadcast of her speech, the media was so moved by her words that her entire sermon aired on prime time.

Mrs. Hamer, a sharecropper from Ruleville, Mississippi, with a middle-school education, was a woman Mississippi and America never cared about. Yet she made the country see her plight, her scars, her fight, what Winona jail cells tried to do to her, and how she continued to march with all the oppressive forces that tried

to stop her nestled in between her toes. She challenged Mississippi and dared America while the president of the United States
shuddered under the might of her song cry. We went to Atlantic
City for America to see us, but with Mrs. Hamer's help, we forced
America to see itself.

If the Freedom Democratic Party is not seated now, I question
America. Is this America, the land of the free and the home of the
brave, where we have to sleep with our telephones off the hooks be-
cause our lives be threatened daily, because we want to live as decent
human beings, in America?

The Democratic Party had no choice but to give us something.
But we didn't lose James, Andrew, Mickey, and more people than
we could count for *something*. We came for everything. They only
offered us two delegates out of sixty-eight, a paltry compromise
that was only symbolic in nature, yet there was a real debate about
whether or not we should take the concession. Then Mrs. Hamer,
Mrs. Devine, and Mrs. Gray spoke.

"We didn't come here for no two delegates. We came here for
sixty-eight and we are either leaving with sixty-eight or nothing,"
Mrs. Devine said calmly.

"And some of y'all telling us to take these two lil measly seats
ain't been in Mississippi with us more than two weeks all summer so don't come up in here telling us what to do," Mrs. Hamer
added, clearly speaking to Dr. King and others who had thought
we should take what was given.

Even if some of us thought the two delegates were enough, it
didn't matter. Nobody was going to go against these three women.
They'd fought as hard as anyone else, and we owed them the final
say. We had come too far not to get what the law of this country
promised us.

I stood out on the Boardwalk where the Children of the Constitution stood next to children of the enslaved in defiance and disbelief, hearing about what had happened inside the convention hall. They were learning the truth about America. It was a communal reckoning with the realization that laws and documents were as immaterial as the justifications for hating someone for the color of their skin. Disenchanted with the ideal of the country's fairness, they would go out into the world with an understanding that would rule the rest of their lives.

The 1964 Democratic National Convention changed America. It cracked the mask, creating a fault line that stretched through to 2016. Nineteen sixty-four gave me a true understanding of whiteness that I wish I had had when I joined the Movement. I learned that white identity is indelibly linked to white supremacy and the degradation, violence, and oppression white people have wrought on America for four hundred years. In order for whiteness to exist as an idea in its current form, it has to embrace white supremacy. Because whiteness is bound to the idea of everyone else being less than. Slavery, lynching, economic disparity, educational inequalities are all part of white identity. Without superiority to the marginalized among them, the idea of whiteness crumbles under the weight of its fallacy.

I've thought for decades about my conversation with Ross Barnett in his office, wondering how someone so blatantly racist could appear so bluntly unaware of the injustices he was committing. I can't stop thinking about his face, the honesty in his questions, the conviction in his bewilderment. It took me years to realize that his genuineness wasn't a contradiction from his racism; it was a feature. White supremacy is an act of reshaping reality. The sheer belief that skin color defines value is necessary for whiteness. It's the same kind of distorted thinking that allowed a segment of the country to believe that Goodman, Chaney, and Schwerner orchestrated their own disappearance and fled to Cuba as part of a communist plot instead of the obvious murderous truth staring the country in its face. The same reality distortion that allows a country to see a cop's knee on a man's neck as he pleads for his mother as a justified act. Or police choking a man to death on a New York street as proper procedure. Or an insurrection at the White House as some harmless act of patriotic passion. Barnett was sincere because he had so dedicated himself to the lies that he was convinced were truths. It was the most cordial conversation I'd have with a white lawmaker in Mississippi, yet it is the one that I can't shake because of how it revealed the true depths of the commitment to white identity.

I entered Freedom Summer with the belief that once this country saw white victims of white supremacy, it would see the error in its violence and change. I underestimated the nature of the monstrosity. I learned too late that white supremacy values whiteness over even white people. I saw Jim Peck's bloodied and scarred face after the beating in Birmingham. I saw Andrew Goodman's and Mickey Schwerner's bodies buried by the KKK. I watched the terror inflicted on white volunteers all through the summer of 1964 because they were threatening the supremacist ideals white folks held the most dear. In the end, they were just inevitable, necessary sacrifices in the pursuit of preserving whiteness.

So many of us went into the Democratic National Convention believing that this country would value the institution of democracy over white supremacy, but we learned that democracy loses its integrity as soon as it no longer serves whiteness above all.

We followed all the rules of democracy in Mississippi. We did what the Constitution says would create a fair playing field for

American voters in this country. We did what we were supposed to do according to the established codes that dictated the way America operated. And as soon as we were able to utilize that law to meet our needs, it stopped becoming the law of the land. The country had no legitimate means to deny us our representation at the DNC. None. So they just . . . changed the rules. The DNC disavowed its own democracy when that democracy was about to serve African Americans.

The 1964 Democratic National Convention, Freedom Summer, and Mrs. Hamer's testimony paved the way for the 1965 Voting Rights Act, which paved the way for Barack Obama to be the first African American president. But the way this country showed its true values and its ability to toss aside its own ideals also paved the way for a Donald Trump presidency. The 2016 election is as much the son of the 1964 Democratic National Convention as the 2008 Obama election.

When Barack Obama became president, many white people believed that he sullied the highest office in America. He destroyed a monument of white exceptionalism. And because a Black man held that office, whiteness required that same office be occupied by a man who lied, hated, and failed his way there. Donald Trump verified the idea of white power after Obama made white folks feel like something less than superior.

Yet, seeing the relentlessness of white supremacy has only strengthened my love and understanding of what it has taken to survive and fight while Black in America. I come from a people who built this country because of slavery and in spite of it. Who have the power to tear down the structures that oppress us and build something new in its place. We had no generational wealth, no political or economic power, yet we walked, rode, and fought together. We were organizers, artists, writers, speakers, who protested, made art, spoke, shot, and loved while facing the empirical force of an entire country and militias roaming its streets. We are a people who resist, not just because we have to but because we desire more. We are not passive riders. We are the force that kept each other alive and saved this country from itself even as it dug its heels into the ground stained by our blood.

We became husbands, wives, mothers, fathers who tried to love our families while squeezing the American disease from our bodies. Some of us failed. Some of us doomed our children while trying to pull ourselves off the ground. All of us loved as best we could. Our Movement persisted in the way we tried to make the world tenable for our children. Mass incarceration. Police violence. Gerrymandering. Redlining. Our Bull Connors and Ross Barnetts became Donald Trumps. Our futures became the legacies we tried to salvage even as we tried to understand the wreckage from our pasts.

But through it all, we were still us. Movers. Black resistance. The undeterred. Describing what we do as fighting against whiteness is insufficient. It's reactionary. We are initiators. We have moved forward regardless of whether the sensation at our backs is bullets or the wind.

● ● ●

I don't just spend my nights thinking about the stories I've experienced or the stories I know. It's often the stories I don't know that keep me awake. It's the families we left behind and what happened to them when we were gone. The mother of four in Greenville who would cook us fried chicken on Thursdays. The factory worker in Hattiesburg who let us use his car even though his white boss knew he was helping out the Movement. The families who risked their lives and had to fend for themselves when the Freedom Summer was over and the white kids went back north. I think about the terror we delivered to their doorsteps and how we could never protect them from it. I think about their bravery when they shouldn't have had to use it.

There's one couple whose names I don't know and who I only saw once from a distance, who stay in my mind, and I can't shake loose. An elderly Black couple in Canton who rode on a mule-pulled wagon to vote in our Freedom Vote Day in 1964, an embodiment of all we fought for and who fought for us. I can still hear the clippity-clop of the mules' hooves hitting the ground, the creaking of wood from their carriage behind them. The man wore overalls over his dress shirt and tie and a wide-brimmed hat to shield his eyes from the sun. He chewed on straw, his jaw muscles bulging from his wrinkled face. She wore a Sunday dress, pink and green flower patterns, and a bonnet. They parked their mule and wagon in a parking spot like it was a car. The couple never quite understood what they were doing or why they were there—"We're here to vote for George Raymond," he said before we had to explain to him that he was just there to register and George was never on a ballot anyway. The couple got out of their wagon, walked past the armed sheriff's deputies who were there to intimidate and take note of the locals participating, to remember who to punish when night fell and the Movement folks went back home. The couple walked into the courthouse, were promptly denied their right to register to vote, and got back in their wagon.

As the man headed away, he nodded in our direction, tipped his cap to the sheriff without blinking, and kept riding. That was the last I saw of them: man and woman, resisting in their own way before disappearing into the Mississippi beyond.

US REDUX

By October 2020, America was 200,000 deaths into a pandemic that would wipe away more than half a million lives. At the same time, the embers of smoke from a summer of police violence were evaporating into the atmosphere—causing us to look to the sky, waiting for it all to rain back down. October 2020 was also the month my dad turned eighty.

We'd spent most of the pandemic having family Zoom meetings to replace the annual Fourth of July visit, the planned trip to Orlando for a week, the Labor Day barbecue. A post-Christmas trip was about to get canceled, too. We were looking at a year without seeing each other. Dad Zoomed us for my kids' birthdays at the beginning of October and I heard a dad I hadn't heard before. The one I wanted when I was a kid.

"I miss y'all so goddamn much . . . I, excuse my language kids. I miss y'all so much," he said, choking away tears. The outlines of his eyes were turning red again. Then he got off the call. My dad had been traveling—running—his whole life, and now he was confined to one space, at home with a spouse for longer than he'd ever been with anyone in one place his entire life. And now he was cut off from seeing the rest of his family, who spent their lives longing for him to finally stop moving. The irony was cruel. And I'd allowed myself to feel something I hadn't given my spirit permission to feel since I was a child: I missed my dad too. He was four hours away but farther from me than he'd ever been.

A couple of weeks later, we Zoomed dad on his birthday. My wife, kids, and I were in our car. "We're on our way to the park but wanted to say happy birthday real quick!" The kids chimed in from the back seat, singing their off-key celebrations. Dad was smiling but I could see the sadness behind it. "I just miss y'all," he repeated.

Suddenly, I slammed on the brakes. "Man, this fool won't get out of the way." I started honking the car horn, screaming at a driver who wasn't there. I kept pretending to throw a fit of road rage. It took my dad a while before he realized the sound of the car horn was coming from outside of his house.

We sat outside all night, obeying our new world laws of social distancing while eating and laughing. "I'm just through the moon right now. I don't even know what to do with myself." It was the happiest I think I'd ever seen him. It was a happiness that I grabbed out of the air and held on to like a hug I couldn't give him.

A central tenet of Americana's particular anti-Black terror is separating Black families from one another. The Black family was never essential, thus it was as disposable as the Black people those families consisted of. Black families, and the unity and love and strength we gained from them, were instead an obstacle to the efficiency of American chattel slavery. Enslaved Black people landed in America separated from one another, parents and children landing on separate corners of the New World.

Black men and women were bred to create more labor, so Black babies were ripped from their mothers' wombs and sold to the highest bidders. After slavery, Black husbands and fathers had to choose between opportunities in northern states and their families back home, leaving many wives, mothers, and children behind as distance and violence made the men disappear. The twentieth century saw the rise in mass incarceration, imprisoning Black parents and separating them from their families. All the while, white America was callously crafting Moynihan Reports and narratives that broken Black homes were a function of some innate characteristic of Blackness that made us incapable of maintaining familial units. Meanwhile mothers, wives, and partners, like Mattie and my mother, had to glue and pray and strengthen and love and fortify in the midst of so much absence.

My dad was supposed to end up as the head of a shattered family full of resentment, distance, and misery. From Mattie to my mother to my sisters to me and all our offspring. The men who pulled guns on him and killed his friends may not have been thinking about my father's descendants, but they didn't have to. Their terror rattled loose the leaves of our family trees. My father was supposed to either die or become so stricken with dread and fear that he'd run from us. We weren't supposed to stand a chance.

I grew up thinking I knew my father, the promise-breaker, the man who loved with his whole heart even if the rest of his being couldn't follow, the workaholic, the runner, the kindest, nicest, cursedly unreliable father I could ever have. I've had to grow to recognize the fight he's had to survive to love me like he has, even when he's fallen short. I've had to learn to forgive the parts of Dave Dennis that became my father and love the parts of my father that were shaped by the Movement. This journey with my father has shown me that both parts of this man, the one I've loved the longest in my life, together make up a complicated, flawed, brave, and wonderful person.

Now more than ever he talks to me about what he wishes he could have done better for me. That he hates what he feels like he became after the Movement. I want to hold him and tell him that he did his best. That I should have thanked him for the lessons he taught me as Dave Dennis. For the parts of who I am that are reflections of him. That while I never searched for my father's approval as a family man or the way I love my wife or raise my kids, I wanted Dave Dennis's approval. I wanted him to feel that his legacy was stronger with every day I strived to be a better man. That I admired the way he stood up for people who couldn't stand up for themselves. The way he stared down a country until it blinked. The way he refused to cower. The way he dreamed of a better world and molded one out of Mississippi red clay. So much of that is what *made* me.

The way we've grown to love each other more fully than we ever imagined is our Movement. Against the odds that kept George Floyd and Eric Garner from watching their children grow old and the destruction that kept Trayvon Martin and Aiyana Jones and Michael Brown and Ma'Khia Bryant from giving their parents grandbabies to love on. We don't love each other simply in spite of what white supremacy has tried to do to us, but we had to claw through rubble, dodge mines, and bandage deep gashes on the way to become father and son because we wanted to give each other the best of what we had. To sit with my father on an eightieth birthday that this country never wanted him to celebrate, in the heart of a virus that wanted to keep us physically distant, is our victory. To watch Dad play Nintendo and card games with his grandchildren, who a few weeks later he'd start having biweekly Zoom meetings with to talk about his time in the Movement; to show them the man I spent my life looking for; to make sure they, too, truly see him. It's all a continuation of the power it took for him to open himself to me so I can transcribe his entire life on these pages. It's the determination to see ourselves for who we are and love each other harder than this country has hated us. We're sitting in a miracle that shouldn't have to be.

Later on the night of his eightieth birthday, my dad finally settled himself from the shock of our surprise visit, took a sip of red wine, and looked off to some other place over the horizon.

"I'm ready. I'm ready for this story to be told. I'm not running from it anymore. I've done some bad things. I've told myself my whole life that I have regrets, but I think if I'd done anything different I don't know that I would be here. With you all. Right now. I can't imagine doing anything to lose this feeling I have at this very moment in my life. This is who I am.

"And I'm okay with it."

ACKNOWLEDGMENTS

DAVID J. DENNIS JR.

To my wife, Krystalyn, nothing I do happens without you loving me like you do. This is our work together. I just want to be worth your love. Our marriage and our family are the two best things I got. I love you.

To Oktober and Max, I can't imagine a world without being your pop. You two are my heroes. Thank you for sharing your time with this book.

To my mother, Carolyn Jolivette, I love you. Thank you for fighting against all the odds and being the best mother I could imagine. None of this happens without you. So happy I chose you.

Erika, thank you for trusting me to tell Dad's story. See, we made it! I love you and our relationship is one of the best things to happen to me.

Andrea and Stacie, you know I love you and always will.

Parrain, you were the first great writer I ever knew. I can't tell you enough how much my life has been made better by having you just one call away.

Uncle Buster, I've felt you with me this entire time. But you already knew that.

To my agent, Marya Spence: you fought for this book when so many others would have given up. This book doesn't happen without your care and dedication. I'm so happy to call you my agent and so beyond blessed to have you as a friend.

My editor, Gail Winston, your patience and love for this book has filled me up. It has been an honor to be edited by you.

Kiese Laymon. You the GOAT and you gave me the blueprint to make loving art. You stuck your neck out for me when you didn't have to. This us.

Imani Perry. You inspire me every day and you wrote things that saved this book from itself.

Gotty: you gave me my first break and were the first person to believe in me as a writer. I'll never be able to thank you enough. Danyel Smith: you taught me so much about writing and how to care for words on a page. You changed my life and I hope I'm making you proud. Justin Tinsley, my brother. Nobody better to be on this journey with. Our books dropping the same day is divine, bro.

To Joel and Chelsi, two of my oldest friends and people who pushed me to be better since we were kids. So thankful to have your friendship.

Mrs. Alix Davis Williams, my eleventh- and twelfth-grade English teacher. You gave me Tim O'Brien's *The Things They Carried* and listened to me envision a book about my dad when I was just sixteen. Not only did you tell me it was possible, you made sure to tell me that you believed I could do this every time we spoke. You changed my life.

Mrs. Lamb, you indulged my absurdity and called it creative, even before I did. The world needs more teachers like you.

Professor Parker, you've been in my corner since you told me that my shirt looked like a rhino taking a dump, and I've cherished every second of it.

Dr. Flanagan, you poured into me so much at Davidson and guided me. Your classes were so integral to changing me for the better.

I'm forever indebted to the elders who sat me at their feet and trusted me with their stories from my childhood to the creation of this book: Hollis Watkins, Bob Moses, Euvester Simpson, Joyce and Dorie Ladner, Mattie Bivins, Charlie Cobb, whose fact-checking and guidance for this book were lifesavers, Ben Chaney, Gene Young, Dr. Anderson, Anita Howard, C. O. Chinn Jr., Annie Devine, Don Hubbard, Jerome Smith, and so many more. I am a child of your Movement because you've loved me enough to let me in.

I'd like to thank everyone who laid their eyes on early drafts and gave feedback to make this better: Saida Grundy, Laura Weber, Sam Cadet, Vann Newkirk, Brooke Thomas, and Regina Bradley. A special thank-you to my therapist, Dr. Tricia Stephens, whose work on intergenerational healing is essential for the work done in this book and for my family.

I'm appreciative of the SNCC Digital Gateway and its unending archive of information. Also, thank you to Malik Bartholomew and John Kennedy at Dillard for their help in gathering information.

Sabrina Ford, your fact-checking and sensitivity reading especially challenged me and made me think critically about how to make this the best work possible. Thank you, Christina Tapper, for putting us together. And for also just showing people like me the way to win by your own rules. I wanna be like you when I grow up.

Thank you to the Heising-Simons Foundation and the American Mosaic Journalism Prize for allowing me the time to dedicate myself to this book like it deserves.

To my Writer's Anonymous GroupMe: We did it. I love y'all.

TSS Crew. RMF.

DAVID J. DENNIS SR.

There are so many people who have had an impact on my life, which has resulted in my being who I am, and who made this book possible. I thank them all from the bottom of my heart.

First, I would like to thank all the people who were part of the extended family that put a floor beneath my feet from my birth until this day. I was lucky to have been born when our Black communities felt like villages. Black people lived together—Black teachers, college professors, business owners, doctors, lawyers, domestic workers and laborers, farm workers, and so forth, all lived together, prayed together, and entertained together. More important, they raised their children together. The children were the children not only to biological parents but of the community. It made no difference if you were part of a single-parent home, which I was—the community looked out for the children. I grew up not knowing who my father was, but I remember having many fathers and mothers—the Black men and women in the village. All had permission from my mother and grandparents to discipline me if they saw me doing something wrong and to share a "T-cake" when I was good.

This extended family culture was the strength and foundation of the Black community and the Civil Rights Movement. After the 1964 Civil Rights Act and the 1965 Voting Rights Act, the white power structure began to attack and destroy this structure, beginning with the Moynihan Report, the Poverty programs, and the developing of expressways and superhighways through the Black communities, especially the economic sections of the Black communities (villages) under the disguise of "urban renewal." After the passing of the 1964 Civil Rights Act, Black people "integrated" and fled their villages to live in overpriced homes vacated by white people. This was the beginning of the execution of a plan to destroy the Black family structure, which was the foundation of the Black power structure. These families make up the people for whom our Movement must persist.

I want to thank all those mothers and fathers who shared their lives with me and protected me and put the wind beneath my wings and who provided housing, food, clothing, and protection to the Civil Rights workers and volunteers during the 1960s. I want to thank all those people who paved the way for us and without whom there would not have been a successful Movement in Louisiana, Mississippi, Alabama, Georgia, or in other states. There would not have been a SNCC, CORE, or SCLC. These people had voter registration drives and education programs before these Civil Rights organizations existed. Thanks to the brave local people from Shreveport: C. O. Simpkins, Reverend Blake, Reverend Blade, Reverend Jones, Reverend McLain, Willie Bradford Jr., Joe Jernigan, the McGinnis sisters, Thomas Peete, Harold and Peter Bayone, Pete Harris, and the Freeman and Harris crowd.

Also, the many local leaders from Mississippi: Amzie Moore, C. C. Bryant, E. W. Steptoe, Hartman Turnbow, Louis Allen, Herbert Lee, D. K. Bivins, Mrs. Woods, Vernon Dahmer, Medgar Evers, to name a few who taught Bob Moses, SNCC, and CORE workers how to navigate the terrain of Mississippi. They made it possible for us to do what we did and for these Civil Rights organizations to exist.

Special thanks to my mom, my grandparents: My grandfather, who taught me that being a man can be painful and will demand much sacrifice and it's not the noise that gets the job done. My grandmother, who had successfully organized her community in the 1950s to demand from the city of Shreveport that sewage and water lines be put on the street where we lived. I found out about my mother's involvement in the Civil Rights movement after she died ten years ago. She was part of a group of beauticians—Mrs. Mamie Love Wallace, Mrs. Berniece Smith, Mrs. Annie Townsend Brewster—and my mother, Mrs. Kizzie Sheppard—in Shreveport. They would travel through Shreveport and the surrounding rural communities—all fully armed—trying to get people to register to vote. I had heard about the beauticians and their work but did not know that my mother was part of the group, and she never told me. I knew that they were all close friends. Also, special thanks to my stepfather, Mr. Aaron Sheppard, who saved my life by stopping police officers from taking me from the house in the middle of the night.

Special thanks to my New Orleans extended family, Rudy Lombard, Edward Lombard, and the entire Lombard family, Oretha Castle, Doris Castle, Julia Humbles, Jerome "Big Duck" Smith, Don Hubbard, William "Big Time Crip" Sonia and his family, Ernest Jones, Raynard Sanders, Paul Sylvester, Fred Johnson, Jesse Cooper Gibbs, Samuel Sepeku, Reverend David Dennis, who everybody thought was my father, Matheo "Flukie" Suarez, and Dorotha Smith.

The Big Time Crip sort of unofficially adopted me and was one of the people who inspired me to go back to college. I worked my way through undergraduate school at Dillard University as a bartender at his bar located on Jackson and Dryades streets in New Orleans. I still consider myself as part of the family. Here was a model of the extended family. Men would caution each other about using profanity if there was a child or a lady within earshot.

I want to also thank my first wife, Mattie Bivins Dennis, for being there during the really hard times of the Movement and who helped me to survive; and our daughter, Erika, for her patience and love and for being able to forgive me for all the birthdays, events, and times that I missed and did not spend with her. I especially appreciate the beautiful family she has: her husband, Brian, who is like a son, and the two grandchildren, Julian and Jalen, whom I love so much.

Special thanks to my second wife, Carolyn Jolivette, and her two children, Stacie and Aundie, whom I adopted, for their support during some of the most difficult times of my life. They were there to help me to rebuild and reconnect to a life that I had left behind. Also, thanks to their children, whom I consider to be my children.

Special thanks to my present wife, who has been my pillar and my rock. She has put a floor beneath my feet that has helped me to soar to heights that I did not think possible. I want to thank her as well for the support and patience with Davy and me in his preparation and writing of this book. Also, during this period she has almost single-handedly managed our nonprofit, the Southern Initiative Algebra Project, which has been extremely difficult because of the pandemic. Thanks, sweetie.

Special thanks as well to Nancy's two children, Jessamyn and Dylan, who are now also my children, for their support and love. They have treated me as a father, and it has been a blessing to have them in my life. Thanks, too, to Jessamyn's husband and friend, Lee Rachels, and their children, Leah and Seth. Grandpa Dave loves you.

Also, special thanks to my biological children, Davy and Erika, who taught me what family is about by being true models. I wish that I would have been the parent to them that they are to their children. Thanks to them for bringing to my life their spouses, Brian and Krysie and four fantastic grandchildren, Julian, Jalen, Max, and Oktober. Each one of them is special.

Also, special thanks to Davy for giving me the opportunity of sharing part of my life through this book. This was one of the most painful experiences I have ever had, and he is the only person I think could have made it possible. There is so much more to tell that would be more painful, and I am blessed to have him with me on this journey.

I want to give special thanks to those lives that touched mine in a special way but did not survive, such as Medgar Evers, James Chaney, Andrew Goodman, and Michael Schwerner. Also, those who have passed on but had a significant impact on my life—Gene Young, Marvin Wilson, Jessie Harris, Jessie Morris, Mrs. Annie Devine, Mrs. Victoria Gray, Mrs. Fannie Lou Hamer, Amzie Moore, Jimmie Travis, James Baldwin, David Baldwin, Mrs. Woods, C. O. Chinn Sr., C. O. Chinn Jr., George Raymond, Oretha Castle Haley, Doris Castle, Thomas Peete, John Lewis, and Richard Haley.

Special thanks to Bob Moses, who has been a part of my life for sixty years. He seems to have appeared in my life when I needed him. I first met him in 1962, when I was at a crossroads in my life as to what my focus should be in the Movement. He came and introduced me to Mississippi. I was at a different crossroads in 1989, when he appeared again and introduced me to the Algebra Project. Thanks, Bob, for being there when I needed you but did not know I needed you. You are a special person to me and to the world.

Then there's my Movement family: Hollis Watkins, McArthur Cotton, Margaret Burnham, Dorie Ladner, Joyce Ladner, Charles McLaurin, Rita Bender, David Goodman, Danny Glover, Charlie Cobb, Ben Chaney, the Moses family—Bob, Janet, Omo, Taba, Malaika, Maisha—Courtland Cox, Hank Thomas, Charles Persons, Myrlie Evers, Robert Polk, and many others.

Special thanks also go to those I call the forgotten or invisible heroes of the Movement, the people who participated in the mass voter registration programs, the Freedom Vote, the MFDP, and the Freedom Summer activities, who housed, fed, and protected the thousand volunteers and the SNCC, CORE, and COFO staff during the summer of 1964, who were never recognized for their contributions and sacrifices. And to the invisible people whose fate we do not know after the summer of 1964, when the volunteers and others left the state and they went back home, many into the back woods of Mississippi. I always wonder what reprisals were taken against them when the cameras left.

Then there is the big one—special thanks to whomever said at the home of Dr. Harris on May 20, 1961, "There's not enough space in this room for both God and fear." That statement opened the door to my future.

I want to make sure that I properly acknowledge the indomitable role of Black women in and beyond the Movement. From Doris and Oretha in New Orleans, Diane Nash in Nashville, the women of the beauty salons in Shreveport to Mrs. Devine, Mrs. Gray, Mrs. Hamer in Mississippi, and countless more, there were always Black women at the front lines. They took the same beatings, were victims of the same violence and the same terror that we faced and worse. Yet they stood taller and more fearlessly than anyone.

This has been true throughout the history of Black resistance.

Black women can save us and pull us to freedom through their sheer force of will. But just because they can doesn't mean we should expect that level of super heroics from them. The rest of us have a task to give as much to and for our Black women as they have given us.

For every Bob Moses, Medgar Evers, or Dave Dennis, there should be a woman who is just as recognized and celebrated for what she did for our freedom. If you know Dr. King, you should know Ella Baker. If you know Malcolm X, you should know Fannie Lou Hamer. If you don't, then that's a failure on all our parts.

I also want to thank the young people who are part of the Black Lives Matter Movement and those who are trying to make a difference for keeping the torches burning and the cry for freedom out there for all to hear, just as we tried to do in the 1960s. Our ancestors continued the battle cry from the time they were brought here in chains. They never stopped, and we have to continue to fight, no matter how difficult the road becomes. We need to rebuild our communities (villages) as our forefathers built them. We have to develop our own. We cannot survive if we depend on the enemy to provide for us.

I also want to apologize to those whom I caused pain and ask for their forgiveness, and I thank them for their patience.

Thanks.

ABOUT THE AUTHORS

David J. Dennis Jr. is a senior writer at *The Undefeated*. His work has been featured in *Atlanta* magazine, *The Atlantic*, the *Washington Post*, and *Huffington Post*, among other publications. Dennis is the recipient of the 2021 American Mosaic Journalism Prize, is a National Association of Black Journalist Salute to Excellence award winner, and was named one of *The Root's* 100 Most Influential African Americans of 2020. He lives in Georgia with his wife and two children and is a graduate of Davidson College.

David J. Dennis Sr. is a civil rights veteran and one of the original Freedom Riders who rode from Montgomery to Jackson in 1961. He served as field secretary for the Congress of Racial Equality in Louisiana and Mississippi (1961–65) and as co-director with Bob Moses of the Voter Education Committee of the Council of Federated Organizations. He helped organize the Mississippi Freedom Summer, the Mississippi Freedom Democratic Party, and the challenge to the National Democratic Party in 1964. He attended Dillard University and earned his law degree at the University of Michigan. In 1972, he co-directed the challenge to the Louisiana Democratic structure that resulted in an African American chairman and a majority African American delegation being sent to the national convention, the first time since Reconstruction. He is the executive director of the Southern Initiative Algebra Project, Inc., a nonprofit organization that works to ensure a quality education for all children, especially children of color and the chronically underserved.